Aryan Cowboys

White Supremacists and the Search for a New Frontier, 1970–2000

Evelyn A. Schlatter

D1481657

UNIVERSITY OF TEXAS PRESS ❧ AUSTIN

Requests for permission to reproduce material
from this work should be sent to:
    Permissions
    University of Texas Press
    P.O. Box 7819
    Austin, TX 78713-7819
    www.utexas.edu/utpress/about/
        bpermission.html

⊗ The paper used in this book meets the minimum requirements of ANSI/NISO Z39.48-1992
(R1997) (Permanence of Paper).

Library of Congress Cataloging-in-Publication Data

Schlatter, Evelyn A.
    Aryan cowboys : White supremacists and
the search for a new frontier, 1970–2000 /
by Evelyn A. Schlatter. — 1st ed.
        p.   cm.
    Includes bibliographical references and index.
    ISBN-13: 978-0-292-71421-2 (cl. : alk. paper)
    ISBN-10: 0-292-71421-1
    ISBN-13: 978-0-292-71471-7 (pbk. : alk. paper)
    ISBN-10: 0-292-71471-8
    1. White supremacy movements—West
(U.S.)—History—20th century.   2. Right-
wing extremists—West (U.S.)—History—20th
century.   3. West (U.S.)—Race relations—History—20th century.   4. West (U.S.)—Politics
and government—20th century.   5. Frontier
thesis.   6. Frontier and pioneer life—West
(U.S.)   7. Messianism, Political—West (U.S.)
8. National characteristics, American.   I. Title.
    F596.2.S34   2006
    305.800978'09045—dc22
                        2006015019

To my parents, without whom nothing would have been possible, and to my sister, who reminded me to laugh.

Contents

List of Photographs

Preface

Fishing in the Abyss

My expedition into the extremist right-wing corners of the white American mind began in November 1992, when Amendment 2 passed in my home state of Colorado. I had just moved to New Mexico to pursue a Ph.D. in history at the University of New Mexico, but I deliberately maintained my voting status in Colorado for a couple of extra months specifically so that I could vote against that legislation. Blatantly homophobic and overtly discriminatory, Amendment 2 ensured that gay, lesbian, and bisexual peoples had no recourse if they were fired or denied housing on the basis of their sexual orientation and stripped them of any basis on which to claim discrimination.[1] Orchestrated by Colorado for Family Values (CFV), a right-wing Christian fundamentalist group based in Colorado Springs, Amendment 2 shocked pundits and progressives everywhere because it had passed (52 percent to 48 percent) in what people thought was a "liberal" Western state.

I knew how the amendment had passed. I had been watching CFV's grassroots campaign for at least six months. It was a masterpiece of spin and organization, employing such catch phrases as "family values," "fairness," and "no special rights" to downplay its exclusionist message. CFV's foot soldiers also knew their target audience. They didn't expend much effort in the heavily populated Denver/Boulder area, considered urban and socially progressive. Instead, they concentrated on smaller rural communities that tended to be more conservative, especially where God and sodomy are concerned.

When the returns rolled in, I felt as though I and my progressive views had been ridden out of town on a rail, like an outlaw whose worldview of her home state was completely transformed for the worst. Barely settled in New Mexico, I had no ties yet to my new home and those I felt to my old had been cut—without my consent, without my participation, without a chance to really draw battle lines. I felt as if the earth had been ripped from under my feet. I had grown up in rural Colorado and graduated from high school in a town of 3,000. The people who had voted "yes" included people with whom I had gone to school, people who had been neighbors. I felt an almost overwhelming sense of sadness that spin had trumped logic and that many of my friends no longer felt welcome in Colorado. The passing of Amendment 2 was thus intensely personal for me. Perhaps not the best reason to pursue a topic of research, but it was the one that initiated my first analyses.

Six months later, I was poring over CFV campaign literature and comparing it to the rhetoric espoused by the 1920s Ku Klux Klan in Colorado. This was when I discovered that, although the targets had changed, the underlying ideological message had not: White America is under attack from outside forces that must be stopped if the greatness of this country were to be maintained. My research became a paper that I presented in 1994, a month after the Colorado Supreme Court ruled 6 to 1 that Amendment 2 was unconstitutional.[2] I still hadn't figured out what I hoped to discover during the course of my work, but I realized something about the American public. CFV had gotten a reputation as a group of hate-filled "fascist," obsessive, mean-spirited religious fanatics lurking on the fringes of American society. I wasn't ready to make that declaration yet, since I felt that CFV and the 1920s Klan knew exactly what they were doing and that they were tapping into extant American historical and social currents.

By early 1995, I was well on my way to researching my dissertation, which dealt with white supremacist groups in the American West. The Randy Weaver and Waco standoffs were adding fuel to a burgeoning militia movement in rural America, and I felt a pressing need to figure out why this was occurring and where the strands of white supremacist ideology in this country came from. Following the horrific bombing of the Alfred P. Murrah Federal Building in Oklahoma City, I began to realize that there was something uniquely American about the white supremacist movement I was studying, that there were links to mainstream conservative rhetoric and ideology, and that there was something about sacred American myths regarding character and identity that indicated to me that the right-wing lunatic fringe really wasn't lunatic or on the fringe. Although I still took a personal interest in the movement because of the elections of 1992, I had come to see that the project was bigger than I and that it resonated across centuries.

Consequently, this journey through the American white supremacist movement has been at once intensely disturbing but also gratifying, if such can be said. I have suffered bouts of depression from reading pages of vile racist, sexist, anti-Semitic, and homophobic rhetoric. I have physically blanched at white supremacist websites that espouse horrific violence against people of color and people of Jewish descent. I have taken showers after archival research, feeling the need to wash imaginary grime from my skin, hoping to erase the effects of hysterical, conspiracy-laden discourse and its stifling bitterness.

But I have also learned deeper lessons. I examine and question the privileges my skin color conveys in American society and culture. I have learned to question many sides of an issue, think about what it means to be white, and understand that painting an opposing viewpoint with an extremist brush can serve to detract attention from mainstream rhetoric that conveys the same messages.[3] I have come to understand, too, that there are very real consequences for the people white supremacists target in their rhetoric. To dismiss their beliefs as "fringe" or "extremist" does not guarantee a cessation of potential violence directed at people of color, Jews, or those among us who are gay, lesbian, bisexual, or transgendered.[4]

And in spite of my own leftist and progressive politics, I have been able to humanize many of the members of white supremacist groups. It's an uncomfortable balance and one I perhaps have not been able to maintain all the time, a dilemma other researchers no doubt have faced. I am completely opposed to everything white supremacists advocate and represent, but I have tried to understand what drives individuals to the organizations and the movement and what larger forces were and still are at play in American culture.

That said, I think the most important thing I have learned during the course of my travels through the topography of white supremacist ideology and history is that I did as much unpacking as packing of my baggage. All Americans are faced with shifting cultural and social situations, economic anxieties, and increased globalization. We need to remember that we are all part of this American community and that solutions to our problems, whether real or perceived, do not lie in conspiracy theories, scapegoating, or rage. After the work I have been doing, though, I can understand why some of us turn to these approaches for answers. However, all of us have a greater responsibility to one another as fellow Americans and, ultimately, global citizens, to address real inequalities in our social and cultural institutions and hierarchies and find workable, community-based solutions. It will require that we look at ourselves, at our core beliefs, and put our history under a microscope. It will also require us to look at the beliefs and stereotypes many mainstream Americans hold and how they can be used in an extremist context. It will be an uncomfortable and, most likely, painful process in some respects. But to ignore the extreme right—to ignore the parts of this country's history that have encouraged this ideology—is to allow it to grow and spread unchecked. The consequences of that, I'm afraid, do not bode well for a united America.

Acknowledgments

A project like this involves a lot of help, whether direct or indirect. I would first like to thank the original members of my dissertation committee at the University of New Mexico, who were very supportive of the work I was doing and offered many suggestions and editorial improvements along the way. They are the late Dr. Robert Kern, whose humor and gregarious character never failed to raise my spirits; Dr. Elizabeth Jameson, my committee chair, who offered guidance with a gentle hand throughout the process; Dr. Virginia Scharff, whose critiques and editing made my own writing better; and Dr. Christine Sierra, whose work in political science strengthened some of the arguments I was making.

Numerous archivists—some of whom have moved on since I conducted my research—aided my long slogs through dozens of files at the University of Oregon in Eugene and the University of Kansas in Lawrence. I want to express my deep gratitude to the staff at both places—especially those working with the Stimeley Collection at the University of Oregon and the Wilcox Collection at the University of Kansas. And, though I have never met her, thanks to Dr. Abby Ferber, whose dissertation about white supremacist rhetoric and gender constructions I read in 1996. Ferber's work made me aware of the Stimeley Collection in Oregon.

A subject like this, I have discovered, takes a lot of psychic energy, and I could not have done it without the support of my friends and colleagues in graduate school who, while I was dissertating, supplied lots of buffalo wings and beer on those Fridays when I felt I was sinking into a morass of conspiracy. I am also grateful to colleagues at the *New Mexico Historical Review*, Dr. Jerry Davis, Tony Goodrich, Dr. Robert Himmerich y Valencia, Dr. Carlos Herrera, Dr. Scott Hughes, Dr. Javier Marión, Jennifer Norden, Dr. Carlos Salomon, and Kim Suina. I also want to extend a great big thank you to my comrade-in-arms Dr. Elaine Carey, my friend, colleague, *Review* buddy, and clear head when I bounced ideas off her during the dissertation and the book-writing phase. Thanks, Elaine!

Thanks to my colleagues at the University of New Mexico Press while I was an acquiring editor and then managing editor: Dr. David Holtby, friend and mentor, who never wavered in his support of any of my crazy ideas and who served not only as a supervisor to me but also as a guidance counselor. Thanks also to Maya Allen-Gallegos, Robyn Mundy, Mike Ritthaler, Kathy Sparkes, Melissa Tandysh, Luther Wilson, Mina Yamashita, and my editorial assistants who took quite a load off my shoulders as I was trying to finish the initial draft for the University of Texas Press: Justin Parks and Sarah Ritthaler. Thanks also to Glenda Madden, for making me laugh when I really needed to, and thanks to everyone at the UNM Press who made coming to work a lot of fun during this process. Thanks also to Dr. Kathy Brosnan and Dr. Sandra Mathews, with whom conferencing was never so much fun!

And to the University of Texas Press: beaucoup thanks for taking me on as an author and for having some faith in this project. Deep thanks to Dr. Lane Crothers, who served as a reviewer and offered some organizational and methodological insights; more, deep thanks to Dr. David Wrobel, who also served as a reviewer for the University of Texas Press and offered wonderful insight and organizational strategies. Both were gracious enough to encourage me to contact them during the revision process if I needed further help. I greatly appreciate your time and energy in reading the manuscript, gentlemen. Theresa May, the acquiring editor for this project, rocks the world, as do her wonderful colleagues and staff at the Press, including Allison Faust, Leslie Tingle, and Lisa Tremaine. Thanks also to Joe Parsons, the copyeditor, for providing more clarity; to Carol Cooperrider, for the fabulous map; and to Mary LaMotte, for the index.

Thanks to Anelke Shulkitas at CORBIS images, who patiently walked me through the process of downloading from their site and who was unfailingly cheerful whenever I contacted her, and thanks to Jorge Jaramillo at the Associated Press, who never failed to respond kindly and courteously to my plaintive cries about images and pricing. A special thanks to Lyn Bayless and the Columbia State Community College library staff for tracking down page numbers.

I must also take time to thank those who offered me deeper insights to the white supremacist right as I was researching both the dissertation and revising for publication. Chip Berlet, a senior researcher at Political Research Associates, answered some of my queries about militias via e-mail and offered his own expertise as a guide. Many thanks to the able staff at the Anti-Defamation League of B'nai B'rith, who sent me their informational packets about certain groups and individuals as soon as I requested them. Thanks to members of the New

Mexico Militia in Hobbs, who were gracious enough to take me out for a steak dinner and then invite me to one of their meetings; members of The Order (currently incarcerated) who corresponded with me and offered polite corrections and assessments of my interpretations and analyses. They are Richard Kemp, David Lane, and Richard Scutari. And thanks to the late Pastor Richard Butler of Aryan Nations, who took the time to respond to some of my e-mails just a year prior to his death. Though I am in utter disagreement with the stances of these men, I do appreciate their willingness to correspond with me.

And finally, my deepest gratitude goes to my family: my parents and sister, without whom I would not be the person I am today and whose support in every facet of this process has led me through some difficult times. Thanks to Taylor, whose doggie humor and personality saw me through both the dissertation and the book. And a billion jillion thanks to Fran, whose good humor and kind nature kept me grounded throughout the revising process. I love you all.

Aryan Cowboys

CHAPTER 1

Introduction: The Ties That Bind

A pril 19, 1995, dawned gray and cold in Albuquerque. I caught the first reports from Oklahoma City around 10:30 A.M. Mountain Standard Time. The news about the Alfred P. Murrah Federal Building was confused. A gas line explosion. A possible bombing. A structural collapse. By noon, the news had confirmed that a bomb had exploded in front of the building, causing a massive collapse and untold deaths. The media voiced suppositions about Middle Eastern terrorists. I disagreed. By 10:00 P.M. that night, no Middle Eastern terrorist organization had claimed responsibility and, based on information I had been collecting for three years, I suspected that the terrorist was right here at home, probably a white man in his twenties or thirties.

The clues piled up. April 19 is the anniversary of the Branch Davidian immolation in Waco (1993). The Murrah Building housed various U.S. government agencies, including a few Federal Bureau of Investigation (FBI) agents. And I did not think Oklahoma City was a likely target for foreign terrorist groups. I had been tracking and researching the American extremist right since 1992 and had a feeling that the terrible tragedy unfolding in Oklahoma City was the product of this movement and its venomous rhetoric that often includes antigoverment sentiment. The nightmare suspicions proved true.

How could this happen? How could an American citizen and soldier kill 168 American men, women, and children? We would like to think that Timothy McVeigh, the man arrested and executed for the bombing, was an aberration, unstable, so we may explain away the horrific occurrence and try to make sense of a senseless situation. On some level, we are correct in these conclusions. McVeigh, however, did not emerge from the background fringes of American society and culture as an anomaly. He is part of an American political and social tradition at least two centuries old. We can locate right-wing (whether extreme or not) sentiment, demonstrations, and organizations throughout modern American history since the eighteenth century. The underlying tenets and ideological expressions of rightist extremism have proven remarkably resilient over time.

What *have* changed are the trappings, packaging, and available technology for extremist recruitment and terrorist acts.

In this book, I will trace and analyze the growth and development since 1970 of certain extreme right-wing groups that are sympathetic to white supremacist doctrine. I have chosen groups that have operated generally in the western United States that envision the region as the eventual site of a white American homeland. I will address how these groups construct "manhood" and "masculinity" and how these constructions reflect popular historical conceptions about "the West" as a symbol of freedom, an opportunity for conquest, and an escape from the conditions of life in modern industrial society. These constructions of masculinity and the West are connected to people's desires to change their situations, desires that reflect their need for self-transformation.

I will also bring into the discussion other strands of American history that have played roles in white supremacist groups and have managed to find expression since the period of this country's founding, which involved westward expansion and the creation of a national identity. These include vigilantism, fraternalism, and political and social extremism (specifically rightist). Historically, these "-isms" have enabled men to group together and attempt to enact local and federal policies that maintain male (generally white) power, whether political, social, or economic.

I am not suggesting that white supremacy *derives* from these historical currents. Rather, I am arguing that these historical traditions have, in some cases, encouraged some white men to enact white supremacist goals. My point is that the foundations of American nationalism, which are based on ideas about "divine mission" and westward expansion, have lent themselves quite handily to exclusionist rhetoric and policies toward nonwhite people. Again, a majority of white Americans neither subscribe to racist beliefs nor run out and join white supremacist groups. However, the very nature of what it means to be "American" can itself provide justification and ideological groundwork for those who do.

I want to make very clear that the personal reasons people have for joining white supremacist groups are myriad. Those who have participated and who still are participating in groups or the movement as a whole come from a variety of backgrounds and households. Most, however, join because they feel somehow "displaced" or "disenfranchised" from society at large. It's a subjective perspective and depends on the person involved. What is apparent, however, is that the movement is largely male.

"Gender is unquestionably an important organizing principle for racist groups," Kathleen Blee states. "Aryan masculinity," she continues, "is venerated as the bedrock of the white race, racist politics as the litmus test of masculine prowess." Assumptions about what it means to be a man are critical in the movement's methods of appealing to white men. Blee noted that throughout American history, "racist groups have trumpeted the idea that white men are in imminent danger of losing their proper economic, political, and social place to undeserving white women and to nonwhite men and women."[1]

The white supremacist movement in the United States is thus all about manhood. More specifically, white manhood and what it means to be a white man in America, whether historically, in the present, or the future. My purpose here is to look at why that might be and what underpinnings in the essence of what it means to be American lend themselves to the existence of white supremacy in this country. I have focused on the West, not just because it's where I'm from personally, but also because I'm interested in how ideas about the West and manhood have historically infused American nationalism and notions about "character," which in turn have found expression in white supremacist rhetoric.

The iconography of "the West" promises a translation of the self into something purer and more authentic. White supremacist groups and their rhetoric are also tied to older patterns of American expansion and nationalism and to recurring patterns of what I have dubbed "frontierism"—the attempt to resurrect an imagined, romanticized past inhabited by white archetypes triumphing over land and human others, often eking out a living by the sweat of their white male Protestant brows.

Primary among popular constructions of "the West" are symbols such as "cowboy," "six-shooter" (guns), and "vigilante." Other constructions include ideas about "frontier" as place, process, and proving ground. Characterizations of westerners (particularly men) include "rugged individualism," "courageous," "strong," and "independent." The list goes on, because we all know and contribute to it. We have seen "Western" films. We are familiar with "Western" novels. From the 1920s through the 1970s, hundreds of nationally distributed feature Western films provided the general American population with a steady dose of big sky country. In 1959 alone, no fewer than thirty-five Westerns ran concurrently on television and eight of the top ten shows had Western themes. John Wayne, as Western hero, became a leading symbol of American masculinity from World War II to Vietnam.[2]

Even during the 1980s and on into the 1990s, "Western"-themed films graced theaters nationwide. Included in those offerings were *Rhinestone* (1984), *Pale Rider* (1985), *Silverado* (1985), *Young Guns* (1988), *Young Guns II* (1990), *Dances with Wolves* (1990), *Unforgiven* (1992), *Tombstone* (1993), *Wyatt Earp* (1994),

Legends of the Fall (1995), and *Maverick* (1995). After 1995, Westerns did not seem as popular at the box office; instead, somewhat edgy "neo-Westerns" and come-dies graced the screen including *Dead Man* (1996), starring Johnny Depp as a man in search of himself; *Wild Wild West,* with Will Smith (1999); and Woody Harrelson, in *The Cowboy Way* (1994) and *The Hi Lo Country* (1998). And Kevin Costner once again returned to the classic good guys versus bad guys Western with his *Open Range* (2003). An intrinsic theme of typical "Western" films and television programs, movies, comic books, and novels such as these is an im-plicit understanding about gender. That is, the West is no place for a lady.[3]

This is a part of Western mythology that continues to resurrect itself from the graveyards of cultural expectations. The "cowboy code," outlined by Gene Autry (ironically never a working cowboy himself), provided ten points by which a cowboy is supposed to live. Those included specifications about conduct, integrity, and even hygiene. A cowboy, Autry stated, should never break his word. He should demonstrate gentleness with animals, children, and the elderly. He should never shoot first, never hit a "smaller man," and never take unfair advan-tage. He must respect women and the laws of his nation. He must be a good worker, help people in distress, and keep clean in thought, action, speech, and body. Cowboys are patriots, Autry enjoined. And they do not harbor racially or religiously intolerant ideas.[4]

Members of right-wing extremist groups, whether they realize it or not, subscribe to most of Autry's rules. That is, they consider themselves the purest of patriots—they are "true" Americans whose government has run amuck. However, all subscribe to racially and religiously intolerant ideas, though most will attempt to justify their position by claiming that they harbor no ill will to-ward nonwhite people. They simply want a whites-only land[5] and white women to bear the next generations of Aryans.

I will explore here how the "West" is a gendered state of mind and how the men who join right-wing extremist groups—especially groups in the western part of the United States—encode and enact popular notions about the "West" such as individualism, masculinity, and escapism. In particular, I am interested in how the rhetoric of white supremacy has historically enabled what I designate a "culture of masculinity" that has existed throughout the twentieth century and reflected "cowboy" mythology in association with right-wing groups.

The "culture of masculinity" within white supremacist groups tends to be Protestant (if there is a religious preference espoused), patriarchal, and very in-volved in displays of physical strength and endurance. Many group members are liquor-, cigarette-, and drug-free. They are expected to marry white women, protect them, and propagate with them. White supremacist men believe that, although white women are "help-mates" and should be trained in the use of weapons in case of emergencies, women's primary responsibility is to home, children, and husband.

Ironically, within white supremacist masculine culture is a paradox: though expected to mimic "cowboy" imagery (rugged and independent), the men involved in the movement are also expected to build communities and families. Abby Ferber notes that women have become more of a presence in the movement, and I would argue that it is precisely because of a stronger emphasis on family. "Women," Ferber states, "also make the movement more accessible and less threatening to the mainstream by creating Aryan coloring books for kids and women's Web sites, and home-schooling their children. They contribute to the seeming ordinariness of life in the movement." Ferber notes, however, that women are rarely in positions of leadership in the movement.[6]

The role of women in the white supremacist right is one fraught with contradictions. Most members of white supremacist groups throughout American history have been and continue to be male. This is not to suggest that women have not been welcomed into the movement or that they are barred from membership. Blee and Ferber have examined the complex interplay of gender and racism, demonstrating that women who join white supremacist groups will act independently and stand up for themselves, but will defend the "natural" role of women—the domestic sphere—in relation to men.

In her work with women who join racist organizations, Blee (2002) argues that nearly all of the women she spoke with did not talk about finally finding an outlet for long-held beliefs. Rather, many seemed to have joined almost serendipitously, and the reasons tended to be aligned more with ideas about "social life" than ideology. Blee also discovered that many women she interviewed did not come from what could be described as racist or intolerant households. In fact, racist beliefs were learned *after* the women joined the groups. Fewer than one-fourth of her interviewees, Blee found, actively sought out white supremacist groups for membership.[7]

Furthermore, those women who are involved seem to experience a wealth of self-doubt about the movement and conditions in the world around them. Many do not seem to "burn with ideological passion" for the cause. Rather, they feel hopeless about societal conditions and the possibility for changing them. Men in the movement talk about their "empowerment," but women give the overall mission of the white supremacist right little chance of success.[8]

Ferber's work has examined the overarching role of men in the movement and how white supremacist groups emphasize the "natural" place of men and women. That is, men are to be the active agents in change and women the domestic support system.[9] However, as she has noted, the advent of the Web has allowed white supremacist groups to appeal to more women and for those women, in turn, to perhaps "soften" the image of racism for a larger mainstream audience.

Blee has argued elsewhere that the Indiana Klan created a women's auxiliary in the 1920s that served as a way to "safeguard" women and "help expand women's legal rights" while at the same time working to preserve white Protestant supremacy. The women Blee interviewed in her study remembered their Klan days as "a time of friendship and solidarity among like-minded women."[10] Women in the organization were expected to conduct themselves in a "respectful" manner, and they were not allowed to hold positions of authority in the Klan. This was something Klan leaders wrestled with: how to define political roles for women while at the same time maintaining male supremacy.[11]

Women here also helped "soften" the Klan's image and, they hoped, make it appealing to a more mainstream following. The overall tenet of the Klan, however, and the white supremacist movement as a whole did not and still has not included women on a level playing field. In other words, though women in recent years (since the late 1990s and early 2000s) have been more involved in the movement and organized white supremacist groups, membership, affiliation, and leadership remain overwhelmingly male. In light of the history of white supremacy in this country and the older mythologies into which it taps, this comes as no surprise.

Although I do not discount the growing membership of women in the current manifestations of white supremacist organizations, or the participation of women historically in these groups, my emphasis here is on men and masculinity and how the movement defines and is defined by ideas about manhood. Women have never held positions of official leadership among white supremacists, and the relationship between men and women in the movement continues to get stuck in this inherent conflict: how to allow women access to political activism while at the same time relegating them to a largely domestic role. The white supremacist right has continually wrestled with this paradox and as long as it does, I would argue, women will never hold positions equal to men in the movement nor will the movement move beyond its primary emphasis on masculinity. Let us turn now to the groups.

The Stage

Since the late 1970s, this country has witnessed a plethora of home-grown so-called white supremacist groups whose members seek to restore the power of white men, segregate races into specific geographic regions of this country, and bring about the downfall of the federal government, which, they believe, is controlled by a secret, powerful cabal of Jewish families and white race traitors. According to these groups, the ultimate goal of "ZOG" (Zionist Occupied Government) is to bring the United States to its knees economically, integrate it with a "New World Order," and place its opponents in concentration camps.

The white race, proponents believe, is the last line of defense against this conspiracy, and they contend that the day of reckoning—the "showdown"—in which ZOG begins its final campaign against them, is upon us. To prepare for this penultimate battle, members of white supremacist groups run secret paramilitary camps, build secluded compounds, conduct survival skills seminars, stockpile food, collect impressive arsenals that include some of the latest military hardware, and spread the word via publications, gun shows, fax machines, phone lines, shortwave radio, and the Internet.[12]

This study focuses on groups based primarily in the western United States that either came west in search of privacy or were founded in western states. Specifically, I examine the neo-Nazi northern Idaho–based Aryan Nations and western-based chapters of the Posse Comitatus. I will also discuss the rise of militias and like-minded so-called Patriot groups since 1992, including Montana's Freemen and the Republic of Texas. I will also address a few smaller groups and several individuals. They include The Order, a paramilitary appendage of Aryan Nations; Gordon Kahl, a Posse sympathizer with ties to North Dakota, Texas, and California; and Randy Weaver, Idaho's best-known white separatist.

Aryan Nations, founded in 1979, was a white supremacist separatist compound whose members advocated self-sufficiency, self-government, and a white homeland that encompasses Oregon, Washington, Idaho, Montana, and Wyoming.[13] Aryan Nations and like-minded groups also espouse a religious doctrine known as "Christian Identity," a modern incarnation of nineteenth-century British-Israelism, alternately known as Anglo-Israelism. Because Christian Identity is integral in understanding white supremacist doctrine since 1960, I will provide a brief history of it here.

In the most general terms, British-Israelism refers to the belief that the British are lineal descendants of the "ten lost tribes" of Israel. It did not become a basis for an organized movement until the second half of the nineteenth century, with two related but distinguishable tendencies at work: either Britain as a nation was specially chosen by God to help realize a divine design in human history, or some spiritually purified portion of it would take on this role—namely, the United States. British-Israelism, therefore, discounted the role of Jews in scripture as

God's chosen people. This belief system made its way to the United States in the latter years of the nineteenth century in the hands of a few male preachers.

Between the world wars, British-Israelism in America began to take on decidedly anti-Semitic and white supremacist overtones as its believers began to conflate the idea of America as the promised land for the true lost tribesmen of Israel (the British) with the notion that Jews had deceived not only people of British descent, but also those of Teutonic descent into believing that Jews are the chosen people. This twentieth-century incarnation of British-Israelism is known as Christian Identity because it fuses biblical fundamentalism (hence the use of "Christian") with the belief that the true "identity" of the chosen people is not Jewish, but Caucasian. This virulently racist interpretation of British-Israelism is, therefore, barely fifty years old, its doctrinal basis established after World War II by a network of independent preachers and writers from whose hands it passed into a variety of extreme right-wing political movements preoccupied with fears of racial mixing and Jewish conspiracy.

Through groups such as Aryan Nations and the Ku Klux Klan, Christian Identity had by the 1970s become the most important religious vehicle for white supremacist orthodoxy.[14] It preaches the supremacy of whites—especially white men. It is virulently anti-Semitic and millenarian in outlook and wholly Eurocentric. Identity has served as a binding force for disparate right-wing groups with white supremacist leanings since the late 1970s.[15] Identity has adherents throughout American white supremacist networks. From modern Klan to Posses, it is common ground between groups, enabling the spread of extremist doctrine across party lines.

The Posse Comitatus (literally, "power of the county"), founded in 1969, "is composed of loosely affiliated bands of armed vigilantes and survivalists."[16] Chapters exist all over the country, and its members devote themselves primarily to tax-protest and an anti–federal government stance. The groups' members also believe that an international Zionist conspiracy is behind such government organizations as the Federal Reserve System and Jewish bankers that seek also to undermine American farmers. Posse groups, like Aryan Nations, infuse their rhetoric with Identity theology, calling for white Christians to defend their homes and families against what they believe is an imminent government takeover orchestrated by Jews.[17] Gordon Kahl, a staunch Posse member during the 1970s and early 1980s, died in a 1983 shootout with federal marshals, subsequently attaining martyr status among Posse members and other right-wing extremists.[18]

The militia movement and its larger umbrella, the Patriot movement, formed as a response to the FBI–Randy Weaver standoff at Ruby Ridge, Idaho (1992), and the FBI–Branch Davidian showdown in Waco, Texas (1993). Some groups include Christian Identity rhetoric in their conspiracy claims. In organization, these groups are most similar to a Posse chapter in that leaders advocate the formation of small paramilitary cells cloaked in secrecy and trained as guerrillas for what they anticipate will be the final showdown with the federal government.[19]

Another aspect of the Patriot movement is the so-called common-law courts movement, which advocates using extant court systems to file bogus liens and claims and thereby wreak havoc in local communities. All deny the legal authority of federal and state governments and seek to create a new system of which they will be the leaders. Traveling teams of instructors hold meetings around the country to show others how to use common-law court tactics to subvert the American legal system.[20] The Montana Freemen and the Republic of Texas used common-law methods against local, state, and federal governments. Many common-law advocates also file bogus claims against their fellow community residents, which creates localized tensions that have the potential to erupt into violence.

In June of 1984, a small cell of the extreme rightist group The Order shot Jewish talk show host Alan Berg to death outside his Denver, Colorado, home. The man ultimately responsible for Berg's death, Robert Mathews, died later that year in a shootout with FBI officials on Whidbey Island, Washington. Mathews had spent most of his life affiliated with right-wing groups, and his beliefs became more extreme as he aged. He began his career as a white supremacist with the John Birch Society during the 1960s and learned survivalism from Arizona's Sons of Liberty. He experimented with tax-evasion societies, and finally came to embrace virulent white supremacist doctrine as a member of the West Virginia–headquartered National Alliance. His last affiliation was with Aryan Nations and The Order, which he founded and recruited from the Aryan Nations compound to fight for a territorial imperative that defined the northwestern United States as a homeland for the white race. When The Order targeted Alan Berg for assassination, they were, they believed, striking a blow for white freedom against an international Jewish conspiracy.[21]

The Aryan warriors of modern paramilitary rightist groups are, they believe, engaged in a monumental Manichean struggle for the very soul of this nation. They seek to prepare—in remote, often rural, areas—for a final battle between the forces of good and evil. Intertwined with biblical prophecies about the return of Christ and the final showdown with Satan, the ideological foundations of many right-wing extremist groups emphasize a millenarian view of history, in which preparation for an impending "end-time" before a thousand years of peace is crucial. Hence the stockpiling, arsenal-building, and compound construction. The nostalgic quest for a mythical and idyllic agrarian past, the search for cultural homogeneity, and preparations for Armageddon are traits of the latest incarnations of rightist groups.

White supremacist warriors believe themselves to be the "last defense" for the white race, the cultural commandos who will lead the country through the twenty-first century following their preordained triumphant battle against the evil forces of the apocalypse. Not unlike some nineteenth-century utopians, these groups' members and their sympathizers search for a new homeland to improve their own lives and initiate a new era. Their aspirations, however, go beyond constructing a personal utopia. In other words, they purport to know what's best for this country and for this world, though the only way to achieve a thousand years of relative peace is by segregating people according to race and ethnicity and minimizing contact among groups.

On Definitions

Defining "extremism" is a tricky matter, because it is a term that can apply to opposite ends of the political spectrum. John George and Laird Wilcox suggest that concepts of a "left wing" and a "right wing" became more clearly defined by the early twentieth century. Popular perceptions associated "right wing" with conservatism, patriotism, racism, nationalism, and religiosity. "Left wing" often implied liberalism, internationalism, collectivism, secularism, and egalitarianism.[22]

"Left" and "right" extremist movements in America have often shared a political focus such as a working impatience with the normal channels for dissent that exist in democratic societies. They have often moved in similar directions, proposing isolationism or perhaps opposition to banking. One constant in attempting to tease out differences between extreme right and extreme left has been the perception of extreme rightist movements as those that rise primarily in reaction to the perceived displacement of power and status that can accompany social and political change, whereas leftist extremism has been perceived as something that impels social transformation by overthrowing old power and status groups.[23]

George and Wilcox's definitions encompass broad tendencies that describe ideological differences between rightist and leftist extremists. We cannot measure to what degree a right-wing extremist subscribes to each of the tendencies, or which are more important than others in the rhetoric because different tendencies take precedence over others in response to national and local events, but most, if not all, of the tendencies exist in the groups' ideological packaging.

Sara Diamond further defines the "preoccupations of right-wing movements" as protecting free market or "libertarian" capitalism, promoting anticommunism, and preserving "traditional morality and supreme status for native-born white male Americans and for the nuclear family." [24] Followers of rightist ideology, according to Diamond, wish to maintain race, class, and gender hierarchies in this country and, specifically, ensure the ultimate supremacy of white, Protestant men over women and men of color.

I should point out here that this study deals with the *extreme* right. Diamond, George, and Wilcox have tended to use "right-wing" more broadly than I do. As Lisa McGirr notes, terms like "radical right" and "extreme" have been applied incorrectly to conservative movements since the 1960s. To do so implies that all conservatives are "extremists" and thus makes it easy to dismiss anyone who claims conservative political or social leanings if one does not share those beliefs. [25]

Conservatives, like liberals and the extreme wings of both ideological milieus, encompass people from all walks of life and backgrounds. Myriad movements exist in the broader context of "conservative and liberal" and extreme right or left. Therefore, I have chosen to use the terms "extreme right" or "extremist right" throughout this discussion in reference to the groups and individuals under analysis. Like McGirr, I have concluded that "extreme" is a word best left to "white supremacist, paramilitary, and fascist fringe groups like the Ku Klux Klan" whose members opt to work outside the democratic political process and who advocate violence to achieve their goals. [26] Some of the groups I examine, like the Republic of Texas, are not overtly racist. Nonetheless, they are antigovernment and at least one chapter has resorted to violence in response to outside stimuli. Consequently, I will use "extreme" in reference to them as well.

I have defined extreme rightist ideology as a belief system that incorporates organized and/or violent reaction (which may or may not involve vigilantism) to an individual or group of individuals whose race, ethnicity, or religious, social, or political beliefs and practices differ from the perceived status quo in the place and time where rightist agitation occurs. I have also included one group—a chapter of the Republic of Texas—in this definition because its members advocated an extreme antigovernment stance that resulted in actual physical violence. As McGirr has also noted, reactions include working outside the normal political democratic process to achieve specific goals. It is a reaction against something that is perceived as "different" and hence a threat to general safety and morality.

Often, that targeted individual or group of individuals is in a numerical minority or a position of lesser social and political power and the rightist reaction develops because of a perceived threat to "how things are" or perhaps as a response to historic beliefs, as in the case of anti-Catholicism and anti-Semitism. Rightist and extreme rightist ideology can operate on political levels, as in the form of political parties during the nineteenth century (and the so-called Populist Party of the 1980s and the current incarnation of neoconservatives in the Republican Party), or it can be expressed in secret societies that may or may not practice vigilantism.

It is also difficult to ascertain degrees of extremism within the boundaries of right-wing ideology. Some extreme rightist groups might support other extreme rightists in some situations but not in others. Some extreme rightist groups might believe that another extreme rightist group simply is not extreme enough or is a tool of the government. Still other extreme rightist groups splinter into separate factions that then mutate into either more or less extreme versions of the parent organization. I do not believe it is useful to develop a scale of "rightism" because, especially since the early 1990s, new groups have appeared and disappeared with remarkable speed on the American landscape that fills all corners of right-wing extremism. Indeed, many people have felt passionately about some social or political issue and espoused an opinion that others could construe as "extremist." But not everyone joins a group or encourages violence as a solution to national problems.

Therefore, in terms of my analysis and for ease of the reader's comprehension, I have chosen groups and individuals whose public rhetoric and literature clearly support white supremacy and/or violence against government officials, people of color, Jews, and gay men and lesbians. In addition, these groups and individuals clearly define themselves as locked in a struggle for control of America, and they choose to demonstrate their cause by joining or associating themselves with organized extreme right-wing groups or touting secessionist antigovernment rhetoric and stockpiling supplies for an impending "showdown" with the federal government and/or other murky antiwhite forces of the apocalypse.

These are groups and individuals who often live and work outside the mainstream and who always look over their shoulders for the long arm of the government they are certain will snatch them and herd them into secret concentration camps. Ruled by conspiracy theories, often paranoid, America's latest incarnation of the extreme right has tapped an old vein in this country's history.[27]

The most extreme rightists advocate injuring and killing government officials, call for a whites-only homeland within the United States (usually somewhere in the West—particularly the Northwest), and support the banishment or deaths of people of color and Jews. In my analysis, the most extreme rightists preach and support violence and perpetrate violent acts to further their cause. The less extreme do not overtly support violence but might subscribe to it as an abstract concept—especially in terms of "Armageddon" or "Apocalypse," in which thousands of people are going to die violently in events that are beyond the control of mere humans.

To justify their views, white supremacists rely on biblical interpretations, racist tracts by members of both early and more recent rightist groups and individuals, and Christian Identity. Further entangled in the rightist web—whether extreme or not—are notions about "Americanism" and what it means to be "American." As I will argue throughout, also intertwined in American nationalism and broader extreme rightist sentiment and organization are ideas about what it means to be an American man and how American nationalism is not only gendered, but also racialized. In this country, white men overwhelmingly populate the images of manhood and masculinity that convey ideas about American character. Broad rightist sentiment and organization has quite a bit to do with a reaction to "difference." But it also has a lot to do with maintaining and expressing Protestant white male authority throughout this country's history in its more extreme manifestations.

Past Tense: Extremism, Vigilantism, and Fraternalism

The best-known right-wing extremist group—indeed, the longest-running—is the Ku Klux Klan. The Klan, however, is not the first demonstration of right-wing sentiment nor are the ideas it has espoused since its first manifestation after the Civil War completely new. Perhaps the earliest documented rightist sentiment is anti-Catholicism, which emerged in Puritan America. Rampant in England before the first Pilgrims took leave of the Netherlands and the British Isles, anti-Catholicism sailed west with its hosts and took root in the burgeoning nationalism of a fledgling America threatened by rival Spanish and French imperial ambitions, both Catholic nations.[28]

Although not necessarily a "crime" to be Catholic in Puritan America, proscription did occur, primarily through legislative action. Most established colonies were not unwilling to restrict church freedoms; limited sanctuary existed for those who subscribed to a so-called secretive and conspiratorial religion. For Puritans in the new Zion of Massachusetts Bay, life in the proverbial garden enjoyed favorable contrasts with the Roman Catholic "cesspool" of Europe. These Puritans sought to build a city upon a hill and fill it with the redeemed who chose to throw off the chains of Old World sinfulness. Catholicism provided images of hell, and these first Puritan settlers despised the Anglican Church because to them, it mirrored the Church of Rome.[29]

By 1740 with the advent of the Great Awakening, Protestant fundamentalist fervor encouraged hatred of Rome and warned Americans of the deadly Catholic threat. Wars against France and Spain fanned rumors of a Catholic conspiracy and painted ominous pictures of Catholic forces amassing in Canada and Florida. During these years, nativism had firmly rooted itself in both religious and conventional wisdom.[30]

The Revolutionary War proved a unifier for "true" Americans and the real test of liberty was whether someone supported the new government or the crown, not whether he or she practiced Catholicism. George Washington went so far as to quash so-called Pope Day festivals in 1775 because he needed Catholic men in the revolutionary army. Catholic France also proved a useful ally in the field against the British. In fact, if not for France's aid, England might have won the war. Even though hostility flared in Pennsylvania and upstate New York in response to Catholics still loyal to the English crown, the provocation was more in terms of loyalism than Catholicism.[31]

Following the war, a greater spirit of tolerance infused the new republic. By 1790, President Washington told clerical and lay leaders of Maryland Catholicism that he expected America to become one of the foremost nations in advancing justice and freedom. He also called for American citizens to remember the patriotism of many Catholics during the fight against England.[32]

His words, unfortunately, did not remove the strain of rightism that leaned toward the extreme that had arrived from the Old World. Three strands of extreme right-leaning ideology found expression by the mid-nineteenth century: anti-Catholicism, anti-radicalism (expressed as a fear of foreign radicals), and finally, what historian John Higham calls "racial nativism." This is what Higham terms "the concept that the United States belongs in some special sense to the Anglo Saxon 'race,'" which offered an interpretation of the source of national greatness.[33] These ideas helped to form the foundations of modern extreme right organization and ideology, one of the loudest expressions exhibited in nineteenth-century "manifest destiny" and violent campaigns against Native Americans.[34]

Organizations dedicated to eradicating certain groups and beliefs from America developed in force during the nineteenth century. These included the anti-Masonic movement, perhaps the first example in the United States of a preservationist antielitist mass movement; it evolved into a political party—one of several new parties offering to cleanse and protect the land from what its members perceived as "evil influences." They wished to "preserve" American values (that they themselves dictated) and were suspicious of elite groups such as the Masons because of their secretive nature.

The anti-Masonic party was active in national politics until 1832, a reaction to "secret" societies and the mysterious disappearance of a stonemason, William Morgan, who was allegedly murdered by Masons. He had been a Mason himself but was in the process of writing an exposé of the group. The anti-Masonic movement first formed as committees in response to Morgan's disappearance. Members of the anti-Masonic party declared that not only was Freemasonry a terrible evil in the country, but so, too, was Catholicism, a similar "secret society."[35]

Another extreme right-leaning political party, the Native American Democratic Association, organized in 1835 after the anti-Masonic movement fizzled. The group argued about whether to focus on Catholics or immigrants as the evil threatening America and instead included both in its platform. They failed in their 1836 election bid, but several other groups formed in response to the rhetoric they espoused. The American Republican Party organized with the image of nativism as the tool to bring about reform on the political and social front. Founded in 1841 in New Orleans, the organization sported a network that stretched to New York by late 1843. Its platform was simple: office holding restricted to native-born white men, Bible-reading in public schools, an extended waiting period for naturalization, the abolishment of corruption from political offices, and the diminishment of foreign influences in the country. The party changed its name to Native American in 1845 but collapsed in 1847.[36]

The next major nativist political force in the mid-nineteenth century was the Know Nothing Party, called thus because when questioned about it, members would say they "knew nothing"; newspaperman Horace Greeley coined the term in 1853. The group had begun as a secret society of white men called the Order of the Star Spangled Banner, but, as soon as the "Know Nothing" name gained widespread use, the society evolved into a political party whose members agreed to attack those who threatened American political liberty and principles.

Eventually capitalizing on Whig support, Know Nothing appeal swept over the elections of 1854. Manufacturers marketed Know Nothing candy, tea, and toothpicks and some buses and stagecoaches sported the coveted name. The elections of 1856, however, brought the defeat of the Know Nothings because of divisions among anti- and proslavery factions within its ranks, a reflection of sectional differences that stretched far beyond the boundaries of the party.[37]

Nativism, racism, anti-Catholicism, and anti-Semitism (more popular among twentieth-century extreme rightists) are unfortunately as old as white settlement in this country. Organized groups such as the Ku Klux Klan had plenty of vitriolic rhetoric and ideology upon which to build their own foundations; it was simply a matter of men stepping forward to organize more groups.

Extreme right-wing groups in this country share not only certain ideological penchants, but also other critical characteristics. Until the early twentieth century, the primary organizers and members of right-wing extremist groups and networks have been white Protestant men. The Ku Klux Klan formed a women's auxiliary during its 1920s incarnation, and some white women are active in Klan, neo-Nazi, and constitutionalist groups today, but their numbers are much lower than those of their male counterparts. Often, they join because of their associative relationships with male members. Most often, they are wives or girlfriends of active right-wing extremist men, and, as we shall see, the right has very rigid ideas about how women are to conduct themselves in the fight against the global conspiracy that threatens the white race.[38]

The Ku Klux Klan and Vigilantism

The Ku Klux Klan (or KKK) first appeared in American history immediately after the Civil War. Formed in Pulaski, Tennessee, in 1865, it consisted of six well-educated but unemployed Confederate veterans. They chose the name based on the Greek word for circle: *kuklos*.[39] Its organizing principles rested on retaining and defending white supremacy from Northern interference and free African Americans. Beginning as a club of sorts for defeated Confederate soldiers, it quickly developed into a loosely knit, secret terrorist network in the Southern states.

By the late 1860s, the Klan had spread a reign of terror throughout Southern and former Confederate border states. Gangs of Klansmen threatened, tortured, and murdered countless people: black and white, women and men. The most common targets were black men and women and individuals involved in contesting or dismantling the foundations of white Southern supremacy. The Klan was particularly expert in using sexual violence and brutality. Klansmen routinely raped and sexually tortured women—especially black women—during household raids. They also tortured, lynched, and sexually mutilated black men and other opponents.[40]

In her study of the the 1920s women's KKK (WKKK), Blee notes that "gender and sexuality were compelling symbols in the two largest waves of the [KKK], those of the 1860s and the 1920s."[41] Each Klan called white Protestant men to protect white womanhood and white female purity. Both the 1860s and the 1920s Klan "dissolved a myriad of social, economic, and racial issues into powerful symbols of womanhood and sexual virtue."[42] Klansmen of the 1860s insisted that white women benefited from the Southern racial state, without which they would be raped and brutalized by black men, who were considered no better than primitive animals.

White women became highly visible symbols through which the Klan could rouse public fears that blacks' retaliation against their former white masters would be exacted upon white mothers, daughters, and wives. The Klan spread the belief that white men were powerless to aid white women who faced frightful sexual violations by black men.[43] Klan propaganda played on not only the fears of women, but also unspoken fears of men. To a Klansman, the abolition of slavery ended white men's sexual access to black women, and it also potentially ended white men's exclusive sexual access to white women.

Blee notes that the Klan's call to defend white women against rape by black men signified a relation of power not only between white men and women, but also between white men and black men. The Klan's emphasis on the threat of black men raping white women served as a warning to both black men and white women about interracial relationships, but underlying the obvious references to potential sexual violation was a deeper threat to white men's sexual privileges.[44] When mobs of Klansmen sexually tortured and emasculated black men, they were, in a sense, validating their claim that masculinity ("real manhood") remained white men's exclusive prerogative. Blee argued that "southern women, white and black, occupied a symbolic terrain on which white men defended their racial privileges." Symbols of white female vulnerability and white masculine potency, Blee notes, "took power equally from beliefs in masculine [power] and in white supremacy."[45]

The 1920s Klan continued to rely on images of white Klansmen protecting white women, but its propaganda also emphasized white men as heads of households and families. Nancy MacLean points out that "rule over one's women was mandated by another staple of the Klan's conception of masculinity: 'honor'; or, as it was sometimes called, 'chivalry.'" MacLean's research demonstrates that "honor" dictated a commitment to protect the virtue of American women. Historically, she states, "honor in fact rested on a man's ability to control the sexuality of his female relations. Their 'purity' was the complement of his 'honor'; hence the Klansmen's insistence on 'the chastity of woman.'"[46]

Expressions of Klan masculinity in the 1920s, MacLean continues, relied more on images of benevolent protectorship than vigilante violence, though the latter was not uncommon. She linked this shift in portrayals to the changing social and political contexts in which the Klan operated. Increasing urbanization and, notably, women's involvement in social and political activism generated a change in how Klansmen attempted to maintain the surroundings they preferred, which encouraged women to stay at home, out of the workforce and politics, and also to keep white men as the pinnacle of an American social and political hierarchy.

Ironically, many 1920s Klansmen were not completely antagonistic to women's suffrage or the idea of women working outside the home. They recognized that white Protestant women must work with their men to achieve shared political and social goals. Nonetheless, "recognition of women by Klansmen was always shot through with ambivalence.... However much Klansmen might try to cooperate with women who shared their social goals, female initiative set them on edge; the undertow of patriarchal prerogative impeded full solidarity."[47] This male ambivalence toward women's roles in social and political circles, as we shall see, remained with rightist groups throughout the twentieth century.

Marauding and violent gangs of nineteenth-century Klansmen conjure images of their contemporary western vigilante groups. Indeed, Klansmen operated as vigilantes in that they were citizens who banded together to combat a perceived threat to their social well-being. They justified their actions to themselves and to their supporters, but as Catherine McNicol Stock notes, "vigilantism in rural America was more often than not a brutal act of violence which, in its broadest manifestation, sought out men and women who threatened the safety and economic stability of their communities."[48]

Throughout American history, Stock argues, vigilantes did pursue criminals, but they also "brought to justice" people whose beliefs and behaviors did not match those of the vigilantes. In the colonial era, vigilantes targeted people whose poverty or perceived laziness threatened the productivity of more established families. In the early nineteenth century, vigilantes targeted such groups as Mormons, who challenged the emerging doctrine of liberal individualism. During the industrial era, Chinese and Mexican people were the victims of vigilante "justice" and miners and lumberjacks were targets of violence when they attempted to unionize.[49] More often than not, people of color, those of the working classes, or people perceived as "deviant" (e.g., Communist) have faced the wrath of vigilante mobs.[50]

The earliest recorded instance of an organized vigilante group occurred in eighteenth-century South Carolina. In 1767, several men banded together to stave off groups of armed bandits who were terrorizing and robbing settlers in the unregulated frontier conditions. The vigilantes, known in the backcountry as the Regulators, employed various strategies to stamp out banditry. Their methods included burning cabins of known gang members and whipping suspected outlaws and their family members. The Regulators often opened fire without warning and killed runaway slaves if it was too much trouble to return them. After their zealous law enforcement, when most of the actual criminals had been rounded up, killed, or had fled, the Regulators continued preying on people who lived on the margins of communities but had never committed a crime. These poorer folk endured Regulator wrath because the latter saw poverty as a result of immorality and a potential threat to the entire community.[51]

Eventually, a full-scale vigilante war developed because another group of citizens, tired of the Regulators, organized and called themselves Moderators. Fortunately, a battle of greater proportions was averted and the two groups called a truce in 1768.[52] Vigilantism as a response to frontier destabilization, however, had only just begun. Between 1767 and 1902, Richard Maxwell Brown notes, more than 326 identifiable vigilante organizations perpetrated at least 729 murders.[53]

In Western myth and also in actual western communities, Richard White points out that it was not uncommon for personal violence and crime to rise to levels that communities refused to tolerate and that appointed authorities could not control. In such instances, groups of citizens (usually male) would band together and "take the law into their own hands"; they claimed to operate outside the law in order to enforce the law itself.[54] According to White, between 1849 and 1902, at least 210 vigilante movements occurred in the American West. In all, they killed 527 people, usually by hanging. The most lethal of these movements occurred in eastern and northern Montana in 1884. It claimed thirty-five victims.[55]

Vigilantes often contended that the breakdown of constituted authority and the rising threat of criminals meant that an armed citizenry had to take control to preserve order. Certainly, some situations existed that justified such an account, but others straddled a far more ambiguous line.[56] Invoking the doctrine of self-preservation and asserting that they were simply observing the right of the people to assume sovereignty when the government proved incapable of doing so (a fundamental doctrine of American republicanism), vigilantes set about overriding legal officials. Ironically, they would imitate said officials when they captured criminals, conducted formal (though illegal) trials of the accused, and meted out justice at the end of a noose.[57] Some vigilante groups merely conducted raids and victimized their targets, without even the façade of a staged trial.

This was the sort of vigilantism in which Klansmen engaged, expressing their ideological leanings through white supremacist violence and self-righteous proclamations. It evolved from a small club into a network of chapters whose members participated in secret, elaborate rituals that required special terminology and costumes that served also to lure new recruits into the fold and impress onlookers. In these respects, the Klan operated as a fraternal order that men who desired to uphold white supremacy in the South could join.

Such male secret societies were common in the last third of the nineteenth century. In a total adult male population of roughly nineteen million in 1896, five-and-a-half million belonged to fraternal groups such as the Odd Fellows, the Freemasons, and the Knights of Pythias.[58] Indeed, the framework of fraternal organizations has informed American extreme right-wing groups since the Know Nothings. A fraternity allows men to feel "part of something," offers support and resources to its members, and encourages a culture of manhood and rituals that further solidify the group. Nothing new in American history, the idea of "fraternity" provides another ingredient in the current white supremacist movement.

Rites of Passage: Fraternalism

Membership in fraternal organizations brought tangible benefits. Businessmen could make contacts, establish credit sources, and gain access to a national network of lodges. Younger, less-established men could socialize with their employers and perhaps make valuable contacts. Often, fraternal life insurance, death benefits, and even lodge charity provided strong inducements for men to join at a time when governmental assistance for any of these benefits was nonexistent. In terms of urbanization and industrialization in the latter half of the nineteenth century, sociological benefits could outweigh even the economic. In an anonymous and perhaps frightening urban environment, fraternal organizations provided cohesive social networks for the men who participated in them.[59]

Mary Ann Clawson argues that fraternalism has been one of the most "widely available and persistently used forms of collective organization in European and American history from the Middle Ages onward."[60] Fraternal organizations, by use of their images of masculinity and craftsmanship, worked to *deny* the significance of class difference and to offer gender and race as appropriate categories for the organization of collective identity.[61] Still, orders existed (and continue to exist) that cater to a specific economic class. Clawson notes that some orders—especially non-Masonic—contained more working-class men than others.[62]

Intrinsic to each lodge or organization were elaborate and involved rituals in which members were expected to participate. Often long and complex, nearly all fraternal rituals required at least an hour to perform, not including the successions of initiatory degrees, which required separate rituals in which only specified members participated.[63] The initiation rituals bound the entrant not only to the members of a local lodge, but also to a symbolic union within the particular order.[64]

Within the rituals and levels of membership of the lodge, the men involved created a highly stratified and hierarchical society in which they willingly participated. Perhaps the greater significance of these orders lies in the fact that millions of men belonged to them. I would argue further that a majority of these organizations limited themselves to white men. Prior to the late nineteenth century, this makes sense, in light of the fact that African American men were enslaved, Asian men were either legally excluded from the country or confined to the western part of the country, and Hispanic men tended to have their own groups. After the Civil War, the imposition of Jim Crow laws further alienated white men from African American men, ensuring that fraternal organizations tended to be race-exclusive. Regarding the rituals enacted in an organization, whether they took place within the confines of a Masonic lodge or around a burning cross, white male participants enacted them with religious fervor.[65]

Fraternal orders also attempted to create a domestic sanctuary outside the home. They were the motherless, wifeless, womanless family in which late-nineteenth-century Victorian-era men could express themselves, ironically, in emotional and spiritual ways with other men without garnering labels such as "effeminate."[66] The orders served perhaps as an alternative church for many men, who wished to escape the confines of evangelical Christianity in which many Protestant women were involved during the nineteenth century.

Evangelicals fought the influence of secret male societies almost since their inception during the early nineteenth century; indeed, the Freemason movement nearly collapsed during the 1820s and 1830s because of unorganized campaigns among evangelical women, who participated in the anti-Masonic movement during those years. Women spoke out against Freemasonry in church meetings and acted in concert to publish anti-Masonic resolutions. Many of these women argued that secret societies such as the Freemasons rendered men impious and led them down a path away from the true word of God, especially since so many of the orders met in pubs and other such places of vice.[67]

The fraternal movement that developed in the mid-nineteenth century, however, had purged itself of alcohol and incorporated rituals that imitated somber religiosity. The orders offered religious guidance and a means for personal transformation, which posed a greater challenge to women who opposed male secret societies on the basis of their affront to Christianity. These reformed orders encroached upon women's role as Christian nurturer. Fraternal lodges, after all, excluded women. Members devised secrets and rituals and threatened each other with punishments if they revealed anything to their wives. Through their rituals, they reclaimed religious authority that had formerly resided in Biblical patriarchs.[68]

During the nineteenth century, formal religion attracted droves of women and quickly became an area of female prerogative. This situation, in which men did not partake as readily in religion and often attended church as reluctant accompaniments of the women in their lives, afforded women unusual power— especially within their own families.[69] By the late nineteenth century, therefore, middle-class men were not participating in religion and were, as one scholar argues, caught in a rising tide of male insecurity triggered by bureaucratization of white-collar professions and fathers' increasing absences from their homes. Urban middle-class culture allowed fewer and fewer opportunities for masculine self-determination and patriarchal control, signaling a reorientation of the meaning of masculinity. The alleged closing of the western frontier, the rise of pacifism, and declining opportunities for the "self-made man" in urban business worlds made the quest for manhood difficult.[70]

Consequently, it seems no mystery why men sought some sort of stability in their pursuit of manhood within the protective confines of fraternal societies. Secrecy remained the best defense against opposition from women and organizations like the National Christian Association (NCA), but fraternal leaders developed new ways to allay oppositional fears. Editors of fraternal monthlies began to address female audiences by including "Ladies' Departments" that featured fashion accounts and recipes in addition to articles that explained how organizations such as the Freemasons accorded with the sentiments of evangelical women. In addition, leaders began to invite wives to attend lectures and banquets (over the strenuous objections of many members) and, most important, societies embarked upon a proposal to introduce women to lodges through the creation of women's auxiliaries.[71]

Virtually no man wanted women to participate directly in the exclusive domain of male lodges or rituals. However, many did see that extending an olive branch of sorts to women might alleviate their suspicions and leave men free to continue participating in their organizations. A leading Odd Fellow, Schuyler Colfax, broached the subject of instituting a Degree of Rebekah—a women's degree—to lessen the prejudice women felt against the Order. He also wrote the ritual for the Degree, which induced women into a defense of the Order. Furthermore, he claimed that few women had actually joined the anti-Masonic movement and instead many had actually supported the efforts of the lodges to exist.[72]

By the 1860s and 1870s, most orders actually followed the lead of the Odd Fellows in devising some form of auxiliary group or ladies' degrees with the exception of the Masonic lodges, which did not officially recognize the Order of the Eastern Star (a women's auxiliary implemented in 1869), but individual Masons sponsored and supported the organization's activities. Indeed, many Masons were appalled by the deceit the Eastern Star's male supporters engendered in the rituals. Conferring such degrees on women, they argued, was calculated to mislead women. Such charges are ultimately true; the differences between women's degrees and the rituals of the male orders were vast, unbeknownst to female initiates at the time.[73] Furthermore, a woman's status in the auxiliaries depended on her husband or father. Female membership in the Degree of Rebekah or the Order of the Eastern Star was limited to the wives and daughters of Scarlet Degree Odd Fellows or Master Masons and if the male relation were expelled from the order for any reason, the woman had to leave the auxiliary, and if a daughter of a member married a nonmember, she had to leave the group.[74]

In addition, all orders banned women from men's initiation ceremonies. The original injunctions on secrecy had been designed explicitly to prevent women from learning about male rituals. The Noble Grand or Worshipful Master of the men's lodge, however, presided over meetings and initiations of the Degree of Rebekah (Daughters of Rebekah) and the Order of the Eastern Star, and men were required to attend the initiations of their female relations. Female officials of the Order of the Eastern Star were given no explanation for this practice when they inquired.[75]

Ironically, fraternal orders managed to reclaim, to some extent, traditional gender roles for middle-class Protestants. Through their revamped organization away from taverns and drunken revelries, they instead promoted moral development. Through death benefits and insurance provisions, they guaranteed financial security for families, a role that men had traditionally fulfilled. And through flattery—especially as depicted in fraternal novels that appeared as serials in monthly magazines—orders assuaged women's fears about secret societies.

The novels' plots often revolved around a disruption of a family and described the calamities that befell its members in the world of men without the guidance of a mother's hand. Through feminine virtue, women protected the home from masculine aggression and materialism, but, fraternal writers warned, women wandering too far from their rightful domestic sphere faced terrible troubles and the loss of their intrinsic womanly assets. The traits that made the heroines of fraternal novels so appealing included beauty, passivity, and naiveté about the world of men. Endangered by unredeemed men, these true women needed the assistance and protection of male lodges and, by extension, their male participants.[76]

Although many lodges implemented women's auxiliaries, women did not participate in any aspect of male ceremonies, whereas men did participate and preside over women's ceremonies. The women's degrees also affirmed the virtues of "true womanhood" and warned women away from encroaching on traditional male pursuits. Male lodge members designed and wrote the ceremonies for women's degrees, so the rituals lacked the dramatic flair of the men's rituals and instead relied on recitations of biblical parables. Women initiates simply affirmed their commitment to these ideals. The women's degrees lacked the dangerous journeys, heroic encounters, and stark representations of death so prevalent in men's rituals.[77]

Despite the fact that deception and strict gender roles enabled the creation of women's auxiliaries, the groups became increasingly popular by the 1890s— approximately 500,000 women had joined them.[78] Certainly, such organizations afforded women the ability to form female networks that stretched beyond the homefront, but they nevertheless remained under the control of their male associates. Women were excluded from the inner machinations of male lodges, but men were expected to attend and preside over women's ceremonies and women's membership hinged not on each other, but on male associations. In the latter half of the nineteenth century, therefore, fraternal societies managed to appropriate middle-class rhetoric of female domesticity and reform in order to reassert ultimate male dominance over both public and private affairs.

When the Ku Klux Klan first formed in 1867, the small group of men did not bill itself as a Protestants-only group. Members had to be white men, however, and they had to profess to uphold the doctrine of white supremacy. This earliest incarnation of the Klan incorporated aspects of both vigilantism (operating outside the law) and fraternalism, in which secret rituals and ceremonies worked not only to bond men to each other and to the cause itself, but also to terrorize the group's targeted enemies. Cross-burnings and night raids in white robes and hoods lent a frightening air of mystery and deadly danger to the Klan, on which it capitalized in its campaigns.

Although the Klan would eventually incorporate rabid anti-Catholicism into its ranks (especially in the twentieth-century incarnation), the nineteenth-century group created a culture with costumes and secret rituals that mimicked the symbolism and ritual of the male hierarchy within the Catholic Church. The Klan barred white women from membership, reflecting larger Southern politics, and the abuse and exclusion of African Americans reinforced an ethos of racial power and invulnerability among Klansmen while the exclusion of white women celebrated and solidified the masculinity of racial politics.[79]

The idea of "white womanhood," however, served as a critical rallying point for the post–Civil War Klan and its violent campaigns. White women benefited from the Southern racial state, Klansmen insisted, because it protected their "virtue" from the lower, more primitive men of color who could not control their animal lusts in the presence of white women. Throughout the writings of the first Klan, the theme of imperiled white womanhood provided a continuous rhetoric of gender roles and true manhood, which was white. Without the Klan, white men were powerless to assist white women who faced potential rape at the hands of former slaves.[80]

This feared assault on white women threatened white men's sexual prerogatives (through competition with African American men for white women) and symbolized the perceived Northern exploitation of the South during the era of Reconstruction. David Chalmers notes that white women stood at the core of Southern white male chivalry and sense of property. Inaccessible to African American men, white women presented the ultimate line of difference between white and black men.[81]

Gender roles play a pivotal role in not only the Klan since the nineteenth century, but also the extremist right in general. Expectations about what men and women should do abound in right-wing rhetoric and continue to play an important role in how men operate within the groups and in their reasons for joining right-wing groups. The Klan's first appearance imitated western vigilante bands in the nineteenth century as well as the rituals and white male exclusivity of many contemporary fraternal societies. After the turn of the century and with the Klan's second major appearance in the United States, the group attempted to appeal to a wider white audience by implementing a women's auxiliary and encouraging a more "family-oriented" atmosphere through picnics and Sunday school sessions.[82]

Klan Resurgence: Twentieth Century

Following World War I, America entered a period of social and economic flux. Urban migration and the expansion of business opened markets for new products. Madison Avenue touted modern conveniences available to most anyone, as options such as credit developed in the 1920s. Mass production allowed many Americans to purchase things like automobiles, which in turn expanded markets for highways and other automobile-oriented facilities such as hotels and motels. The service economy entered high gear during the 1920s. Women finally won the right to vote, and suddenly generations of youth discovered life away from nuclear families and farms as a shifting economy opened urban service and factory jobs.

Times like these, which involve rapid social and economic change, are ripe for right-wing movements and groups because rightist ideology rests on the premise that change is "bad" and to cure social ills, it is best to return to "traditional" values—that is, a social hierarchy that places white men at the apex. Typically spouting ideology of nostalgia and warnings of a dire future because of the social changes that come with rapid economic expansion, right-wing organizations attempt to reassert white hegemony by hearkening back to what their members see as the "good old days."[83]

The Klan gained prominence again in the wake of World War I, riding a wave of revisionist sympathy for the Confederacy and a profound sense of discontent and anxiety among many American residents. The Klan in the 1920s was not primarily a Southern terrorist organization. It branched out and preached a mutifaceted program based on "100 percent Americanism" (native-born white Protestant Americans) and militant Protestantism, and it enlisted recruits in every section of the country. Histories of the Klan argue back and forth over the past seventy years about the type of members the group attracted and whether it was predominantly a rural or urban phenomenon.[84]

The Klan became a movement that transcended rural, and often class, boundaries in pursuit of local and national issues. In other words, Klansmen found commonalities across these lines in pursuit of 100 percent Americanism.[85] Because of differences in local issues, the Klan expanded its bashing repertoire to include Catholics (because of their perceived loyalty to the pope rather than the United States), "subversives" such as communists (in the wake of the Bolshevik Revolution of 1917 and the Red Scare in 1919), and "intellectuals" (because of their association with movements such as communism and socialism) in addition to obvious targets like people of color.[86]

This twentieth-century incarnation of the Klan would have repercussions throughout the century. No longer was the Klan an isolated Southern phenomenon organized in response to a specific event (Reconstruction). Rather, as its 1920s development demonstrates, it tapped into deeper white Protestant concerns that had continued to simmer within the melting pot of American history—remnants of Puritan millennialism and belief in Manifest Destiny.

With the end of the war, the United States had entered the messy realm of world politics. The Great War was, in a sense, this country's coming of age. Improvements in industries and transportation—planes, trains, and automobiles—linked Americans internally and to the rest of the globe. City populations swelled with natives and immigrants alike, seeking part of the American dream. Corporations expanded, consumers consumed, science and medicine increased research, and a frenetic sense of discovery jockeyed for expression with a nostalgic longing for a mythic, simpler past.[87]

Arnold Rice argues that the decade 1920–1930 suffered from the effects of World War I in profound ways. First, during the war, antialien and, by extension, anticommunist campaigns created an atmosphere of hostility and tension between Americans who considered themselves "native born" versus new immigrants. Second, Rice claims that racial antipathies increased because of the migration of African Americans to northern cities in search of better-paying war industry jobs. In addition, African American men who served as soldiers in the armed forces brought their experiences abroad back to the States—including ideas about liberation. Consequently, groups like the Klan capitalized on the feelings some whites had about so-called "uppity Negroes." And third, the old American evangelicalism seemed to disappear in the wake of modernism and the expansion of consumer markets.[88]

Regardless of how postwar turbulence and the rise of a culture of prosperity interacted to spawn the first twentieth-century Klan, historians generally agree that this manifestation found great support among both disaffected rural and prosperous urban Anglo Protestants.[89] Although overall Klan ideology and goals may have been generally the same, Klan members themselves came from an array of social and educational backgrounds and were undoubtedly drawn to the organization for a variety of reasons. Like many local political organizations, Klan chapters expressed regional differences and concerned themselves with localized, as well as national, issues.[90]

Virulently anti-Catholic, anti-Semitic, and anti-immigrant as well as anti–African American, the 1920s Klan couched its policies toward its perceived enemies in a rhetoric that extolled Christianity, the Constitution, and the duties and responsibilities of the white race to uphold both. The Klan made its reappearance in 1915 under the direction of William Simmons, an Alabama-born Methodist pastor enamored with fraternal organizations (he was a member of several, including the Masons), which no doubt played into his interest in the Klan. Not much is known about Simmons, who was tight-lipped about his past. He had served in the Spanish-American War, but had not advanced to the rank of "Colonel," which is what his Southern friends called him. Simmons himself was tall and lanky, capable of "fire-breathing" preaching in a deep voice, which no doubt lent itself to bringing supporters into his fold.[91] He himself was apparently

"Colonel" William J. Simmons, Grand Wizard of the second incarnation of the
Ku Klux Klan, which he re-formed in 1915. Here Simmons is attending a House
committee investigation of the Klan probably in October 1921. Courtesy of the
Library of Congress, LC-USZ62-104018.

the son of a man who had been an officer in the Confederacy, so he always
dreamed of re-forming the Klan.[92]

Two events occurred in 1915 that fed the fire to reorganize a group like the
Klan. D. W. Griffith released his film, *Birth of a Nation,* which garnered national
attention and glorified the Confederacy during the Civil War (and painted African Americans as monsters) and Leo Frank, a Jewish pencil factory manager,
was convicted in Atlanta after he was accused of raping and murdering a thir-
teen-year-old white girl. Evidence pointed to a janitor at the factory, but such
did not save Frank from a death sentence. After the conviction, more evidence
came to light further exonerating Frank. The judge commuted Frank's sentence
to life in prison, but a lynch mob intervened and carried out the death sentence.

Because of intense media coverage, Frank's case garnered widespread attention. When Simmons restarted the Klan on Thanksgiving of that year, he did so in
an atmosphere that seemed supportive of such activities, given the sensationalism
surrounding Griffith's film and Frank's death. At Stone Mountain, Georgia,

Simmons and sixteen hooded men re-formed the Klan. It was at this meeting that cross-burning was officially introduced into the Klan's repertoire. Simmons formally declared himself "Grand Wizard" of the "Knights of the Ku Klux Klan," and he apparently got no argument. Under his leadership, which was absolute, Simmons directed the Klan until the early 1920s.[93]

The phenomenal success of the 1920s Klan had to do with its differences from its earlier predecessors and the context in which it formed. It drew its membership from small business owners, professionals, merchants, skilled laborers, and land-owning farmers. In other words, it went after the middle class, which joined in large numbers (between 3 and 6 million) in such states as Indiana, Kansas, Oklahoma, Colorado, and Oregon. Simmons himself enjoyed only limited success in his first five years, and in 1920 he hired professional organizers. Edward Y. Clarke and Elizabeth Tyler launched a recruitment effort that belied anything Simmons had been able to conduct. Clarke and Tyler deliberately targeted extant fraternal organizations like the Masons for recruits. They were quite successful. In addition, free publicity as a result of Congressional hearings and sensational articles published by the New York World made many Americans aware of the group and its goals.[94] By the early 1920s, Klan ranks could boast more than a million members.[95] Clarke, a former journalist and fraternity organizer, had been promoting a festival in Atlanta when he met Tyler, who was handling publicity for the "Better Babies" hygiene movement. The two formed a business—the Southern Publicity Association—and their clients included the Anti-Saloon League, the Red Cross, and the Salvation Army. In June of 1920, Simmons met with them in hopes of giving his group the boost it needed.[96]

Simmons signed a contract with Clarke and Tyler that granted the publicists a phenomenal eight dollars of every ten-dollar initiation fee. Clarke billed himself as imperial kleagle, head of the Propagation Department, and within a few years, the two publicists had met with incredible success. They felt that Simmons was only reaching out to a small market with his appeals for men to join a mystical society that dedicated itself to protecting Southern "order," patriotism, and racial superiority. Instead, Clarke and Tyler turned the Klan into a traditional nativist crusade that assailed all nonwhites and Catholics and the links between "foreigners" and the Catholic Church. With this new advertising campaign and an organized approach to recruitment that involved dividing the country into target areas, Clarke and Tyler brought in more than a million men within the first three years of the 1920s.[97]

The Klan's incredibly rapid growth resulted from the sale, literally, of mystical fraternalism, as well as the traditional attraction of nativism. Clarke, Tyler, and

Simmons also developed elaborate costumes (robes and hoods, among other paraphernalia) that created a market for the manufacture of such items. In addition, they created a publishing company to print Klan magazines and newspapers. Overall, however, the romance of a secret society proved a huge draw for men just as it had in the nineteenth century; Clarke and Tyler's managerial expertise merely capitalized on extant sentiments in a postwar, consumer-driven society.[98]

In 1922, a coup of sorts occurred in Klan ranks. Dissatisfied with the direction the Klan was taking, Texas dentist Hiram W. Evans wrested control from Simmons, who had been ill for some time. Evans named himself new Imperial Wizard and began foisting the Klan onto the national scene, involving itself in local and national politics. Evans went after organized labor (which he viewed as terribly leftist) as well as big business, which he viewed as "anti-worker." He also reached out to women, but with a caveat. Women should participate in the Klan to "restore" traditional values to America, but they should not participate in politics or the workforce.[99]

Evans also touted what he passed as "American" values, but he blatantly stated that white supremacy was the answer to the country's ills. "In the future as in the past—the hope and destiny of the nation rests in white supremacy." To Evans, white supremacy would "preserve the doctrines of popular liberty which lie at the foundation of our government, these ideals which are enshrined in the republic and our free institutions."[100]

Often declaring themselves in favor of stringent law enforcement—particularly pertinent in this age of Prohibition-generated crime—the Klan appealed to white Protestant men in search of answers to the chaos they saw around them every day. The Grand Dragon of Colorado's Klan, for example, claimed that the Klan had "a responsibility and an obligation hitherto without precedent in the history of our country," indeed, "an obligation written with an unseen hand, deep in the heart of every individual klansman [sic]." Calling upon the American patriotic spirit, the Grand Dragon invoked it by stating that a Klansman should be devoted to "his God, his country, his home, and his fellow men."[101]

Mantled in these traditional symbols of Protestantism, the 1920s Klan posed as bearers and saviors of what Robert Goldberg dubs "old time religion."[102] The Klan promised to unite Protestants in a moral crusade that would combat the purported evils of evolution and restore faith in God, the Bible, and Christian fundamentals. Large donations to Protestant churches and heavy recruitment of ministers maintained the veneer of religiosity that accompanied the Klan during the 1920s while cries for law and order appealed to more secular-oriented individuals. Klansmen also vigorously attacked the "moral laxity" sweeping the

Aerial view of a Ku Klux Klan parade down Pennsylvania Avenue NW in Washington, D.C., 13 September 1926. The Klan enjoyed remarkable success during its second incarnation, roughly 1915–1928. By the time of the Great Depression, Klan influence would wane as a result of several internal scandals and changing economic situations. Courtesy of the Library of Congress, LC-USZ62-59666.

country: new styles of clothing, sexually suggestive dances, and tantalizing motion pictures were sapping America's strength and encouraging a general social and moral decay. Many Klansmen vowed to work diligently at not only banishing "loose women," roadhouses, and heavy petting joyriders, but also at restoring decorum and decency in their communities.[103]

By 1925, the Klan boasted more than a million members nationwide, with strongholds in Indiana, Oregon, Texas, and Colorado. The Klan also held enormous influence over local governments in those states as well as others, including Alabama, Mississippi, and Georgia. Ultimately, the 1920s Klan may have been a victim of its own success. As it expanded nationwide, it became more difficult for Evans to maintain control over individual chapters and chapter alliances in other states. Infighting between Evans and his underlings helped fracture the Klan, and a series of scandals in the organization brought it extremely bad press.

The worst of those may have been the rape and subsequent death of a woman named Marge Oberholtzer. Oberholtzer worked in an Indiana program to combat illiteracy in the 1920s. In 1925, she was kidnapped and repeatedly raped and brutalized by Indiana Klan Grand Dragon David C. Stephenson, who was also the money behind such political figures as Indiana's governor, Ed Jackson. Oberholtzer survived the attack but attempted to kill herself afterward while still Stephenson's hostage. He foiled her first attempts, but her third (mercuric chloride poisoning) left her vomiting blood, so Stephenson had some of his supporters drive her to Indianapolis, ostensibly for medical treatment. On her deathbed, she fingered Stephenson as the attacker. A doctor who examined her noted that the wounds the Klansman had inflicted on her made it appear as if she had been attacked by a "pack of wolves." [104]

Stephenson was arrested and convicted of second-degree murder. He was sentenced to life in prison but was granted clemency in 1950. Arrested again for a parole violation, he was freed in 1956 and moved to Tennessee, where he died in 1966. This incident spelled the end of the Klan in Indiana during the 1920s, and the ripple effect created such bad press that other Klan chapters began to fold. Moreover, by the late 1920s and early 1930s, Americans' concerns had shifted to the everyday battle for economic survival rather than Klan activities.[105]

The Klan lost members in droves during the Great Depression. Nonetheless, the advent of the Civil Rights era during the late 1940s and into the 1950s would see its reformation and reestablishment in a renewed push for white supremacy.

Just prior to World War II, three strains of American right-wing extremism took root. From these roots sprouted the many branches of the profligate extreme right so apparent since the 1980s.

Beyond the Klan

In 1933, an embryonic neo-Nazi group modeled after Hitler's Brown Shirts formed under the auspices of William Dudley Pelley. He called his group the Silver Legion, though they are better known as the Silver Shirts. Pelley had been a writer and journalist for magazines during the late 1910s and early 1920s. He had worked for the Associated Press in Russia during the 1917 Revolution, and his experiences in that country colored his views about Soviet peoples to the extent that he was alarmed at the possibility of the rise of a workers' state, which he was certain would lead to American bolshevism.[106]

Pelley turned to writing romantic novels and movie scripts, but in 1927 he retreated to the California mountains and apparently underwent a mystical religious rebirth in which he claimed to have made contact with the occult and heard voices from other worlds. He also began leaning toward apocalypticism, writing about a "time of troubles" that would lead to the redemption of the human race. Pelley claimed that Christ would return during his lifetime, and he took to reporting various sightings. By 1931 he was claiming that the worst reincarnated demon souls lived in Jewish bodies, through which they were wreaking chaos on the nation. These demons also controlled President Herbert Hoover—the same demons who had engineered the Great Depression.[107]

Two years later, Pelley founded his Silver Legion, which openly supported Hitler, cooperated with the pro-Nazi German-American Bund, and launched a vicious anti-Semitic campaign. Members had to be at least eighteen and were required to wear a specified uniform (consisting of a service hat, blue corduroy trousers, leggings, a tie, and a silver shirt upon which a letter "L" was stitched on the left breast). They were also expected to participate in elaborate hierarchies.[108]

In 1940, Pelley claimed to have 25,000 members, but membership had actually declined before that. Most of the Legion's activities centered in a few urban areas: Minneapolis, San Diego, Los Angeles, Seattle, Chicago, and the industrial areas outside Cleveland. In 1942, President Roosevelt charged Pelley and others with violating the Espionage Act because they had distributed information aimed at subversion of the United States armed forces. The prosecution inflated Pelley's influence, though his defense was weak. Sentenced to fifteen years in prison, Pelley ended up a martyr for the right as a result of the attention he had received at his trial.[109]

A second strand of right-wing extremism unraveled on the Kansas plains. Gerald B. Winrod, a Protestant fundamentalist minister, preached to a large and militant following across the Midwest. Through the pages of the *Defender* (his popular publication), he propounded the virtues of Nazism and fascism and the patriotic groundwork of both, along with anti-Semitic myths. Unlike Pelley, Winrod claimed that his anti-Semitism was rooted in Biblical prophecy. Winrod had been preaching since the age of twelve, following his mother's miraculous recovery from terminal cancer. The great masses of Jews, he claimed, were unaware of the sordid Jewish plot to rule the world; nevertheless, the Jewish elite, he argued, was responsible for the trial and execution of Jesus as well as the persecution of early Christians under the Roman Empire. The early Jewish elders composed the *Talmud*, according to Winrod, which was the precursor to the *Protocols of the Learned Elders of Zion,* the text that "proves" an international Jewish conspiracy.[110]

Winrod placed the myth of the international Jewish conspiracy at the center of a revived Protestant fundamentalism that embraced the Ku Klux Klan. Winrod preached fundamentalism and combined it with politics to run as a Republican for the Kansas State Senate in 1938. He finished third, with strong support from Mennonites and former Klan counties. In 1942, he met a fate similar to Pelley's. The Roosevelt administration charged Winrod with sedition in its attempt to undo the nativist right.[111]

The third strand of modern rightist extremism developed with Gerald L. K. Smith, who is the most important link between the fascism of the 1930s and the white resistance groups that sprang up during the 1970s. Smith's roots were in Wisconsin, where he began a career as a fundamentalist minister at age eighteen. In 1933, he was among the first to join Pelley's Silver Shirts. He eventually ended up in Shreveport, Louisiana, preaching at the First Christian Church. Ideologically, themes in his preaching shifted from storm-trooping to rural radicalism; he eventually left the church to work for Huey Long, the flamboyant and larger-than-life governor of Louisiana elected to the U.S. Senate in 1930. Smith served Long as an organizer for the "Share Our Wealth" campaign and earned a reputation as a rabble-rouser and a fiery speaker.[112]

After Long's assassination in 1935, Smith made an unsuccessful bid for power in Louisiana. He then attempted to develop a national third party with Francis Townsend, a physician who wanted to provide a pension plan for the elderly, and Father Charles Coughlin, the nationally known radio personality who became a virulent anti-Semite. The collaboration bore fruit with the Union Party, which ran William Lemke unsuccessfully against Franklin Delano Roosevelt in 1936.[113]

Following Lemke's defeat, the Union Party crumbled beneath the egos of Smith and Coughlin. Smith moved to New York after the election and created the Committee of One Million, dedicated to combating the evils of the New Deal and communism. Unsuccessful in New York, Smith moved to Detroit, where he met Henry Ford, though the full extent of the pair's relationship remains historically unclear. Nevertheless, Ford fueled Smith's belief in a worldwide Jewish conspiracy by supplying him with copies of the *Dearborn Independent*'s series on the International Jew.[114]

In the late 1930s, Smith sought the Republican nomination for the United States Senate in Michigan but was soundly defeated. During World War II, he was a strong isolationist and staunchly pro-German; he continually denounced Roosevelt and the New Deal and attempted to involve himself in every presidential campaign he could after the war. A friend of Wesley Swift, Smith came to embrace Christian Identity by World War II, further solidifying his anti-Semitic views and conspiracy-ridden beliefs. Smith lived until the late 1970s, certain that an international Jewish conspiracy would bring about the eventual downfall of the United States and possibly the world.[115]

Throughout his life, Smith insinuated himself into mainstream politics at the highest levels. Ever the orator, Smith also turned his hand to writing, churning out forerunners of today's direct-mail fundraising letters and espousing nativism, elements of populism, and nationalism. He remained politically active most of his life. In the end, Smith and his supporters provide a bridge from past to present. From Smith's anti-Semitic preachings and Christian Identity leanings, modern white revolutionaries such as the new Klan (since ca. 1970), Aryan Nations, and the Posse Comitatus have emerged and coalesced into a widespread grassroots social and political movement that has tapped into such American traditions as nativism, xenophobia, and racism. None of this is new. What *is* new is the proliferation of such groups since the late 1980s.

In Chapter 2, I will set the stage for the links between white supremacist doctrines and older traditions of American constructions of nation and nationality. I will historically contextualize Manifest Destiny and how the doctrine of American expansionism echoes through the extremist right.

In Chapter 3, I will discuss the Hayden Lake, Idaho–based Aryan Nations since its origins in 1973 and Robert "Bob" Mathews' terrorist spin-off, The Order. I will examine how Aryan Nations leader Richard Girnt Butler came to establish the compound (once known worldwide for its summer "Aryan World

Congresses"), how its members performed "masculinity" as "Aryan warriors," and how earlier ideas about American westward expansion and the "frontier" play into modern expressions of white supremacist ideology.

With regard to The Order, I will provide a brief biography of Mathews, how he ended up in Washington state, and how he attempted to develop a so-called White American Bastion, or white homeland, in the Pacific Northwest. Tantamount to this discussion is the rise of "survivalist" culture since the Vietnam War and how some white men have been trying to fight and win Vietnam in other arenas—e.g., through the pages of novels, through movies like *Rambo* (1983) and magazines like *Soldier of Fortune,* by participating in paint ball "wars," and, in some cases, by joining white supremacist groups.

In Chapter 4, I will set the stage for the Posse Comitatus and provide a background to rural protest movements and Populism in the American West and Midwest. I will also sketch the historical and social circumstances that surrounded the farm crisis of the 1980s, which spurred the growth of some extreme right groups. I will address the history of the American agrarian myth and its role in rural America before and after the farm crisis. I will trace the development of the Posse Comitatus with specific emphasis on the Midwest and West. The Posse Comitatus, as a rurally based movement, used the farm crisis as a means to recruit farmers in desperate straits into its ranks across the West and Midwest. Not only did the Posse propagandize the importance of farmers to the moral and social fabric of America (thus falling back onto images of the Jeffersonian yeoman farmer bringing settlement to the wilderness), it also relied on vigilantism (or the threat of it) in an attempt to empower its members in its war against the federal government. As an example of one man's war against ZOG, I will discuss Gordon Kahl, a farmer and Posse member who died in a 1983 shootout with federal law enforcement officials.

In Chapter 5, I will trace the development of the 1990s "Patriot" and accompanying militia movement as a response to the 1992 standoff on Idaho's Ruby Ridge between Randy Weaver and the FBI and Bureau of Alcohol, Tobacco, and Firearms (ATF). The movement also grew as a result of the deaths that occurred when David Koresh's Branch Davidian compound in Waco, Texas, burned to the ground in 1993 during a standoff with FBI and ATF officials. I will examine how "Patriot" groups preach vigilantism and rely on a culture of masculinity that emphasizes the paramilitary warrior to recruit members and build cohesive fighting units.

The two examples I will examine involve the 1996 and 1997 standoffs that involved the Montana Freemen and the Republic of Texas, respectively. I will discuss how the government changed its tactics to deal with right-wing extremists and what effects that had on the local communities and extreme rightists as a whole.

Ultimately, I hope to convey that the white supremacist movement is something that is not as much on the "fringe" as we would like to believe. Its ideology has evolved from earlier ideas about American nationalism, "character," and a sense of "mission" that defined westward expansion during the nineteenth century. These ideas about what it means to be an American and especially an American man continue to resonate in current political debates about "family" and "traditional values."

America's loss in Vietnam also played a crucial role in the formation of white supremacist groups since 1970. During the late 1970s and early 1980s, a culture of survivalism developed as a means—especially for men—to fight battles (paint ball) or prepare for them (stockpiling, paramilitary militia training). This survivalist culture, as James Gibson notes, seems to be a response to America's loss in Vietnam and a way for men to prove somehow that they are men by going to battle. Since the military fell into so much disfavor after Vietnam, some American men have sought to create other battles and other training grounds in order to enact a rite of passage that perhaps their fathers and grandfathers had—military service and/or going to war.[116]

Other American men seek their battles—their "frontiers" to conquer—within the ranks of white supremacist groups. Here, they can be the cowboys and the warriors that serve as the archetypes of American culture and character. They can learn how to protect their heritage, their race, and their women. Here, in essence, they can learn how to be men.

CHAPTER 2

Missions, Millennia, and Manifest Destiny

In 1996, Richard White asked what we should make of the current "weirdness in the West." He referred to the Unabomber, the Freemen, militias in Arizona, Montana, and Washington, the bombing in Oklahoma City, the county independence movement, Aryan Nations, and the more extreme fringes of Wise Use.[1]

What, indeed, are we to make of all this extremist activity? White made a crucial point in his assertion that the federal government, a demon to all extreme right groups, is particularly hated and visible in the West. Western states are full of national forests, national parks, Indian reservations (held in trust by the federal government), military bases, and areas managed by the Bureau of Land Management.[2] After 1960, White argued, the West (as a region) began "to show a greater preference than the North or the South for more individualist solutions to economic and social problems." The burgeoning conservative West, White continued, thus sees its ancestry not in the history of federal development in the region, which is a more accurate perspective, but rather in terms of archetypes: "the isolate, armed male, the courageous homesteading family, the poor but industrious immigrant."[3]

In line with White's assessment, during the 1960s an important development in postwar American political culture (with roots in western Texas) was the rise of what Jeffrey Roche calls "cowboy conservatism." It was characterized by a set of ideas that celebrated individual freedom and community responsibility, "traditional family values," Protestantism, patriotism, and entrepreneurial capitalism. Cowboy conservatives stressed the importance of individual freedom from government restraint but promoted their community-shared values, especially with regard to issues that dealt with race and morality.[4]

What interests me here is how White's archetypes found expression in the extremist right. Roche notes that cowboy conservatism incorporates symbols and myths of the frontier West in its ideology—particularly where individual freedoms and government interference are concerned—but how did they end up as a framework for some white supremacist groups?

Perhaps religion can provide a bridge of sorts. Patricia Nelson Limerick notes that, to many white Americans, "belief in the mythic Old West has come to resemble belief in more conventional religious doctrines."[5] She notes that, for believers in conventional religious doctrines, the "Old Frontier" (her designation) is the nation's creation story, "the place where the virtues and values of the nation were formed."[6] However, as Limerick notes, the stories of the "Old Frontier" are filled not with preachers and churches, but with outlaws and gunslingers, of free-wheeling men battling sheriffs and posses, of individuals up against the forces of government. The church, after all, represented respectability that would eventually work to tame the wild West and thus put an end to all that fun and adventure.[7]

The reality of colonization and the brutality that often erupted between differing human cultures as the lines of "frontier" pushed westward were only muted in the guise of religion, which served to advance the message of white encroachment into traditionally Indian and Hispanic strongholds. Miriam Horn noted in 1990 that most damaging to Native Americans was what she referred to as "the white cult of individualism," which seemed to allow white colonists to explain and excuse policy and behavior toward Indians. "The mythic West," Horn continued, appears to have "a tenacious hold on the national imagination."[8] We're coming, the preachers and missionaries said, and you'll see that's how God intended it. Consequently, religion provided a justification of sorts for outlaw glory days of the "Old West."

The extremist right also uses its own interpretation of Protestantism to justify its treatment of those among us who are not white, not heterosexual, or who are Jewish. Proponents claim that what they say and what they do are sanctioned by God, that in fact God gave white people dominion over land, water, and nonwhites. After all, was it not white Puritans who established the "city upon the hill" when they arrived in the New World? And was it not white people who settled the West and brought both coasts under the control of the American government? Did not these white people "tame" the wild areas and create a mighty nation from the raw materials therein?

The history of the West is rife with images of these tamers—these "pioneers"—slashing their way through thick forests, building sod houses on barren plains, circling the wagons in the face of imminent Indian attack. Limerick notes that the use of the word "pioneer" is so prevalent in current American lingo that it has, in a sense, lost its relation to the westering Americans who took it upon themselves to build in untrammeled sections of the country.[9] David

Wrobel further notes that the word "frontier" has come to signify progress and promise rather than a period of time in which people pushed westward in this country, looking to build new towns.[10]

We may nowadays invoke imagery of "frontiers of medicine" and "pioneers in civil rights," using "frontier" and "pioneer" to go along with virtually anything that seems new. We all know what these terms mean, but we don't associate them immediately with, for example, hardscrabble Norwegian Americans building sod huts on the plains of North Dakota. However, if a phrase like "pioneer roots" or "pioneering Americans" enters a discussion, I'd wager that an image of wagons fording a river might come to mind or perhaps an image of the "olden days," in which most Americans were rural and used outhouses would come to mind faster than an image of a "frontier in medical science." It is these images of "pioneers" and "frontiers" that the extreme right employs when it talks about the duties of whites with regard to their "heritage." The extremist right deliberately uses terms such as "pioneer" within the context of the American creation story to garner support from potential members and paint themselves as simply pro-American rather than extremist.

The rhetoric espoused by the formerly Idaho-based Aryan Nations (the compound is now defunct) leader Richard Girnt Butler, for example, echoes older patterns of American expansion and nationalism and recurring patterns of what I dubbed frontierism in the Introduction. Such rhetoric describes a romanticized mythological past in which white archetypes, usually male, triumph over the landscape and nonwhites through Protestant values and hard work. In this "restored" United States, the current federal government would play little or no role and each Aryan individual would be responsible instead to local governments. It is not that far an image from Jefferson's idealized communities of independent yeoman farmers dotting the American landscape, with no interference from the federal government.

White addresses the hatred and suspicions extremist groups harbor for the federal government, and the nostalgic yearning for a mostly fictional past, but he does not consider the crucial role that race plays in much of the current "weirdness." Whatever eruptions of extreme right activity catch media attention, they are not something new in American history. The federal government may be a major target of current rightist agitation, but far more sinister to members of the right is the alleged international Jewish conspiracy that drives the government to perpetrate evil against the white race. Consequently, many members of the militias, Freemen, and Aryan Nations that White mentioned have put much effort since 1970 into stockpiling food, weapons, and medical supplies in preparation for a showdown with the forces of darkness (the federal government and its Jewish leaders). They have also spent a great deal of time creating an ideology about white male warriors battling nobly in the approaching apocalyptic encounter and working on pseudo-military maneuvers in isolated areas, many of which are in the West.

Examples are particularly vivid in some Aryan Nations literature, as in a 1981 newsletter article entitled "The Sword on the Land": "No one knows exactly the day or hour of the 'sword' coming to America. I personally have the feeling that it will be at the time of complete economic chaos, so long planned by the jew [sic]." From that same newsletter, Roy N. Eddy, in "Evacuation Part I," addresses his article to "the members of Aryan Nations who have had little or no experience in walking or hiking long distances with or without a pack. When the balloon goes up, all members of our organizations are expected to immediately leave their homes, if they are located in any of the critical areas, and move as quickly as possible to their predesignated survival areas." [11]

Behind all the bluster and the threats and the self-righteous anger lies a genuine fear of the future and often deep paranoia about "what's *really* going on in America." The world of the extremist right is one filled with shadows and conspiracies, frustration, and a frenetic sense of mission, often inextricably tied to millennialism. Among white supremacists, a sense of loss and an almost wistful attempt to resurrect America "as it used to be" pervades groups' rhetoric.

The theme of "race war" appears in white supremacist literature at least as early as the 1960s. George Lincoln Rockwell, founder of the post–World War II American Nazi Party, claimed that "there's going to be a battle of Armageddon, and it's going to be not between communism and democracy, but between the colored millions of the world and the small but elite corps of white men." In yet another publication put out by the Euro-American Alliance, the author stated that "this is a holy struggle for the White Race, for Western Civilization and Christianity, and for our America." In 1986, the Arizona Patriots "made ... white supremacy into a jihad, or holy war, that portrays Jews as the source of all evil." [12]

Intrinsic to this rhetoric and the emotions it is supposed to convey is the role white men are to play in the impending Armageddon. In white supremacist rhetoric, the new world, born of blood and fire, will be white-run and operated, and it will be segregated according to race. Most of the United States will belong to the white race, and white men will fill all positions of leadership.

Apocalypse ... Now?

In 1983, the following quotation appeared in the *Inter-Klan Newsletter and Survival Alert:*

> *On the men of this Order hang the hopes of our folk for life's existence. They are the vanguard of the coming new era and new Order; they are the pioneers who will lead the White Race out of the depths of its present dark age and toward the unexplored heights above—heights reserved for Aryan man, and Aryan man alone.*[13]

The quotation conveys an immediate sense of purpose and power to its readers. It is intended to stir the hearts of white Protestant men into some kind of action in the face of the coming dark age—the collapse of civilization—because from the ashes of what was will rise the new age and its victorious surviving citizenry: the white race.[14]

In addition to the writer's dark apocalyptic hints, he refers to the men of this Order ("Order" here referring to the growing group of white men who had become involved in the Aryan warrior's cause) as "pioneers" who would "lead the White Race" into a new age—into the "unexplored heights" beyond the dark age. As I will demonstrate in this chapter, white supremacist ideology since 1960 has tapped into two deeper but prevalent strains of American sociocultural folklore. One of them is millennialism—the belief that a thousand-year messianic kingdom on earth will follow Christ's Second Coming. The other deals with Manifest Destiny and images of "the West" as ways to define American character.[15] The two are sometimes difficult to draw apart.

Beginning in 1990, I began following various media—mainstream, Christian (mostly Protestant), leftist, rightist—for signs of what I dubbed "millennium freakout," which came in mild or wild forms: mild forms exhibited by people who made reservations at New York's Plaza Hotel at least ten years before the year 2000; wild forms expressed in small groups of people stockpiling for "the end" and perhaps engaging in violent acts in an attempt to draw out the forces of "evil" with which they are supposed to wage war before the peace. To every apocalyptic millenarian, there is always an evil that they, the good millenarians, must combat or escape.

The year 2000 is a cultural artifact, connecting religious and secular forms of the apocalyptic. Many people were drawn into images and dark statements about the year 2000; many felt compelled to prepare for "Y2K"—a vast computer meltdown that would allegedly occur because original programmers had neglected to ensure that the machines could understand the flipping of a new numerical millennium. No American was untouched, whether he browsed *National Enquirer* at the checkout stand or she read *USA Today* on the train to work.[16] Most of my friends and colleagues sheepishly admitted that they had stockpiled a few gallons of water and cans of food "just in case." In case of what? Oh, they said, in case a computer glitch shut down the power grid. If such were to occur, we would have far worse problems than simply sitting at home in the dark, I thought. Still, I made it a point to have my own extra cans of food, gallons of water, bags of dog food, and rolls of toilet paper stashed in my pantry. Just in case.

Millenarianism is not something that exists entirely on the fringes of either the right or the left. Nor is it something only fundamentalist or evangelical Christians profess or a bizarre cultic activity or a solitary descent into madness. The end of time—that is, the belief that such a thing is possible and that the present world as we see and experience it will come to an inevitable end—hovers in various world belief systems and has for centuries.[17]

During the Middle Ages, European millenarian sects and movements waxed and waned in response to troubled times, whether natural disasters (the Black Death) or oppressive rulers.[18] By the late Middle Ages, Western social preoccupation with the theological millennium joined forces with active demands of the oppressed factions of society. By the seventeenth century, millennialism (the belief that change coincides with the millennial time demarcations) had become popular in England and France and had entered the mainstream of Western religion and philosophy. Curiously, the long-term effect of this social acceptance was to dilute the strength of millenarian doctrine but also to inject it wholesale into Western society. As the millennium came to be understood in terms of the gradual unfolding of scientific knowledge and human potential, it was regarded as less and less imminent. Eventually, elements of millennialism and millenarianism found passage to America, where they coalesced into rhetoric and ideology that viewed the New World as the "New Jerusalem"—the "redeemed society."[19]

The colonizing venture to what would become America began at a time of intense apocalyptic awareness in England—an aura that seemed to lend the mission itself a certain sense of finality. The Puritans who migrated to the New World shared the millenarian hopes of those who remained in England.[20] Millennial expectations receded in England after 1660, but American Puritans discovered prophetic meaning in their own history. When the political situation in England stabilized in the late seventeenth century and the sense of apocalyptic crisis abated, New England Puritans began to develop a more provincial mythology of the new American Israel.[21]

Boston minister Increase Mather speculated in 1676 about America's prophetic destiny as a forerunner of the New Jerusalem. Boston political leader Samual Sewall shared Mather's conviction when he wrote in 1697 that America might be "the seat of the divine Metropolis" in the millennium. From cosmic visions to rather mundane events, New England prophecy writers, like their English counterparts, found apocalyptic meaning in current events.[22]

Increase Mather's son Cotton inaugurated a period of apocalyptic expectation in America, the force of which did not diminish until after the Revolutionary War. Cotton Mather himself pored over texts that dealt with prophecy, writing often on the subject in his diaries and proclaiming that Christ's kingdom would initiate an era of economic justice and social harmony. Mather's musings and sermons garnered disagreement and opposition from other ministers, such as Benjamin Coleman, who warned listeners to take with a grain of salt any linkages between prophecy and current events.[23] Spilling out of the pulpit, ideas about when, where, and how Christ's kingdom would eventually develop fueled lively debates among colonial Americans.

The Great Awakening that swept the colonies in the early 1740s brought apocalyptic speculation to the forefront of public discourse. Renowned minister Jonathan Edwards began a journal on the subject and offered various reflections on prophecy, though he refused to set dates. He did believe the millennium was fast approaching, as the Reformation represented to him the Fifth Vial of Revelation (as described in the Bible) and the world was therefore operating in the Sixth Vial, the last one before the "end." Through revival, prayer, and missionary effort, no doubt the prophesied Age of Grace would dawn.[24]

A large body of prophetic writing also surrounded the French and Indian War (1754–1763), with the French Catholic enemy cast as Antichrist, marking a shift in apocalyptic belief. Edwards and others during the Great Awakening had interpreted America's spiritual history apocalyptically and viewed the millennium as a product of the gradual spread of Christianity. With the French and Indian War, those who wrote and spoke of the approaching apocalypse began to frame it in military and political terms. Thus, by 1760 few New England ministers were drawing clear distinctions between God's kingdom and the goals of their own political community.[25] By the late 1750s and early 1760s, many ministers who preached about the French and Indian War also celebrated the millennial implications of American expansion into the then-western territories, merging political and religious ideologies.[26] This idea would resonate into the eighteenth century. We see, therefore, that millennial beliefs have influenced American religious and political thought and also that American political and social history has often been interpreted within the context of millennial beliefs.

During the Revolutionary War, patriot prophecy writers, like their predecessors, again linked contemporary events to ideas about the millennium and apocalypse. They identified British leaders, including King George III, as the Antichrist. The prophecy writers framed the conflict with England as a conflict between the forces of righteousness (the future America) and the devil (the British). With the approach of American independence, themes of national mission were increasingly linked to talk of an independent American state. The idea of the United States as the principal seat of a millennial kingdom thus combined the biblical symbolism of the Anglo-American Protestant tradition with a new revolutionary nationalism.[27]

American Patriots could be viewed as the vanguard not only of a new country, but also of a new sacred kingdom within the context of Protestant theologies. Consequently, the colonization era of this country tied events to dark warnings of apocalypse, using the latter to galvanize believers in a variety of religious and political causes. Disagreements about the form and timing of the end of the world, however, have also existed and created varying perspectives and arguments.

By strict definition, the term "millenarianism" refers to the biblical millennium, a one-thousand-year period after history ends. Many Christians believe this will be a time of peace and plenty but they differ with regard to how this era will be brought about. For some believers, Jesus will return to usher in and rule the kingdom. This interpretation is referred to as "premillennialism." For others, the millennium will come about purely through human intervention; Jesus will not appear until the final phase of the unfolding drama. This belief is "postmillennialism."

Apocalyptic millenarianism emphasizes the importance of cataclysmic events as the necessary preface to the new (and better) world. Believers of apocalyptic millenarianism within the Christian tradition are by definition premillenarians, since Jesus is supposed to return to bring about the thousand years of peace. Most American premillenarians, however, are not apocalyptic. The difference centers on imminence—that is, on whether the apocalypse is perceived to be looming and immediate action is imperative. Apocalyptic millenarians view themselves as actors in the impending chaos. American premillenarians who are not apocalyptic hold to the idea that the rapture will allow them to escape the worst of the apocalypse and that they will not be involved in the events.

Finally, "revolutionary millenarians" are those apocalyptic millenarians engaged in either a nonviolent quest to revolutionize an existing religious tradition or a movement that may resort to violence in an effort to upset the status quo. In so doing, they actually *force* the end.[28] They turn their beliefs into action, creating an apocalypse.

Twentieth-century white supremacists fall into the apocalyptic millenarian camp. I would argue that many are also revolutionary millenarians of the type who would use violence to upset the status quo. Members of these groups justify their actions by emphasizing white men's "duty." They have a "duty" to lead the white race into the coming battles of the ages. They have a "duty" to govern hearth and home. They even have a "duty" to find white women with whom to start white families. It is considered part of God's "design" (and justified in the torturous interpretations of Christian Identity) that the white race will reign victorious over a world that has gone to "hell in a handbasket" as a result of Jewish machinations.

In 1980, the Aryan Nations code of conduct instructed white men to "never forget" that they are Christians fighting for their race, responsible for their own actions, and "dedicated to the principles which made our people great in the sight of God." The code further declared that white men were never to surrender in the battle and that, ultimately, they would survive as long as they maintained their duty as white men.[29]

Although it might seem strange to think about white supremacy as a "duty," the concept of Anglo-Saxon "duty" has deep roots in American history and intellectual discourse. Reginald Horsman notes that between 1815 and the mid-1850s, an American Anglo-Saxon ideology bolstered the power and protected the status of the existing white population. In addition, this Anglo-Saxon ideology externally justified American territorial and economic expansion, while internally it emphasized that the American republic was a white Anglo-Saxon republic. Whites who weren't Anglo-Saxon would be absorbed within the existing mass, whereas nonwhites would be excluded from any equal participation as citizens.[30] How non-Anglo-Saxons who immigrated to the United States and decided to stay responded to these pressures, whether expressed in media, legislation, or interpersonal relationships, is a history of conflict and concession, of a constant jockeying to maintain ethnic heritage and also identity as "American." Many of us don't think about how social pressures and outright coercion have worked to create a national identity, yet force is an intrinsic aspect of our history as Americans.[31]

Manifest Destiny, a term coined by New York newspaperman John O'Sullivan in 1845, was a nationalist doctrine that proclaimed a national destiny for a united citizenry.[32] O'Sullivan first stated in 1839 that "we may confidently assume that our country is destined to be the great nation of futurity." He continued, "in its magnificent domain of space and time, the nation of many nations [the United States] is *destined to manifest* to mankind the excellence of divine principles; to establish on earth the noblest temple ever dedicated to the worship of the Most High—the Sacred and the True" (emphasis mine). Waxing poetic and perhaps a bit prophetic, O'Sullivan finished with a flourish, stating that "America has been chosen" for "this blessed mission," and the country's "high example shall smite unto death the tyranny of kings, hierarchs, and oligarchs, and carry the glad tidings of peace and good will where myriads now endure an existence scarcely more enviable than that of beasts of the field."[33]

O'Sullivan's rapturous declarations with regard to the new nation caught hold in American popular culture. The concept was (and still is) elastic enough to encompass other aspects of "mission." By the mid-1840s, a facet of Manifest Destiny that proved immensely important in the wake of strained relations with Mexico was an emphasis on regenerating "backward" peoples. It was a "duty" to do so and a mission to which white Americans should aspire as they pushed the boundaries of the country westward.[34]

Paradoxically, the United States was not a united country, in spite of all the clarion rhetoric about equality and individual freedom. Deep sectional differences existed between North and South, and arguments raged as to whether the institution of slavery should expand into western territories. White points out elsewhere, correctly, that Manifest Destiny assumed that Americans wanted the continent no matter who was already living on it, but most of the people living in the territory that expansionists coveted were not white.[35] Which brings us to a set of problematic questions: If "Americans" wanted the continent, who would fill that definition? Who was an "American"? Where did Native Americans and people of Spanish and Mexican descent—who were already living on the continent—fit in this expansionist doctrine?

Errand into the Wilderness

No one was white before he/she came to America. It took generations, and a vast amount of coercion, before this became a white country.

—James Baldwin[36]

The concept of a distinct, superior Anglo-Saxon race with innate abilities that would enable it to perfect governmental institutions and achieve world dominance was a product of the first half of the nineteenth century. The seeds of those ideas, however, took root in the sixteenth and seventeenth centuries.[37] Horsman argues that English immigrants to American shores in the seventeenth century brought as part of their religious and historical heritage a clearly delineated religious myth of a pure English Anglo-Saxon church.[38]

In the seventeenth and eighteenth centuries, they shared with their fellow English believers an elaborately developed secular myth of the free nature of Anglo-Saxon political institutions, which implied that all rational beings could participate and that the political institutions were ordained by a higher power. By the time of the American Revolution, those who called themselves Americans (i.e., whites of English descent) were convinced that Anglo-Saxon England before the Norman Conquest had enjoyed freedoms they had lost under Norman control. Notably, since the sixteenth century, both on the European continent and in England, Anglo-Saxons had been firmly linked to the Germanic tribes described by Tacitus.[39]

Emphasis on the Anglo-Saxons as a strong branch of the Germanic genealogical tree continued as one thread of the political arguments of the seventeenth century. Ultimately, the conflict between English royalty and those who opposed it allowed the fusion of two myths—the myth of a pure Anglo-Saxon church that developed in the sixteenth century and the myth of a free Anglo-Saxon government (a government not beholden to outsiders) that developed in the seventeenth century.[40]

In the wake of the Glorious Revolution (1688), a "Whig" view of the past held that a golden age of government existed in England prior to the Norman Conquest. The conquest eroded English liberties, but a long struggle ensued for the restoration of good government, the foundation of which was the Magna Carta and the seventeenth-century victories over the Stuarts. As a result, the perception of England as a nation with a continuity of law and institutions stretching back for more than a thousand years inhabited by freedom-loving Anglo-Saxons took hold among England's inhabitants, though not all accepted it.[41]

In the seventy years after 1660, the myth of Anglo-Saxon England flourished in English politics, fueled by a rise of Anglo-Saxon scholarship, particularly at Oxford. In these years, a group of preeminent scholars, including George Hickes and Francis Junius, encouraged the study of the Anglo-Saxon language and its sources. They did nothing to correct the prevailing myths about "freedom" and its links to Anglo-Saxon institutions, and their linguistic studies served to expand interest in links between the Anglo-Saxons and other Germanic peoples. Under their teachings, ideas about the pure and superior nature of Anglo-Saxon institutions percolated in intellectual discourse. Consequently, the eighteenth-century English view of Anglo-Saxons was a mythical one, produced by two centuries of religious and political conflict, reinforced by images of Germanic peoples propounded by Tacitus, and, in turn, elaborated by post-Reformation writers.[42] Later, American white supremacist groups would express a reliance on these ideas as part of their efforts to claim white European ancestry and celebrate the superiority of that supposed heritage.

Settlers in America—colonial English folk—absorbed this mythical view of the English past, but they differed from the English majority in that the colonial English leaned more toward a minority English viewpoint: the English constitution had not been cleansed of religious and political abuses since the Conquest. During the mid-eighteenth century, English radicals (Real Whigs) appealed to the burgeoning "Americans" who were becoming more dissatisfied with their relationship to the English political establishment. By the time of the American Revolution, many English descendants ("Americans") welcomed the views of English radicals who were asking for a reform of the English system to *restore* its "pristine Anglo-Saxon vigor."[43]

This idea of "restoring" is a crucial one in the modern white supremacist movement. It is a driving force behind much white supremacist rhetoric. The United States, they have held, is in dire straits and if only things were as they were "before" they went bad—i.e., before the various social movements since the 1950s—America would be a great country once again. Many white supremacists see themselves as "true" patriots, fighting another revolution that will free whites from the insidious hold of Jews and nonwhites.

Historically, through the very act of revolting against England, the generation of Americans of English descent believed that they were reinforcing their links with their Anglo-Saxon ancestors in separating from the government of Great Britain, which was a corrupt entity and allegedly nothing like its great and pure pre-Norman institutions. This, coupled with contemporary scholarship in both England and America, confirmed the archetypal Anglo-Saxon myth. In addition, the political and religious struggles and the historical revisions that lent the myth credibility provided for the English and for Americans of English descent a perspective that led them to racialized explanations for the course of history.[44] In other words, Anglo-Saxon whites were the pinnacle of historic achievement and, by extension, Anglo-Saxon white Americans were working to ensure this proud legacy.

By the time of the American Revolution, new tendencies in European thought had laid the foundations for different interpretations of what seemed to be the persistence of free, democratic government among Anglo-Saxons. Older ideas that suggested Germanic origins of the Anglo-Saxon love of freedom and democratic government gave way to certain elaborations that found tentative voices in the second half of the eighteenth century. A new Aryan interpretation of the Anglo-Saxon past transformed respect for Anglo-Saxon institutions into a racialized interpretation of English and American success. By the nineteenth century, the secret to Saxon progress lay not in institutions, but rather in blood.[45]

Edward Saveth notes that some acclaimed historians of the early nineteenth century capitalized on these myths about Anglo-Saxon freedoms and institutions, spreading them through their own writings, which were often disseminated to the American public and picked up by the next generation of historians. The so-called Teutonic Hypothesis claimed that English and German institutions derived from ancient Teutonic tribes they called "Aryans." Some of these Aryans migrated to Greece, thus forming Greek, and later Roman, civilization. Eventually, they ended up in the part of Europe we know as Germany, and their ideas spread with them throughout the continent.[46]

The Teutonic Hypothesis received its fullest development from the work of Herbert Baxter Adams, who was based at Johns Hopkins University. Under his direction, the hypothesis took on another dimension: the United States was simply another homeland for the beliefs and institutions of these ancient Aryan peoples. This first generation of American scientific historians (Adams and his colleagues and students) found meaning in the American past as they perceived it in light of the Teutonic Hypothesis and also through the belief that acquired national characteristics were inherited and intrinsically "racial." Race became a cultural and political determinant and convinced other historians using the comparative method in their work that this view about the American past was "scientific."[47] The perceived superiority of Anglo-Saxon and Protestant Americans, which almost all early nineteenth-century historians accepted essentially on faith, spread into the larger political arena, and helped create what Saveth calls the bond between Teutonism and the Whig-Republican understanding of American history.[48]

By the late nineteenth century, ideas about how the American environment had helped shape national identity and character entered historical research and eventually public discourse. Social Darwinism—"survival of the fittest"—contributed to the expanding notion that Anglo-Saxons were "chosen people" who had survived the rigors of the American wilderness. Saveth writes that "the hazards of life in a new land, the obstacles of frontier and forest to the push westward were interpreted as selective factors which made for the development of a superior national type."[49] Only the strongest could survive such rigors, so it seemed to American scholars and researchers who bought into social Darwinism that those of Anglo-Saxon descent were the best of the best.[50]

As a rule, Saveth argues, "those who applied the principle of natural selection to American development asserted confidently … without examination of the actual character of the frontier experience, that the wilderness brought out the best in men and in institutions." Saveth notes that, in most—if not all—cases, the best men were Anglo-Saxon. That is, they were white.[51] Logically, then, it follows that American whites are the group imbued with the special mission O'Sullivan described in 1839.

Ideas about a "special destiny" fit in neatly with contemporary American discussions about Manifest Destiny, the ideological driving force behind westward expansion in the United States.[52] Among American white supremacist groups since 1960, ideas about a "special destiny" for Anglo-Saxons have created a sense of "mission" among group members. As we will see in later chapters, this "mission" involves an Aryan resurgence across the United States that will literally "take back America" from nonwhites—Aryans have been preparing to fight another "frontier" battle.

One of the tools white supremacists use to fight this battle is Christian Identity. As strange as the earlier incarnation of it, British-Israelism, might have seemed to many Christian Americans, the teachings nevertheless attracted a substantial audience in this country because there was no shortage of Americans convinced that their country was destined to fulfill some kind of millennial role and that the history of Israel carried a template for the pattern of American destiny. Anglo-Israelites linked biblical prophecy with American fulfillment (not unlike other contemporary organized religions in the country such as Mormonism, which prophesied that the lost tribes would return to an American Zion in the end times). In the hands of American preachers, and without a central organizing doctrine, British-Israelism diffused through a mishmash of patterns and individuals.

The processes through which Identity evolved and adopted this doctrine are complex and beyond the scope of my inquiry here. Suffice it to say that the key events involved contacts between anti-Semitic British-Israel figures such as C. F. Parker and Clem Davies in Vancouver, British Columbia (where a thriving British-Israel community developed prior to World War II), and the West Coast cadre of Identity figures associated with one Gerald L. K. Smith (who would become a mentor to the Aryan Nations founder). Among these Californians were Wesley Swift, Bertrand Comperet, and William Potter Gale, all of whom would play important roles after World War II in the emerging American white supremacist movement through their teachings and writings.[53]

Smith's influence was so important that two generations of Identity teachers were associated directly with either his Christian Nationalist Crusade (Swift, Gale, and Comperet) or his youth movement. Smith himself shared Identity exchanges with Wesley Swift, who Smith credited with opening up Identity hermeneutics to him.[54] Under the auspices of Smith and his followers, the world of Christian Identity was soon to gain wide currency in the world of the American extremist right. In the post–World War II era, Identity adherents included members of conservative Protestant churches and disaffected Protestant premillennialists.[55]

The transition from Protestant premillennialism to Christian Identity was not difficult to make, since a heavy dose of apocalypticism infuses Identity doctrine, which is not that different from the end-of-time beliefs of Protestant fundamentalism (with the exception of the belief in "rapture"). Many fundamentalists believe that in the end times and the dreaded seven-year period of the Tribulation (including war, famine, and disease), they as believers will be "raptured" to heaven, safe from the ravages of the "End of Days" and right at Jesus' side. Identity believers have no such hope of supernatural rescue. Instead, the only certainty is a belief in the individual's ability to persevere and survive not only by the grace of God, but also through adequate preparation—hence the Identity believer's emphasis on urban and wilderness survivalism.[56]

Christian Identity as a belief system in this country effectively melded the foundations of British-Israelism with the insidious tenets of a myth predicated on a worldwide Jewish conspiracy. Part of Identity's resilience—indeed, of the staying power of a mythical conspiracy itself—is that, because it is based on rumors and misconceptions, it is very difficult to disprove, especially to those who truly believe.

"Go West, Young Man"

In 1918, Emerson Hough wrote about the idea of "frontier" with a wistfulness, stating that "there is no word in the English language more stirring, more intimate, or more beloved" and that the idea of "frontier" carried "all of the old Anglo-Saxon command, *Forward!*"[57] Frederick Jackson Turner had declared the frontier "gone" when he read his famous (infamous, perhaps) essay at the American Historical Association meetings in Chicago in 1893. According to Turner and his reading of census data, the frontier no longer existed as of 1890 because of increased settlement. There were too many people, it seemed, to call that line of white westward expansion a frontier any longer.[58]

Turner's essay didn't garner much attention at its original presentation, but years after the fact, it has demonstrated quite a long shelf life as Americans have struggled to understand what exactly the frontier is and how it has created and been created since someone thought to link it to westward expansion. Hough's view of the frontier probably echoed the sentiments of many Americans, who perhaps associated the West with "the old hope of a real personal liberty and ... a real human advance in character and achievement."[59]

Horsman suggests that, by the mid-nineteenth century, ideas about race and racial hierarchy extant since the early part of the century found fertile ground in American political and intellectual discourse.[60] The peculiarities of the American experience and the existence of white, Asian, black, Hispanic, and Indian peoples within the continental boundaries of the United States influenced the development of American thought on race. While the relationship between Whites and Blacks formed a crucial and terribly resilient core of American history, Native Americans during the nineteenth century were of particular importance within the context of an expanding and aggressive nation. "In dealing with the Indians," Horsman argues, "the United States began to formulate a rationale of expansion which was readily adaptable to the needs of an advance over other peoples and to a world role."[61]

Since the second half of the nineteenth century, American expansion has served as a foundation and shaper of "American" character and identity.[62] Certainly, I am not suggesting that all white Americans have subscribed to overt or covert racism. Individual politics are much more complicated than that. I *am* suggesting, however, that American domestic and foreign policy is itself predicated on assumptions about the alleged superiority of white, Protestant Americans and these assumptions justified territorial expansion. As a result of official policy, ideas about what constituted an "American" were tied to the rhetoric of Manifest Destiny, which tended to favor white Protestants.[63]

Manifest Destiny pushed white America westward and provided reasons and "rights" to do so. It also provided the foundation for the construction of a cultural myth about American character that still resonated at the beginning of the twenty-first century. That cultural construction is the "frontier," and it has proven an able traveling companion for white Protestants. Richard Slotkin contends that the myth of the frontier "is our oldest and most characteristic myth, expressed in a body of literature, folklore, ritual, historiography, and polemics produced over a period of three centuries."[64] According to the frontier myth, the conquest of the wilderness and accompanying subjugation or displacement of Indians who originally inhabited it have been the means to an achievement of "our national identity, a democratic polity, an ever-expanding economy, and a phenomenally dynamic and 'progressive' civilization."[65]

Originally called upon to explain and justify the establishment of American colonies, the myth was used to account for economic growth and the expansion of a nation state once those colonies had substantially grown. The myth was also touted as a reason for a distinctively "American" approach to the socially and culturally disruptive processes of modernization.[66] Slotkin further notes that between 1815 and 1870 the United States experienced a period of relatively steady and rapid economic expansion, shifting away from an agrarian-based to an industrial-based economic system. Even the destruction wrought by the Civil War could not deter the economic growth of the nation as a whole. This economic expansion coincided with dramatic geographic expansion, according to Slotkin, and these two arenas of expansion became linked in American historical mythology. Consequently, the westward movement of American population has been interpreted as a cause—or even as *the* cause—of American economic development.[67]

Slotkin also notes that, in the literary mythology of the Jacksonian era, a two-tiered representation of America juxtaposed "masculine" and "feminine" worlds. The juxtaposition found its largest expression in the opposition of the male frontier to the female metropolis.[68] The frontier myth, according to Slotkin, contrasted an active white male citizen with a passive female nonwhite laborer who lived in cities. In so doing, the myth thus devalues men of color and all women, touting the white male who left the city to seek his fortunes out west as the quintessential American.[69]

Gendering of the frontier myth occurs in many American cultural influences. Henry Nash Smith discusses the ways in which frontier ideology has influenced American literature since the eighteenth century, especially as expressed through the Caucasian cowboy.[70] Smith further notes that "the character of the American empire was defined not by streams of influence out of the past, not by cultural tradition, but by a relation between man and nature—or rather ... between American man and the American West."[71]

At the turn of the nineteenth century, when the United States was involved in the Spanish-American War, Theodore Roosevelt became an icon of "manliness" for his military service, life out West, and his own image-making. Gail Bederman points out that Roosevelt felt as if the United States was "engaged in a millennial drama of manly racial advancement" and that American men needed to "prove their virility, as a race and a nation" through a life of work and physical challenge in the advancement of "civilization."[72]

Clearly linking white American manhood to racial conflict on the eighteenth-century American frontier, Roosevelt called for the subjugation of "inferior" races as necessary. Applying principles of Social Darwinism to his historical analysis, he constructed the frontier as a site of origins of the American race, "whose manhood and national worth were proven by their ability to stamp out competing, savage races."[73] Roosevelt wrote and lectured widely between 1894 and 1901 on Rudyard Kipling's "White Man's Burden," in which white men had a responsibility to go forth into the world and conquer uncivilized races. To not engage in imperialism was "unmanly" to Roosevelt, and these ideas were often echoed in contemporary American popular culture.[74]

Bederman notes also that when members of the American media dubbed Roosevelt's regiment the "Rough Riders" prior to their departure for San Juan Hill in Cuba during the Spanish-American War, they were demonstrating that they understood the historical connections Roosevelt always drew between Indian wars in the American West and his virile imperialism in Cuba and the Philippines. "Rough Riders" was a term long used in adventure novels to describe western horsemen.[75] Michael Kimmel further notes that, during the last thirty years of the nineteenth century, degrees of manhood corresponded to race. The most manly men thus were white, given the perceived superiority of the white race.[76]

Consequently, white manhood could be expressed through American imperialism, and the development of settlements across the western landscape were reflections of American ingenuity and the men who brought them. Turner linked the development of American institutions to how Easterners (that is, whites headed west) adapted to and developed towns and political and social structures in wilderness areas.[77] This process, according to Turner, literally *created* Americans. The very idea of frontier and the accompanying mythology that has grown in its wake have shaped how many white Americans perceive their cultural and racial identity as uniquely American.

Whether we define the frontier as a place, a process, or a predicament, it has salted the stew of American "character" and continues to serve up social and cultural definitions of what it means to be "American." It is here—on the borders of what *is* and what is only *wished*—that the white supremacist movement attempts to re-create, on the one hand, the alleged glory days of Protestant agrarianism and the noble yeoman farmer and, on the other, the rugged individualism of the archetypal white frontiersman. The frontier is a proving ground in American myth, a place *and* a process where boys go to become men—indeed, where men go to become "Americans." As an added bonus, one can gain access to the frontier in twenty-first-century America through movies, television, literature, video games, and magazines, which offer heaping helpings of it for public consumption.[78] You no longer have to make a physical pilgrimage to prove yourself out West.

Far more insidious than obvious frontierist references or romantic ideas about westward expansion are notions of American "character" that remain embedded in American soil and psyche since their sowing in New England colonies. In and of themselves, these notions resonate with the essence of "frontier," whether one conjures images of cowboys and Indians or not. Invariably, all one has to do is mention "red-blooded American" and the image that jumps to mind is that of a white man engaged in various masculine pursuits such as settling the West, building a city, surveying a landscape studded with oil derricks, going to war, or perhaps riding a horse into the sunset. The essence of this "American character," no matter the medium through which it is expressed, is itself a frontierist construction, and its archetype encodes race (white), gender (male), and place (frontier—out West).

The very foundation of "American character" thus incorporates a triad of "-isms": racism, sexism, and frontierism. I am not suggesting that all white Americans historically subscribed to the less welcoming strains of Manifest Destiny and a sense of "mission." White people are no more prone to –isms than any other human group. Interpersonal interactions are always complicated, and hundreds of thousands of white Americans historically did not and still do not subscribe to the –isms that have influenced the formation of American national identity.

What I am suggesting, however, is that the ideology of American nationhood and subsequent genesis of an "American character" have loaned themselves— perhaps inadvertently—to the creation of hierarchies of human beings, at whose pinnacles stand white men. Consequently, there is nothing all that mysterious about why American white supremacist groups developed and have continued to exist in a land that ostensibly extols "liberty for all" and "equality." The mystery lies in why we as Americans have not really deeply examined our own dearly held beliefs about ourselves in order to understand or address a much darker and divisive side of who we are as a nation.

By not doing that, all three of these –isms continue to find expression in white supremacist groups, some of which have taken up their own version of homesteading. In 1973, one of these homesteaders, Richard Girnt Butler, would arrive in Idaho, seeking refuge from the world without.

CHAPTER 3

Armageddon Ranch

Homesteading on the Aryan Frontier

Eve was seduced; now our whole race is seduced. But we have a nation to broadcast the truth to our people. Two-thirds of our race will die, according to the Bible—because of the antichrist, famine, disease, warfare, whatever. Bad times are coming.

—Pastor Richard Butler, leader of Aryan Nations[1]

In 1973, Steve McQueen and Ali McGraw starred in *The Getaway,* "Tommy" premiered in London, Pink Floyd released *Dark Side of the Moon,* and the Watergate "Plumbers" were convicted of burglary. The Vietnam War, though technically over, hadn't ended. The battlefields of Southeast Asia remained lodged in the men and women who had been there and in the imaginations of those who hadn't. This war robbed Americans of an inheritance through which national character had created and re-created itself: military victory. Transformed from victors to victims, from heroes to killers both on screen and off, Americans in the wake of the Vietnam War faced a presidency rocked with scandal, a military in disarray, and cultures of protest seeking an end not only to the war but also to perceived white male dominance in American institutions.[2] The Vietnam War and the decades it encompassed brought about profound and unprecedented changes in American culture and society.

The U.S. defeat in Vietnam brought the post–World War II era of unrivaled American political and military power in international affairs to an end. But the failure resounded all over the world, challenging a country that had always celebrated war and the warriors who participated in it. Post-Vietnam America suffered a crisis of self-image. No longer "winners," what role could Americans fulfill? Specifically, with the failure of warriors, what place did men—and in particular, white men—have in the formation of American character, which had always relied on white male archetypes for definition?[3]

Arnold Isaacs maintains that the Vietnam War "has lingered as a symbol and metaphor for everything that troubled Americans."[4] World War II, by contrast, was an ugly but "necessary" engagement, in which there were clear military and civilian goals and widespread popular support. Vietnam taught its American participants that the world is ultimately absurd, that there are no clear lines between good and bad, and that policymakers don't always make the best decisions. Vietnam is a powerful symbol of damaged ideals. The war created a loss of trust and unity in America, as it shattered shared myths and common values.[5]

Veterans who served in Vietnam came home to a very different situation than their World War II predecessors. Many have complained that they felt silenced when their tours were over, and many have spoken of a profound sense of alienation. Isaacs interviewed dozens of Vietnam veterans in an attempt to understand how their experiences differed from other American wartime involvement. In the past, he notes, American society shared blame and responsibility with those who fought in wars. The country refused to do so wholeheartedly for Vietnam, leaving the blame to the veterans, the responsibility for failure to those who fought.[6]

In the late 1970s, the Carter administration granted amnesty to men who dodged the draft for Vietnam. In 1979, a survey conducted of hundreds of veterans who had served in Southeast Asia demonstrated a profound sense of cynicism and alienation from the culture around them. Many veterans were also furious at President Carter for "excusing" those who balked at serving their country. It seemed like another blow to veterans who had come home to a very different context than their fathers did at the end of World War II.[7]

A turning point of sorts for Vietnam veterans came on January 20, 1981. On that date, 52 American hostages returned from Iran after 444 days in captivity. The homecoming of these Americans stuck in the craws of many veterans, who felt they had been denied the welcome of those hostages, who weren't subjected to active combat. The hostages hadn't volunteered to take up arms for their country, but they were being honored in parades and the media. Veterans began speaking up with regard to their experiences in the war, demanding recognition for their work in Asia. Less than two years later, a Vietnam veterans' memorial was dedicated in Washington, D.C., and a steady stream of movies appeared that painted veterans in a more heroic light.[8]

The rifts in American society that appeared with the Vietnam War, however, remained. Unlike World War II, in which the average American soldier was twenty-six, the average age of a Vietnam soldier was nineteen. Millions of middle-class, better-educated men managed to escape the draft during the Vietnam era, using college deferments or other methods that the Johnson administration approved. These included lowering military qualification exam scores. As a result, younger working-class men who were not yet college-educated were caught in the draft or easily qualified for military service even with low scores.[9]

Military experience was also different during the Vietnam War than it had been in World War II. In the latter, American men shipped out as complete units. The men who went to war together had trained together, creating a strong bond between them and, thus, effective military cohesion. In Vietnam, men often shipped out individually and were air-dropped into hotspots as needed. They did not often train as a unit. They were instead dropped into a situation not knowing their comrades or the military objectives for the area. As a result, soldiers often felt no immediate bond to their units or commanding officers; they hadn't had the opportunity to work closely with them and establish a rapport. In addition, the armed forces had become increasingly bureaucratized since the end of World War II. A system of rewards was imposed on the military that transformed senior officers from military leaders into bureaucratic managers. The more bureaucratic an officer, the less inclined he was to risk his neck out in the field with the grunts. Shorter tours of duty for officers also put enlisted men at risk. Shorter tours precluded officers from building cohesive military units and kept them from getting more combat experience. The less experienced the officer (which was common), the greater number of enlisted men under his command who died. Resentment of enlisted men toward officers in Vietnam reached unprecedented heights.[10]

Back on the homefront, the advent of television brought the war into many American households. Media influence helped fuel distrust of U.S. policy in Asia and also magnified divisions between those who supported the war and those who did not. Isaacs notes that the peace movement, though activist and politically motivated, "had no real political roots" and thus did not offer a true radical alternative to conventional two-party politics. A class difference existed between those who fought in the war and those who fought against it; men from lower socioeconomic strata were more often shipped out while middle- and upper-class men and women were engaged at home in activism.[11]

Because the peace movement was not deeply rooted, real political change stalled and liberals of the era were subsequently saddled with a lasting image of cultural radicalism. Conservatives, for their part, were seen as mired in nostalgic myths that disregarded changes taking place.[12] The war had also definitively altered American politics, creating two camps: liberal and conservative. It's a hobgoblin that has dogged liberals for more than thirty years. Because antiwar protests were associated with liberals, conservatives have consistently used a liberal "straw man" to denigrate their opposition, painting all liberals as "unpatriotic" and "anti-American" should questions about government policy arise. Conservatives, however, have had to contend with their own Vietnam baggage;

they are often viewed as reactionary and are frequently dismissed as "old" and "stuck in the past" by opposition forces. In the space between these two opposing ideologies has risen since the 1980s what Brian Balogh refers to as an "expert" culture. That is, rather than focusing on solutions to problems, people who call themselves "experts" on the topics under discussion (with regard to foreign and domestic policy) make pronouncements in support of their causes, creating an echo chamber of policy and ideology that bounces around American media. The end result is a loop argument that condemns and attacks the other side, whether liberal or conservative, rather than offering viable answers or compromises.[13]

Vietnam thus fundamentally altered how Americans view themselves and their fellow Americans. It changed how we as a society view our military, how we view our government, and how we view dissenters. In the rifts that Vietnam exacerbated, a small segment of the population sought answers to growing concerns about the direction of the country as a whole in a conspiracy-laden world.

Some white American men—lacking confidence in the government and the economy, faced with changing relations between the sexes and races, uncertain of their own identities or futures—perhaps began to dream about the powers and features of another kind of man who could retake and reorder the world. The hero in all of these victorious fantasies was the paramilitary warrior. As he fights in the "New War," he symbolically wins the battles of Vietnam in Third World countries across the globe. He returns America to an imaginary golden age, a time before Vietnam, before feminism, and before civil rights.[14]

It is no accident that modern paramilitary culture dates back to the mid- to late-1970s. Expressed in movies such as *Rambo*, pulp novels such as *The Executioner* series, magazines like *Soldier of Fortune*, games such as paintball, the growing popularity of military-style automatic weaponry, and the establishment of privately run combat training schools, American paramilitary culture gives men a substitute for war and the rite of passage into manhood that war has traditionally provided.[15]

As Randy Shilts has noted, "For many thousands of years … [b]oys [have gone] to war to prove they are men. Some anthropologists assert that this is one reason why wars exist in the first place: so men can have a venue in which to prove their manliness." He pointed out that there were "fewer proving grounds so sure as combat" and that participation in war can cause one to shed childhood insecurities and it can create a place for the individual in the broader network of community and nation. Shilts argued that this process did not "establish manhood so much as personhood. However, in the United States in the middle of the twentieth century, to be a person meant to be a man." Part of the Vietnam legacy included changing public perceptions of the military—violent and bad, when for centuries it was the lure of the military that would turn boys into men. Shilts further stated that, throughout American history, the institution most devoted to the ideology of masculinity has been the military.[16] Participating in paramilitary culture after the Vietnam War offers men a chance to be modern-day frontiersmen—men who, like lone cowboys, right wrongs and can stand tall in their righteousness.

Unlike America's traditional image of the hero in post–World War II movies, the hero of this "new war" is not a member of conventional military or police units. Instead, because of political and bureaucratic restraints and ineptitude, he fights alone or with a few comrades. The mythological fighting powers of the American man are released, consequently, by fighting *outside* the system.[17] Another key to this paramilitary culture is the fact that *any* man can participate because it lies on the outside of society and thus doesn't require a full-time occupational commitment. Furthermore, in the mythology of the New War, the U.S. government and the political power structure across the country are painted as weak, immoral, and corrupt. The system, therefore, no longer has legitimate moral authority.[18]

Intermingled with the literature and films indicative of paramilitarism are themes that embrace survivalism and apocalyptic visions of social collapse or nuclear war. The emergence of this paramilitary subculture blended an interest in state-of-the-art armaments with preparations for survival in a disintegrating world. The paramilitary warrior had to kick enemy butt *and* save American survivors in the wake of social and political chaos or nuclear annihilation.[19] For its part, apocalyptic prophecy works because it feeds off itself. By pinning current changes or major events such as wars and environmental, economic, and political changes to the millennial myth, apocalypticism can be neither proved nor disproved; it comes down to a matter of belief.[20]

This paramilitary dream culture mined from American folklore and ideologies about the "frontier" and rugged individualism held its strongest appeal until the late 1980s when, not coincidentally, the dissolution of the Soviet Union effectively ended the Cold War. Who was the enemy now? What menace did communism and evil empires present after the wall was down? More important, what was a white guy to do?

Aryan warrior in modern military garb, indicative of the paramilitary subculture that developed in the United States following the Vietnam War. To his left is the Aryan Nations insignia and to his right is the Ku Klux Klan standard. The teardrop shape in the center of the Klan cross represents a drop of blood, indicative of the purity of the white race. With regard to the Aryan Nations symbol, which is heavy with Christian Identity overtones, the crown signifies "Yahweh's" (the Father's) sovereignty over all things; the three jewels on the crown represent the Holy Trinity; the shield is a symbol of Christian faith (as interpreted by the group); the two-edged sword represents the Lord's truth; the "revolving resurrection cross" centered on the sword is indicative of the white race's return to righteousness; the "cross of Jacob" (the diagonal lines through the center) symbolizes the "blessings of Israel" (prior to Jews); the three stripes on each of the diagonals represent the twelve tribes of God's racial nations and inheritance in His kingdom; the square in which the symbol floats is indicative of the "divinely appointed four-square formation and order" commanded by Yahweh for the armies of the "true" tribes of Israel. Eventually, the "new Jerusalem" of the white race will be four-square with twelve gates (for each of the twelve tribes of the racial nations). The colors are red, light blue, gold (the crown and cross) and white. I found information about what the insignia means at the Twelve Aryan Nations website, located at www.twelvearyannations.com. The image is from the now-defunct *Inter-Klan Newsletter and Survival Alert,* which circulated among white supremacists during the late 1970s and early 1980s. Courtesy of the Wilcox Collection at the University of Kansas Libraries, Lawrence, RH WL D1953 no. 4 1984.

The Great White North(west)

The warmer-climate community just hasn't found the colder climate that attractive. It's an area of America that has simply never attracted the Afro-American or the Hispanic.
—Idaho Congresswoman Helen Chenoweth (R), on why the U.S. Forest Service should stop trying to recruit minorities for jobs in her district.[21]

The Idaho panhandle's northern stretch holds the kind of scenery one might see in an Imax theatre. Thickly forested and mountainous, sparsely populated in many areas, it is the kind of place one might envision as the perfect summer camp-site. Almost forty percent of Idaho is blanketed by forests and sixty-three percent of the land is federally owned.[22] The total population of Idaho in the 2000 census was 1,293,953. According to the census, 1,177,344 of those people are white. There are 15.6 people per square mile in the state, compared to the national average of 83 people per square mile.[23]

To the east sits Montana, a state whose own beauty has been broadcasted to the country in movies such as *A River Runs Through It* (1993) and *Legends of the Fall* (1995). Montana boasts fewer than six people per square mile, with a total population, according to the 2000 census, of 902,195. Of that, 817,229 are white.[24] The western half of the state is more forested than the eastern, which is mostly grassland used for agriculture and ranching.[25]

To the west sits Washington, forested along the eastern border that it shares with Idaho's panhandle. The most recent population count for Washington, in 2003, found that 6,131,445 people live in the state. Nearly eighty-two percent of them are white.[26] More than half of Washington is forested and most is still rural, boasting roughly 2–10 people per square mile, depending on the county.[27] It is the kind of place where you could live without seeing another human being for days on end, where you can't see the trees for the forests. It's the kind of place Theodore Roosevelt would encourage young (white Protestant) men to go to discover the great West and, in the process, their manhood.

Like many pockets of the West, Idaho has proven an effective hiding place for those who wish to disappear; many parts of it remain inaccessible to the outside world. Many people have chosen to live there for these reasons—spectacular views, clean air, pristine lakes, rivers and streams, and the rugged grandeur of its landscape. The northern reaches of Idaho's panhandle, known for all of these things, has also garnered media attention since the mid-1980s because some of its inhabitants have moved there specifically to get away from the reach of the federal government, from nonwhite people (among whom they include Jews), and from what they claim is a brewing international conspiracy. Idaho harbors some of the most famous white supremacists in recent memory.

Richard Girnt Butler and Aryan Nations

The Aryan Nations compound was located just outside the northern panhandle's Hayden Lake. It existed from its founding in the early 1970s until 2001. Richard Girnt Butler was born in Colorado in 1918. A former Lockheed engineer, he moved from southern California to Coeur d'Alene in 1973. Soon after, he founded his Identity-based Church of Jesus Christ, Christian, and the compound quickly followed.[28] In 1970, the population of Idaho was around 713,000.[29] Butler found that encouraging, especially coming from a heavily populated area of the West Coast.

As a young man, Butler and his parents resettled in Los Angeles after the Great Depression. Butler studied aeronautical engineering at Los Angeles City College and served in the armed forces during World War II. Following his military stint, he returned to California troubled about what he felt were wrong turns America was making with regard to political and social policies. He landed a job at Lockheed as an engineer and, during the years following World War II, came into contact with retired colonel William Potter Gale, an Identity proponent and organizer of other rightist groups like the Posse Comitatus. By the mid-1960s, Butler was a hardcore Identity follower. Through his work as national director of the Christian Defense League, he developed a working relationship with well-known Identity pastor Wesley Swift and attended his congregation until Swift's death in 1971, at which point Butler declared his ministry the direct successor to Swift's.[30] A longtime supporter of racist beliefs, "Pastor" Butler has supported the "Northwest Territorial Imperative"—the goal of establishing a whites-only "homeland" (a "national racist state") in the northwest United States that would include the states of Idaho, Washington, Oregon, Montana, and Wyoming.[31] According to the National Network of Libraries and Medicine for the Pacific Northwest region, this area has the largest land mass in the United States but is the least populated, even in the early twentieth century.[32]

Why Idaho? "'Aryans are Nordic in their blood,' Butler claimed. "'North Idaho is a natural place for the white man to live.'"[33] It was also a reasonably inexpensive place for the white man to live in the early 1970s. Land was available for $200 an acre and Butler may have found a better audience for his Identity leanings than he had encountered in southern California. James Aho notes that "a substantial minority of Kootenai [KOOT-nee] and Shoshone County residents are descendants of Confederate states loyalists" who had migrated to those counties to work the mines in the Silver Valley in the early part of the twentieth century.[34] The Anglo-Israel movement had already made inroads in the Pacific Northwest by 1970, and several retired Church of Jesus Christ, Christian, congregants were living near Coeur d'Alene.[35]

By the early 1970s, some prominent Identity spokesmen had begun to settle in the Idaho panhandle. Aho argues that they came because Idaho seemed to offer respite (at least temporarily) from police surveillance as well as a preexisting system of mutual aid and moral support. Among all these kindred spirits, these men of Identity dreamed about establishing a pure, Aryan nation.[36]

Since the fledgling Identity movement had already made inroads in the Pacific Northwest by 1970 and several retired disciples of the Church of Jesus Christ, Christian, were living near Coeur d'Alene,[37] Butler began to push for a white homeland. And the backbone of any Aryan state, Butler counseled, is agriculture and the farmers who make it happen.[38] Without an infrastructure predicated on the yeoman farmer, an Aryan state was untenable. Butler's compound, however, wasn't situated in the best place for agriculture (especially large-scale) and presumably, he and his compound colleagues didn't plant much of anything green. Why, then, did he place such emphasis on it?

Butler may not have been a farmer himself, but he knew what fields to plow for recruits to his ideology. The American farmer was, as Henry Nash Smith has pointed out, a collective representation, a poetic idea that defined the promise of American life.[39] The image was a dominant one in the nineteenth century,[40] but here it was again, resurrected in the twentieth century as the anxiety wrought by uncertain economic times and big government inspired many to look to a mythic past for answers.

Butler understood this, just as he understood the importance of symbols in his movement. On the one hand, he needed proud Aryan warriors willing to take up arms for the movement. And on the other, he needed proud Aryan men willing to work on farms for the movement. He touted the values of God, work, and agriculture, though he may not have had much to do with tilling the soil or working the land during his twenty-seven-year tenure at the northern Idaho compound. And in the late 1970s and early 1980s, when Butler was spending a great deal of energy in pushing his compound and ideology, America's family farms were caught in a deepening economic crisis.

Consequently, Butler demonstrated his sympathy for family farmers losing their farms by touting the importance of agriculture in America. At the same time, he couched his message in such a way as to garner interest in his movement from farmers either already displaced or in danger of becoming so. But-

The Aryan Nations compound near Hayden, Idaho. Here it stands deserted on 22 May 2001, after leader Richard G. Butler lost a court battle and, as a result, ownership of the compound. Note the printing press standing near the front door. Aryan Nations was able to produce its own literature for dissemination in its early days; the advent of computers made this much easier. Internet millionaire Greg Carr (Prodigy, Inc.) purchased the compound. Copyright © Associated Press.

ler's Aryan state needed farmers, so he was willing to provide the land for them if they joined the movement. The more people who participated, the greater the chances for the White American Bastion to come to pass. Simply put, Butler was looking for homesteaders.

His compound, which Butler himself touted as "the international headquarters of the White race," hosted annual white supremacist summer festivals called "Aryan World Congresses" (or the World Congress of Aryan Nations). As many as 200 people from a variety of white supremacist groups attended the gatherings, which included workshops on paramilitary training and networking opportunities. The compound's location provided two major advantages: first, it was located in a remote area of northern Idaho, which made it difficult for law enforcement, counterdemonstrators, and media to access; and second, its setting by its very nature provided a rugged, unspoiled outdoor experience that resonated with the separatist and survivalist leanings of many white supremacists who attended the congresses.[41]

During the early 1980s, Butler undertook projects to encourage further settlement and conversion to his cause. He initiated an Aryan youth academy in an attempt to inculcate Aryan Nations philosophy (including no drinking or drugging) in local children, and he tried to appeal to young men and women (skinhead gatherings) through racist music festivals held each April (to coincide with Hitler's birthday). By the late 1980s, Butler had established Aryan Nations sub-chapters in several other states and had begun prison outreach programs.[42] Specifically, Butler was active in recruiting white prison inmates through his newsletter "Calling Our Nation." He regularly corresponded with inmates and disseminated racist and anti-Semitic literature to them, trying to convince them to come to the compound and do battle for the Aryan homeland once they had served their terms. In 1987, Butler's Aryan Nations began providing financial and administrative support for a prison outreach newsletter edited by inmate David Lane, one of the men involved with The Order, who was sentenced to life in prison for civil rights violations in the murder of Denver radio talk show host Alan Berg.[43]

Though not necessarily an idea that originated solely with Butler's cohorts in Idaho, the quest for a "homeland" for "dwindling numbers of Aryans" has consumed a great deal of the literature. Whether in the form of dire warnings or advertisements for land co-ops in rural areas, white supremacist groups advocate

Pastor Richard Girnt Butler, center, leader of the Idaho-based Aryan Nations. He and other Aryan Nations members engage in Nazi salutes as counter-demonstrators at an Aryan Nations rally attempt to shout them down on 3 July 1999. About eighty members of the group had marched into Coeur d'Alene, Idaho, during an annual meeting at the nearby Hayden compound. Copyright © Associated Press.

a white stronghold within the United States and that area is usually somewhere relatively difficult to access via conventional means. Donald Clerkin, for example, founder of the Milwaukee-based Euro-American Alliance, called, as early as 1976, for the creation of a white "training base" named "Europolis" that would have to be situated in "rough country, country not easily accessible to our enemies."[44] Idaho's panhandle offered such a place in 1973 — three years before Clerkin issued his call.

Even though Butler had advocated a white homeland since the compound's inception, the media did not take an interest in him or his rhetoric until Berg's murder in June 1984. Butler denied that he knew the extent of The Order's activities, though the group has been definitively linked to Aryan Nations. Following Berg's death, Aryan Nations started making the news with stories like "Aryans plan NW homeland," in which Butler was quoted as saying that he was "pleased with the discussions about forming a territorial sanctuary in Washington, Oregon, Idaho, Montana and Wyoming."[45]

In recognition of Butler's plan, one author who called himself "Fafnir" stated that "[a]t Hayden Lake, a determination was agreed upon to build the Racial Nation within the boundaries of the existing political State."[46] Remarkably, Butler's quest for a racial homeland did not change for more than thirty years. Someday, if his dreams are realized, he wrote that "pure-blooded white people—an estimated 33 million Americans who claim roots in the twelve Aryan Nations—will abandon most of the continental United States to live in an all-white Republic in the Pacific Northwest.... Hayden Lake will be the capital."[47] In his Republic, only whites would vote, own property, and bear arms. There would be loans without interest and no taxation. Jewish people and other "hybrids," as he referred to nonwhites and mixed-race people, would be "repatriated" from the territory.[48]

Butler also contended that places like northern Idaho are popular destinations for white people because of their rural character and the lack of people of color. In a 1996 interview with journalist Mike Sager, he compared America to a house. The walls, doors, and windows provide protection from the elements, but if the man of the house allows anyone to come in and sleep wherever they like, then soon the house will be overrun. That is why, Butler contended, "people are leaving the cities and coming to places like this [Idaho]. The only thing that will protect the white race from the storm is being with their own kind."[49]

In this white Pacific Northwest–based homeland, with the Aryan Nations compound as the capital, Butler believed that every individual had certain responsibilities predicated on strict social expectations that, in turn, were predicated on even stricter sex roles. In the white homeland, each sex was to have specific duties to perform within the family and within the community as a whole.

The rhetoric of Aryan Nations has contended that the foundation of this state, "like any state," is its farmers and agriculture. "The countryside produces men for the nation, and has been through the generations the eternal source of national strength."[50] Land settlement, with the creation of farm holdings for family inheritance, "is the aim of an Aryan State, rather than the movement of population to the towns and cities."[51] Property ownership would be subject to public control and operated in the national and racial interest, though private ownership would remain in name. However, "since all ownership is regarded as trusteeship for the nation, under God, exploitation must be effectively ended. There shall be no taxation on homes or farms of citizens."[52]

Aryan nationalism advocated a system in which "all men are producers," with the exception of children and the elderly, who are to be cared for with "State help and allowances."[53] For their part, women are to have one major responsibility and that is children—bearing them and caring for them. "A creed of Aryan women is this: 'We serve the life of our people. We regard our household tasks as a means for achieving and maintaining the physical and spiritual health of the nation.'" An Aryan woman, furthermore, brings "true love and affection, and a happy, well-run home to refresh and inspire her man."[54] An Aryan girl, for her part, must educate herself with regard to her future role as a wife of an Aryan man and mother of Aryan children. In Butler's vision, "there is a world of man and the world of woman. Nature ordained that man should be the guardian of the family and protector of the community." Women were to focus on family, husband, children, and home.[55]

Aryan men, meanwhile, were to serve as protectors of their race (specifically white women, children, and the homeland) in addition to working as farmers and industrialists in the so-called White American Bastion. Some would be called upon to serve in an elite capacity:

> *[These] men of the true Order are of the best the Aryan race has produced in this generation. In them is combined fiery passion and icy discipline, deep intelligence and instant readiness for action, a strong sense of self-worth, and a total commitment to the cause.*[56]

White people, in a sense, allowed bad things to happen because they hadn't lived up to God's expectations. They allowed awful things to come to pass, such as "curses" that included "women's lib, homosexuality, and wars."[57] The Aryan race was not superior, Butler contended, because its members advocated that it was. It was superior because "God so ordained it; it is a fact of history."[58] And the guardians of the white race—the guardians of the white future—are Aryan men.

In October of 2000, Richard Girnt Butler left the twenty-acre Aryan Nations compound for the last time, losing it as a result of a civil suit filed in early 1999.[59] The suit was filed by Morris Dees of the Southern Poverty Law Center on behalf of Victoria Keenan and her then-teenaged son Jason, who claimed they were assaulted July 1, 1998, when their car backfired as they were driving down the dirt road that passed the compound.

The suit alleged that after the backfire, several Aryan Nations guards piled into a pickup truck and chased the Keenans' vehicle down the road. Members of the group allegedly fired an SKS assault rifle, among other firearms, at the car. At some point during the chase, the Keenans veered off the road into a ditch, after which they were surrounded by Aryan Nations members, who allegedly grabbed Victoria Keenan's hair and struck her on the arm and struck her son in the back with a heavy object before detaining them at gunpoint.[60]

The court ruled in favor of the Keenans and awarded a 6.3 million dollar judgment. After nearly twenty-five years at the compound, Butler was out of a home and nearly bankrupt. He still had some benefactors, however. Vincent Bertollini and colleague Carl Story were operating the white nationalist 11th Hour Remnant Messenger out of Sandpoint, Idaho. They had been financially supportive of and on friendly terms with Butler since 1990. Bertollini and Story had moved to northern Idaho, above all, because "98 percent of north Idaho's population is of the Adamic [descendants of the biblical Adam] White Aryan people."[61] Butler, a widower since 1995, and his German shepherd Fritz moved into a house in nearby Hayden that Bertollini purchased for him.[62] He died in his sleep September 8, 2004, at the age of 86.[63]

In March 2001, the Keenans sold the compound to the Carr Foundation, a human rights group based in Cambridge, Massachusetts. In May of that year, the foundation began dismantling the compound with plans to convert it into a retreat.[64] However, Greg Carr of the foundation had stated earlier that they would probably turn the land over to firefighters, who could use the property for a training exercise, and then sell parcels as pasture.[65] Ironically, Butler's compound would finally see use as agricultural land.

Butler had not only lost the compound in the court battle; he had also lost the right to use the name "Aryan Nations."[66] He thus adopted "Aryan National Alliance," though his website is still available as "Twelve Aryan Nations."[67] In addition to the legal battles and subsequent loss of the compound, miniwars

Aryans Awake!

Join with
Aryan Nations
in the Battle for
Christ, Race, and
Nation!

Before God our Honor!
"For there is no more sacred duty... no higher law to
obey, than the battle for the existence of our Racial
Nation..." RGB

ARYAN NATIONS, P.O. BOX 362, HAYDEN LAKE, IDAHO 83835

Crusading imagery on an Aryan Nations flyer, circa early to mid-1980s. White
men are encouraged to go to battle for the future of their race and to bring about a
white nation. Courtesy of the Wilcox Collection at the University of Kansas Libraries,
Lawrence, RH WL Eph 2097.9.

erupted among Aryan Nations officers and group members over who should succeed the pastor as the rightful leader of the neo-Nazi organization.

Butler originally appointed Ray Redfairn of Dayton, Ohio, to succeed him as national director, but in September 2001, the two apparently had a falling out. August Kreis, based in Ulysses, Pennsylvania, then announced plans to build another Aryan Nations compound, but his plans later fell through because of a lack of funds. Kreis had been an officer (Minister of Information and Propaganda) in Butler's Aryan Nations, but Butler denounced him, as well. For their part, Kreis and Redfairn claim that Butler was no longer a recognized leader of Aryan Nations after the compound's demise, though he was to be regarded as the founder of the group.[68]

At the end of 2003, the dispute continued to seethe as Redfairn and Kreis were at odds. Kreis appointed fellow Pennsylvanian Charles Juba as the "national director" while Butler and Kreis continued to run dueling websites claiming that each is the true Aryan Nations.[69] As of June 2005, the Twelve Aryan Nations website was touted by an Arkansas branch of Aryan Nations as the "World Headquarters" of the group. Kreis' website is under "Aryan Nations" (aryan -nations.org). This website billed Kreis as the "national director," and the contact address is in Lexington, South Carolina. The address on the Twelve Aryan Nations banner is Lincoln, Alabama, both far from the pristine Idaho wilderness Butler proclaimed as the future capital of an Aryan homeland.

And so the compound once stood, a lone outpost on the ideological frontier of white supremacy, where soft white men could transform themselves into hardened Aryan warriors and their Aryan women could stay at home churning out future Aryans. Life at Aryan Nations became a prep course for rough, violent conditions that would coincide with the millennium's end. It was a regimented existence, often strict (a military-style hierarchy in place), and demanded adherence to the rules and regulations of Aryan ideology and Christian Identity. Other requirements included outreach—extending the message to like-minded others. Each Aryan who joined, after all, was another hand to help carve a white homeland out of the northwestern landscape.

Aryan Nations operated as a frontier vanguard—a fort—with ideological leanings that echoed the rhetoric of Manifest Destiny and hoped to establish a foothold in hostile territory. Ultimately, Butler's mission—to carve a white homeland/homestead out of the northwestern forests and plains—failed. His message, however, resonated with others who took even more extreme action.

Charles J. Juba, director of the branch of Aryan Nations based in Pennsylvania following the loss of the Idaho compound, stands second from left in front. He is flanked by Josh Webster of Alabama and Barbara Kreis, age ten. Her father, August Kreis, stands behind her. Kreis' chapter of Aryan Nations lists contact information in South Carolina. Barbara Kreis raises her arm in a Nazi salute; the "88" on her tee shirt symbolizes the eighth letter of the alphabet, which is "h." Together, "88" means "hh," or "heil Hitler." The Aryan Nations insignia appears on Juba's left lapel and Webster's left arm. Webster also sports the Klan logo on his left breast. This photo was taken on 25 September 2004 at a neo-Nazi rally at Valley Forge National Historic Park in Pennsylvania. Copyright © Associated Press.

Trails West: Robert Mathews and The Order

At the Aryan Nations compound, rituals that emphasize men's physical strength and bravery were performed on special occasions—generally Aryan World Congresses, holidays, and initiation rites. These rituals included cross-burnings or elaborate knighting ceremonies in which a man was welcomed into the Aryan Nations fold and took a warrior's oath. Or they might have involved secret "brotherhood" meetings not unlike those enacted in fraternal organizations earlier in the twentieth century.[70] Like those organizations, rituals and ceremonies in white supremacist groups serve as a social glue. They foster a feeling of inclusiveness among their participants—a sense of belonging to something bigger than the self.

They also provide a sense of mission and loyalty and, ideally, a willingness within each participant to carry out duties and responsibilities in the group.

Whether he consciously understood this about group dynamics or not, Robert J. Mathews, leader of The Order, used rituals, ceremonies, and stirring martial rhetoric that often included references to Nordic mythology to inspire the men in his organization to carry out robberies and murders during the early 1980s. Wives and girlfriends of the men of The Order often provided locks of their hair as talismans and symbols of what the struggle was about. Furthermore, the oath to be a member of The Order was taken in a group setting, the group surrounding a baby or child (always female), in recognition that the Aryan man's duty was also to ensure the survival of Aryan women.[71] Women, for their part, were not to engage in the struggle. They were to ensure the comfort of an Aryan man at home and provide him children.

In Mathews' last letter, written shortly before his death in an FBI/ATF stand-off in 1984, he spoke of how he suspected he would soon die. He expressed no fear of that. He claimed that "the reality of life is death" and the worst his enemies could do is "shorten his tour of duty in this world." He signed off with the statement, "for blood, soil, honor, for faith and for race."[72]

Mathews exemplified what Butler attempted to convey through his rhetoric about male Aryan warriors. He referred to a "tour of duty," a military term, but also referred to his responsibility—his duty—to sacrifice himself for the future of his children and ultimately for the white race. In Mathews, the frontier myth melded neatly with white supremacist rhetoric and ideas about Aryan manhood. Under Mathews' direction, the group called The Order (sometimes referred to as "The Silent Brotherhood" or "Die Brüderen Schweigen") would involve itself in robberies and, eventually, much worse.

Best known for the 16 June 1984 assassination of Jewish talk-show host Alan Berg, The Order was perhaps the first white supremacist group to put into action the rhetoric of race-cleansing that organizations like Aryan Nations advocated. Under Mathews' leadership, The Order committed several robberies throughout the Pacific Northwest during the early 1980s and ran a counterfeiting operation. With the money from these crimes, Mathews ensured that his small paramilitary army was funded. He also made donations to other white supremacist groups and traveled extensively throughout the United States on networking trips.[73]

The revolutionary actions of The Order were shocking but not unprecedented in the American right wing. During the 1960s, the paramilitary organization the Minutemen, headed by Robert DePugh, set off various leaflet bombs, including one that exploded prematurely near the White House. DePugh and members of

Robert "Bob" Mathews at an Aryan Nations rally in Spokane, Washington, in June 1983. Copyright © Bettmann/CORBIS.

his group were arrested and indicted several times on weapons violations, which included the discoveries of massive stockpiles of guns, ammunition, and survival gear.[74] The Order, however, was different from its predecessors because it was so well organized and operated effectively as an underground terrorist cell.

The Order was a millenarian revolutionary movement that challenged ZOG (the so-called Zionist Occupied Government of the United States), confident that through the power of God it would ultimately emerge victorious.[75] After a crime spree that included an armored car hijacking on a highway and Berg's murder and then the fiery death of Mathews on Whidbey Island, Washington, The Order's ultimate goal—a White American Bastion in the Pacific Northwest—remained unrealized. Nevertheless, Mathews became a martyr for the white supremacist movement, and his story is pivotal to that of the group he founded.

Robert Jay Mathews—known as "Robbie"—was born 16 January 1953 in Marfa, Texas. The family moved to Phoenix in December 1958. Mathews' oldest brother Grant was diagnosed with schizophrenia in 1959, so Mathews and his older brother Lee grew to rely on each other rather than their parents, who were completely absorbed with Grant and his condition. Largely left alone, Mathews joined the John Birch Society at age eleven, much to his parents' consternation. They thought he was too young to engage in such politics. Nevertheless, Mathews maintained his membership. He entered high school and went on a clean living kick that included physical fitness and healthy eating. Nor did he smoke or drink; he would continue this regimen for the rest of his life.[76]

During his high school years, Mathews converted to Mormonism. Many of his fellow students in Tempe were Mormons, and he admired their clean-living, conservative lifestyle. Mathews' parents were not pleased with their son's decision, but relented, apparently afraid that if they didn't, he would rebel in other ways. Through his Mormon network, Mathews also fell in with supporters of tax resistance. This, coupled with his extreme anticommunism and hatred of Russia, led him to begin criticizing the U.S. government and the ways in which he thought foreign and domestic policy were playing into the hands of the enemy.[77]

Eventually, Mathews decided that he wanted to go to West Point after high school, but the My Lai Massacre in Vietnam occurred just before he was to take the qualifying exam. This event soured him on becoming a soldier. Nevertheless, he took the exam to appease his parents, but scored too low in math, losing a chance at the military academy. In 1971, Mathews' parents received notification that their son would not be able to graduate from high school because of an incomplete in an economics class that he had refused to attend. The teacher, Mathews felt, was an advocate of "creeping socialism."[78]

When he was around nineteen or twenty, Mathews joined the Sons of Liberty, an Arizona-based paramilitary group that advocated underground resistance to the government. The Sons of Liberty believed that Jews were responsible for income taxes, which were part of a master plan to control this country through economic dependence.[79] Details of what happened following his stint with the Sons are scarce, though Mathews claimed that the IRS had "shot at him" and that he had gotten into trouble with the FBI. In January 1974, he was placed on six months probation for tax evasion. He then went to work at the Magma copper mine in Superior, Arizona.[80]

Drifting and dissatisfied, Mathews made a decision to try his luck elsewhere in the country. One story goes that he closed his eyes and put a finger on a map one day. Upon opening his eyes, he saw that his finger rested on Metaline Falls, Washington, a town of about 200 people in the northeastern corner of the state.[81] This part of Washington abuts northern Idaho and shares its neighbor's rugged, forested topography. Mathews fell in love with the place and made plans to save some money and buy land. He landed a job at the Bunker Hill Mine and prepared to settle down. Mathews' father helped his son make payments on sixty acres and even helped the younger man clear the land—after he had gotten Robbie's promise that he was through with the white supremacist movement.[82]

In 1976, Mathews married Debbie McGarrity, a woman who had responded to an ad he had placed in *Mother Earth News*.[83] In 1977, Mathews' parents and brothers, Grant and Lee, moved to Metaline Falls to live with him (now "Bob") on his land. Mathews' parents had their son's promise that he was no longer involved in white supremacist extremism, so the move was a decision they made happily.[84] Mathews, however, had not made good on his promise. He had continued to ponder the fate of the white race, and by 1980 he was corresponding with the National Alliance, a neo-Nazi organization based in Virginia. Through his Alliance contacts, he found out about Butler's Church of Jesus Christ, Christian, at Hayden Lake, about three hours east of Metaline Falls.

It was through the Alliance and its leader, William Pierce, that Mathews discovered *The Turner Diaries*, which seems eerily reminiscent of the later actions of The Order.[85] Pierce wrote *The Turner Diaries* under the pseudonym of Andrew MacDonald. He was the leader of the white supremacist group the National Alliance (the largest neo-Nazi organization in the United States), based in Mill Point, Virginia. A former physics professor who taught at Oregon State University from 1962 to 1965, Pierce ended up back in his native South as head of the Alliance. In the mid-1980s, he purchased land in Mill Point and moved the headquarters of the group from Arlington. He died in July 2002.[86] The Order's members, though fans of *The Turner Diaries*, used other books as so-called personal bibles. Mathews' tract was William G. Simpson's *Which Way Western Man*, whereas ideas for tactics came from *The Road Back*, a manual of guerrilla warfare.[87]

In *The Turner Diaries*, the main character, Earl Turner, records his exploits as a white man at the end of the world. He joins an underground group called the Organization in the early 1990s, which wages guerrilla war by attacking banks and Jewish-owned stores for funds. The elite core of the Organization is a smaller group called the Order. Members of the Organization murder Jewish conspirators, African Americans, and law enforcement officials, striking fear in America's "Zionist overlords."

One of Turner's first projects involves the destruction of the FBI's national headquarters with a truckload of homemade explosives. Another Turner project is to flood the American economy with counterfeit money before taking control of a nuclear arsenal and using it to attack Israel and selected Zionist targets in Russia. Turner and his followers stockpile a huge collection of weapons in Pennsylvania as the revolution unfolds, and they take these arms and attack the Pentagon, where Turner dies a martyr's death. By 1999, according to the book's epilogue, the dream of a white world becomes a reality.[88] That was what Mathews wanted to see.

He became more outraged during the early 1980s by the things he saw going on around him. The economy, he thought, was in shambles. Industry important to the area like logging and mining were laying people off. And worst of all, the Farm Crisis was hitting family farmers extremely hard. Mathews had managed to collect a small following of men and convert them to his views, but the early 1980s spurred him to greater action. He was interested in building not only a homeland, but also a following. To fuel a movement, he knew he needed money, so he and his comrades began planning robberies to funnel money into their own coffers for guns and supplies and also to other like-minded groups for whatever they needed to further the movement and the revolution of the white race.

By 1982, Mathews had adopted Butler's ideas about the White American Bastion and began working hard to publicize it. He ultimately wanted to sell the Pacific Northwest as a "natural" territory for white families (clean air, clean water, few nonwhites). Through sheer force of numbers, the Bastion would be able to exert the economic, social, and political influence that Mathews thought the country lacked. He put ads in white supremacist newspapers and printed pamphlets using the press at Aryan Nations. One featured a White American Bastion banner under which two white men—one a Viking warrior and the other a caped pioneer-type—faced each other in a pine forest. And, like that pioneer, Mathews began constructing more cabins on his land in preparation for the tides of people he expected who would come to settle their homeland.[89] Despite all of his time, money, and energy, only one couple moved to the Northwest to join his efforts.[90]

Mathews also targeted his recruiting efforts at farmers and independent truckers because, as he saw it, "from the beginning of this nation to the present, the yeoman farmer has been a symbol of the Aryan work ethic—the living monument to masculinity." Mathews spoke of his recruiting efforts among farmers and ranchers, "a class of our people who have been hit especially hard by the filthy lying Jews and their parasitical usury system."[91] He was well aware of the Farm Crisis and may have found some welcome listeners to his rhetoric. Mathews felt that urban living corrupted people and that the only way to revitalize the body and mind was through the soil. That is, through working it and harvesting its bounties. Consequently, he took it upon himself to raise farmers' interest in his movement, since he needed someone to help him create an agricultural infrastructure in the White American Bastion. Few, if any, did.

Mathews was growing increasingly frustrated with what he perceived as the inaction of other white supremacist groups. He decided to take more drastic action to further his goals. During the early 1980s, white men were constantly coming and going at Mathews's homestead, drawn by his charisma and willingness to help many of them financially. He would put them to work on his land, preparing more sites for living quarters.[92] Richard Kemp and Richard Scutari, two members of The Order who are now serving long sentences for their involvement in the crimes of the group, informed me that Mathews was extremely generous with his time and money. Kemp, who was one of the youngest members of the group, said that he felt sometimes that Mathews was a "father figure" to him and others who felt displaced by the American economy and what they felt were antiwhite policies in affirmative action.[93] Mathews was beginning to make a name for himself in larger white supremacist circles through his tireless advocacy for the movement and his generosity of spirit in any venue for the cause.

In September 1983, The Order made its initial appearance. Mathews gathered eight men willing to work with him, and they met in the barracks on Mathews Acres, where Mathews conducted an elaborate ceremony that involved the circle of men standing around one of the men's baby daughters. They swore an oath "upon the green graves" of their sires, upon the children "in the wombs" of their wives, and "upon the throne of God almighty." In the oath, Mathews and his followers declared their "sacred duty" to do whatever necessary to deliver white people "from the Jew and bring total victory to the Aryan race." They declared that they were in a "full state of war" and would not rest until the enemy had been "driven into the sea."[94]

Once Mathews assembled his inner circle, he launched his money-making ventures, which began with small-time robberies and culminated with armored car heists. Like the fictional character Earl Turner, he also spearheaded a counterfeiting operation. Also like Turner's Organization, Mathews' Order fully intended to kill the enemy. Alan Berg, well known among extremists for his bombastic, anti–right wing opinions, was the second (and last) victim of Mathews' master plan. The first was Walter West, a member of The Order who other members felt "talked too much." According to journalists Kevin Flynn and Gary Gerhardt, Order members Richard Kemp and James Dye took West deep into the Kaniksu National Forest of northern Idaho, where Kemp hit him over the head with a sledgehammer, though the blow didn't kill him. Randy Duey then shot West in the forehead. David Tate accompanied the small group.[95]

Berg was shot to death outside his Denver home in a hail of automatic weapon fire in June 1984. Bruce Pierce was the shooter; he was accompanied by Mathews and David Lane, whom Berg had taunted as "sick" when Lane called into his show at an earlier date to challenge him. Order chief of security Richard Scutari was implicated as the getaway car driver, but his involvement in the Berg murder couldn't be definitively proven.[96]

The Order began to unravel when the FBI found a gun that was registered to one of Mathews' group and that Mathews himself had accidentally dropped during an armored car heist outside Ukiah, California. FBI agents traced it to The Order member who had purchased the gun in Montana and, through his name and phone records, discovered the link to the radical right and consequently to Berg's murder.[97]

On 6 December 1984, with the FBI closing in and Order members on the run, Mathews fled to Whidbey Island off the coast of Washington State, where he barricaded himself along with comrade Ian Stewart in an uninhabited summer home. Through an informant who had been a sometime member of The Order, representatives from the FBI, ATF, and SWAT surrounded the house and tried to negotiate with Mathews. A few members of The Order who had already been captured tried to talk him out of the house, but Mathews' response was that he would only surrender if parts of Washington, Idaho, and Montana were set aside as an Aryan homeland.[98]

Stewart surrendered the next day, leaving Mathews alone in the two-story house. At one point, agents tried to sneak in after Mathews faked a suicide (one shot and a low moan). The Order leader opened fire from a second-story bathroom but did not succeed in hitting anyone. He also fired through the roof at a helicopter hovering overhead the evening of the second day and shot at agents in the woods. Finally, law enforcement decided to lob M-79 Starburst flares into the house, hoping that the ensuing flames would bring Mathews out.[99] They didn't. Mathews died December 8 in the fire the flares created.[100]

Following Mathews' death, Order members were summarily rooted out and brought up on charges that included counterfeiting, robbery, racketeering, and murder. The group is now defunct, but its members are still considered heroes of the white supremacist movement and receive frequent mention on rightist websites. The members of The Order who are still in prison are referred to as "political prisoners."[101] Most are still involved in white supremacist causes.

Robert Mathews exemplified ideal Aryan manhood. The consummate frontiersman, he worked hard to clear his land and prepare it for agriculture, he studied racist tracts diligently, stayed active in spiritual pursuits, and he married a white woman who believed that women should stay home and produce Aryan children. He lived "cleanly," apparently never drinking, smoking, or swearing, and he worked out constantly. He abhorred television, though he apparently liked to watch Clint Eastwood and Charles Bronson movies when he stayed with friends who had VCRs.[102] He recruited other Aryan men for his group and he initiated a plan that, he believed, would result in "freedom" for whites in the Pacific Northwest. To Mathews, the revolution had begun. The race war that signaled the apocalypse in *The Turner Diaries* was coming to pass and The Order's members were the shock troops.

Like Richard Butler of Aryan Nations and white supremacists across the country, Mathews believed in rigidly defined gender roles. He spent most of his time with men, conducting the business of men: tactical battle strategies in the New War. He was a product of the Cold War and Vietnam; his was a world of things gone terribly wrong, in which "true" American values were lost in a sea of debauchery, corruption, and miscegenation. Like other New Warriors, Mathews and his associates stockpiled the latest in military-style hardware. Order member Bruce Pierce, for example, used a .45 caliber submachine gun equipped with a silencer to shoot Alan Berg.[103]

Mathews established a miniature "homeland" of sorts in the Pacific Northwest for his white "kinsmen," a place of safety and rebirth in the wake of the coming race war, a place of large forests and, in many cases, sparse population. Here Mathews homesteaded, clearing his land and constructing his houses and outbuildings not unlike many people a hundred years before his arrival. He was aware of a "frontier spirit"; he incorporated it into the rhetoric behind his White American Bastion.

The men who made up his band of Aryan warriors—many culled from the Aryan Nations compound—were examples of Gibson's New War.[104] Many had been in trouble with the law or perhaps simply felt that they "didn't fit in anywhere." Most either couldn't hold regular jobs or had low-paying jobs, and a few were military veterans. All were looking for something that would put their skills to use and that might also make them feel as if they were "worth something." Mathews' charisma and his sense of mission provided his followers with goals and a sense of purpose: planned robberies, counterfeiting, and stalking and killing Alan Berg.

For example, Order member Denver Daw Parmenter II was an ex-military man who was born into a military family. He served in the army from 1970 to 1973 as a clerk-typist at a NATO installation in Turkey. After his honorable discharge, he moved to Bellingham, Washington, where he served as a clerk and administrative assistant to the vice president of finance at Western Washington University. Deciding to attend college, he moved to Cheney, near Spokane, to attend Eastern Washington University (ESU), where he washed dishes and did janitorial work to make ends meet. He was active in fraternities and gained a reputation as a financial "whiz kid." Parmenter married his girlfriend in 1981 and graduated with a degree in political science and economics, but the only job he could get after graduating was as a parts manager at an equipment company in Spokane. Parmenter apparently battled alcoholism, which indicates that he was struggling with some demons.[105]

Fellow member Randolph George Duey met Parmenter at EWU. He was a better-than-average student, but, because he continually switched majors, he racked up credit hours but never graduated. He was also an Air Force veteran who, in addition to taking classes, taught survival skills at Fairchild Air Force Base outside Spokane. He ended up getting a full-time job with the U.S. Postal Service before he joined Mathews' group and began to explore different spiritual and political beliefs, which eventually led him to Christian Identity.[106]

Gary Lee Yarbrough, for his part, grew up in a violent household in Arizona. By the time he was eighteen, he was in trouble with the law for grand theft. In 1973, he was given the option of joining the Marine Corps or doing time. He chose the Marines, but quickly went AWOL and began serving 5–8 years in Florence, Arizona. It was through Butler's prison recruitment that Yarbrough was introduced to white supremacy. After his release, he headed to Idaho, where he eventually met Mathews at the Aryan Nations compound.[107]

Mathews offered the chance for these three and the other members of his gang to "be real men." As Aryan men, they had certain responsibilities and duties to each other, to white women, and to the white race. Mathews was very clear about this and himself served as an example of Aryan manhood. Like Butler, he had gone to the Pacific Northwest seeking a place to homestead, seeking his own frontier. Like Butler, he had spent most of his life steeped in the rhetoric of the extremist right and lived his life according to the tenets he expounded. Mathews also developed survival skills through his tenure with groups like the Sons of Liberty, who would spend days and nights training for Armageddon in the deserts and arroyos of Arizona. In The Order, he incorporated his ideas about the coming apocalypse and his expectations of his men.

The Order is therefore significant in the history of American extremism because it was the first of a new kind of white supremacist organization—a sophisticated terrorist operation with cells, safe houses, fake IDs, and communication blinds.[108] A product of modern survivalist culture that developed in the wake of the Vietnam War, The Order's members, like soldiers going to battle, prepared to fight the New War so that a new frontier could be established in the wreckage of doomsday. Mathews and his band of followers are but one manifestation of a white male paramilitary culture that emerged after the Vietnam War. Their message, though extreme, merely amplified already extant underlying tenets of white male dominance that the feminist and civil rights movements challenged in the 1960s and 1970s.

In the face of this challenge, some white men found a sense of mission and purpose in white supremacist groups like The Order and Richard Butler's Aryan Nations. The ideology and rhetoric of these groups lay claim to a frontier heritage that is embedded in ideas about American "character." Butler's Aryan Nations and The Order did not necessarily refer to themselves as cowboys and they certainly did not limit themselves to fighting Indians. They did, however, tap into the foundations of American "character," which relies on frontier imagery. Firmly rooted in that imagery is a white male archetype, pushing ever westward, seeking new homelands and new beginnings.

CHAPTER 4

From Farms to Arms

Populists, Plowshares, and Posses

[W]hat really is the truth is that here in the heartland of rural America,
and the heartland of the entire American Nation, sits the heart and soul
and, if you will allow me, the conscience of the Nation....
—North Dakota Governor George Sinner, speaking at a 1987 Congressional hearing with regard to problems facing American farmers

To hear Governor Sinner tell it, American farming seems to rest on an intimate, almost spiritual relationship between farmers and soil; farming is a foundation of American character.[1] As I have argued, perceptions of the "West" rest on images of men—white and Protestant—riding the range, driving wagon trains, and building towns on the "frontier." However, ideas about the "West" also rest on images of Thomas Jefferson's yeoman farmer. Though not as adventurous or romantic as, say, The Virginian, farmers and agriculture nevertheless have spawned their own cultural mythology that still resonates in the beginning years of the twenty-first century.

In this chapter, I will discuss this "agrarian myth" and its lasting hold on American perceptions of the West and, by extension, the nation. I will also discuss the tradition of what Catherine McNicol Stock calls American "rural radicalism," with particular emphasis on late-nineteenth-century Populism and its ideological relationship to late-twentieth-century populist sentiment.[2] The rise of right-wing extremism in rural America (here, those rural areas west of the Mississippi River) has its roots, like other manifestations of the right, in earlier American history.

Twentieth-century rural radicalism, like its predecessors, was a response to external forces that included economic pressures and environmental conditions. And, like the big "P" Populism, late-twentieth-century rural radicals sought answers to their plight in action, in reaching out to people in similar situations, in railing against "big government" and "big money." Where Populism and populism diverge, however, is in a rhetorical twist difficult to untangle from its historical roots. The populism of the late twentieth century, sprouting in the fields of discontent originally sown by the Vietnam War, preaches exclusion rather than inclusion. It is ultimately not a language of community, of coming together for the common good of the country. Rather, it places blame for American social problems and agricultural failures on shadowy figures that are part of an international Jewish conspiracy working against the interests of white people.

As we shall see, the agricultural crisis of the late 1970s and 1980s encouraged the growth of right-wing ideologies and groups such as the Posse Comitatus, which, along with other groups like it, is an expression of American agrarian/frontier mythology and results of that mythology. Like the lone cowboy, the struggling or triumphant American farmer (usually male) stands as an icon of the West and, by extension, of America itself. Embedded in the cowboy and the farmer are both freedom and self-sufficiency, two pinnacles of mythic American "character." Implicit in these symbols, however, is the image of a white, Protestant man setting down roots on the western frontier. The question thus is not how long the roots are, but rather what sort of trees have sprouted.

Big "P" Populism and Its Little "p" Descendants

In the final decade of the nineteenth century, a wave of rural radicalism swept over southern and western portions of this country in response to a variety of economic and environmental stresses. The movement evolved into a third political party and took the name "Populist," or "People's" Party.[3] The Populists enjoyed some success in implementing their program, which would come to fruition more so during the Progressive Era and beyond.[4] They also proved significant in western politics for three reasons. First, the Populist Party represented a regional political movement in which people in the West and South joined together in a challenge to economic dominance of the Northeast. Second, it raised the issue of the West's economic subordinance to the Northeast and demanded solutions that involved political intervention on the part of the federal government in terms of national and regional economies. Third, the Populist Party represented a political revolution in the West as farmers attempted to wrest political control from small-town elites.

Big "P" Populism evolved, broadly, because capitalists reaped the wealth that farmers created. Farmers, however, argued that they received nothing in return. Though western and Southern Populists might have been vague about the identity of these capitalists and the money power they represented, they were nonetheless specific about its abuses and local agents: railroads, because of a high rate structure that discriminated against agricultural shippers; middlemen who controlled grain elevators and profited more from storing farmers' products than farmers got for growing them; bankers and mortgage companies that charged exorbitant interest rates; and a gold standard that caused steady deflation.[5]

What Populism managed to accomplish with these umbrella issues was the unification—however temporary—of diverse interest groups all struggling for the common good. Robert Larson's work on Rocky Mountain Populism notes that in different states, different local interests converged under the Populist aegis in an attempt to make their voices heard and bring about change. These interests included miners, farmers, livestock owners, and labor unions (not necessarily mutually exclusive).[6] Larson also notes that local Populist movements could incorporate nativist and theological issues; Montana included an anti-Chinese plank, Colorado Populists also exhibited some anti-Chinese sentiment, and Utah's theocratic framework encouraged cooperation between farmers—the Mormon influence may have dissuaded open agrarian uprising. Wyoming Populists were not as engrossed in the free coinage issue and instead were drawn into range wars between large and small livestock holders, while Colorado Populists emphasized the silver issue, because of the state's strong silver industry.[7]

Peter Argersinger further notes that the western Populist movement drew from different cultural traditions that included rural protest and religion. Participants often framed their appeals in evangelical language and invoked moral imperatives to attack industrial capitalism and an unresponsive polity for permitting such injustice to remain unchecked.[8] The People's Party, he continued, was "more an uneasy coalition of former opponents temporarily united through dissatisfaction, distress, hope, and hard politics than a unified and cohesive political party."[9] Nevertheless, 1890s Populism was an expression of agrarian revolt that coalesced into a viable third political party and did include diverse interests in its platform.

The party itself emerged from the Farmers' Alliance in Kansas, which managed to sweep the state in the 1890 elections. Populists captured five congressional seats in Kansas and 96 of 126 seats in the state legislature. Kansas also placed a Populist in the United States Senate. In neighboring Nebraska, Alliance candidates captured the legislature, while in the Dakotas they made a few inroads.[10] These victories spurred the formation of a national Populist Party in 1891. The first convention met in Omaha in 1892, where delegates nominated James Weaver for president and adopted a platform that included a graduated income tax, an eight-hour working day, and immigration restriction. The Populist Party phrased its interests in national terms, but the first skirmishes were local, as Larson notes.[11] Regardless, the issues that Populists addressed had implications that reached far beyond the agricultural and manufacturing sector of the United States.

The Omaha Platform had very specific planks and resolutions that included calls for stronger government regulation in some instances. In the platform, the People's Party condemned the demonetization of silver and called for free and unlimited silver coinage at a ratio to gold of sixteen to one. The party also affirmed the power of the federal government to create and distribute money through a subtreasury plan (in which smaller regional treasuries would be situated to better manage local monetary affairs). The platform suggested a system of postal banks in which to keep money that would be secure from economic downturns. In addition, the platform called for government reclamation of land that was unused by railroads or other corporations or "foreign-owned." As an extension of this reclamation, the unused land was to be opened only to "actual settlers" so it could be put into production use. Furthermore, railroads and telephone and telegraph lines should be nationalized to ensure access for working and poorer Americans. Populists also called for a graduated income tax and demanded that the federal government expand to stop poverty and oppression in the nation.[12]

The series of resolutions tacked onto the Omaha Platform included reforms that, like some of the platform's planks, would find further expression during the Progressive era and beyond. These included calls for an eight-hour workday, direct election of senators, the implementation of the initiative and referendum, tax reductions for producers, the formal limitation of the president and vice president to two elected consecutive terms, and immigration restriction.[13]

In the elections of 1892, many western Populists fused with the minority party in a given state or locality (usually the Democrats) to defeat the majority party (usually the Republicans), though the types of alliances varied.[14] Local fusion brought some immediate political success, but weakened the overall organization and effectiveness of the Populist Party. It was difficult, thus, for Populists to enact legislation they supported, particularly since Republicans continued to control at least some branch of most state governments.[15]

Four years later, the People's Party would face a crossroads and ultimately, its demise. Politically, when William Jennings Bryan ran for president on the Democratic ticket in 1896, he may actually have inadvertently thrown a wrench into the nascent machinery of the People's Party. Bryan made free coinage of silver at a ratio of sixteen to one with gold one of his primary issues—a major aspect of the Omaha Platform. Bryan delivered his famous (or perhaps infamous) "Cross of Gold" speech at the Democratic convention, where he was trying to get the Democratic nomination for president against the Republican William McKinley.

Bryan had basically stolen Populist thunder; he took a Populist issue but was carrying it as a Democrat, which threatened to reduce the effectiveness of the Populists as a viable third political party.

Indeed, the Populist Party had already felt some strain from a growing split within its ranks. Some Populists felt their issues would be better handled were they to merge (hence the name "fusion Populists") with sympathetic Democrats. Other Populists, like the 1896 Populist nominee for president, Georgian lawyer Tom Watson, advocated a "middle-of-the-road" approach. That is, steer clear of both major parties and don't fuse with either. The Democratic Party had tried to sabotage the Populists since their inception, and the Republicans didn't seem to truly support western or Southern farmers or workers. Watson lobbied to schedule the Populist national convention before both Republican and Democratic conventions so as to prevent any attempts at fusion with the major parties. He was unsuccessful and watched with perturbation as Bryan spouted Populist sentiment, garnering much support from fusion advocates. Bryan received the Democratic nomination for President *and* the Populist nomination—the fusion Populists had carried the day during the hectic conventions of 1896 and had seemed to subsume their party in the Democratic fold.[16]

Watson received the Populist vice-presidential nomination but Bryan ignored him, working instead with the Democratic nominee, Arthur Sewall, a probusiness candidate. Watson lashed out at Sewall and Bryan as well as fusion Populists. As punishment for his attacks, the Bryan/Watson ticket was removed from many Southern states, though Watson managed to poll twenty-seven electoral votes on his own. Ironically, Watson's later years, in which he ran for president as a Populist in 1904 and 1908, saw him completely reverse his stance on many inclusive views he previously advocated during his early Populist years. He became extremely racist, supported the Klan, and, as he made more money, denounced socialism, from whose ranks many Populists had come. Watson would eventually be elected to the U.S. Senate in 1920; a cerebral hemorrhage killed him in 1922 at the age of sixty-six.[17]

Bryan, for his part in the 1896 election, managed to carry almost every state west of the Mississippi. However, the single-issue campaign took Populists away from much of their 1892 platform. William McKinley won the election because he carried the states east of the Mississippi and north of the Ohio, where most of the population and electoral votes were centered. As a result of these elections, and because Populists were divided among themselves on the issue of fusion with other parties, they could not reorganize effectively and never again would be an important factor in western politics, though aspects of their platform would persevere and later become aspects of American farm policy.[18]

The Populist movement may have run into trouble also because it differed in political and social emphases in different parts of the country, making it difficult to organize under one definitive banner. In the Rocky Mountain region, because of the importance of mining, Populists emphasized silver coinage. In the South, cotton was a major factor in the regional economy, so issues related to cotton production took precedence over mining. In the Midwest, a major crop was wheat, and like the South, Populists in the Midwest emphasized wheat's importance and, consequently, agriculture, though all regions in which Populism became important emphasized other issues (including local control over railroad prices) in addition to the big ones.[19]

What is important here is not that Populism as a third party ultimately failed, but rather that it tapped into extant American symbols—the rugged individualist working man and Jeffersonian yeoman farmers—and fueled a radical political and social rhetoric whose overall message was progressive. It was the first movement in modern political history to insist that the federal government had some responsibility to ensure the common good and address problems created by industrialization.[20] Ironically, nearly a hundred years after its election successes, another Populist Party would emerge, not as a progressive movement, but rather as a right-wing call to arms, using imagery that included visions (reminiscent of its earlier namesake) of a noble agrarian past, small towns, and opposition to big bankers. Other small "p" populists would also start banding together in groups such as the Posse Comitatus and the American Agricultural Movement to protest government and banking policies in rural America. Where the Populists of the early 1890s attempted to coalesce and move forward as a collective, those of the 1980s emphasized differences among groups and scapegoated others in an attempt to appeal to white, middle-class or working-class Protestant Americans willing to accept the message of exclusion.[21]

Some scholars would argue that it wasn't much of a stretch for 1980s Populists to fall into racist and exclusionary rhetoric; their earlier predecessors drew from a similar vein. Richard Hofstadter argues that early Populists embraced conspiracy theories about a secret international money power and often referred to that power as "Jewish."[22] Hofstadter is careful, however, to point out that references to international Jewish bankers and other anti-Semitic conspiracies were more a "rhetorical device" and not a part of the official Populist platform.[23] Still, the idea of an international money conspiracy run by Jews did appeal to some

Populists in the 1890s, fueled perhaps by the overall jingoism of the age. After all, the Spanish-American War was looming, fueling American foreign policy in and attitudes toward Latin America.[24]

Walter Nugent, writing in 1963 (about the same time as Hofstadter), states that, contrary to some historians of Populism at work during the 1950s, the movement as a whole was not specifically racist, anti-Semitic, or exclusionary. He notes that there were individuals who participated in the movement who may have held these views, but the overall goals of and issues supported by the People's Party did not advocate racist solutions. Nugent attributes the earlier interpretations of Populism to the McCarthy era and the Cold War, which may have fostered conspiracy theories that authors projected onto their work about Populism.[25]

Later historians of Populism, such as Robert Larson and Lawrence Goodwyn, writing in the 1970s, seemed to take Nugent's view. Individual racists and anti-Semites existed in Populist ranks and may have incorporated nativist sentiment in a few local platforms, but the party and the movement as a whole could not be characterized by such.[26] Other recent studies of Populism conducted during the 1990s and early 2000s emphasize local histories and the anticapitalist and anti-industrial nature of the movement as a whole.[27]

However, a strain of exclusion and nativism that some Populist individuals espoused did inform 1980s Populism. Individuals in the movement during the late nineteenth century did buy into conspiracy theories as they sought to undo the power of monied interests and further the rights and dignity of farmers and working classes. Hofstadter notes that an 1895 manifesto signed by fifteen leaders of the Populist Party claimed that an international gold ring was conspiring against Populist attempts to bring back silver coinage.[28] The 1980s Populist Party and small "p" advocates would latch onto conspiracy theories wholeheartedly. In the more recent example, the platform would explicitly emphasize the conspiracy and the role of Jews therein. For Populism, exclusionary rhetoric moved from back rooms to front parlors in the ninety years that separate the original from the spin-off.

Westward, Hoe! The Agrarian Myth in American Culture

The 1980s Populists—they called themselves the Populist Party—did not necessarily subvert the ideology of their predecessors. Rather, the more modern version tapped into the same traditions—rural radicalism and evangelical tumult—but put them to different use. Michael Kazin suggested that an embryonic populist rhetoric composed of two different, but not exclusive, rhetorical strains existed in antebellum America. One was a pietistic impulse inherited from the Protestant Reformation that was continually revived through "Great Awakenings" and the other involved a secular faith acquired from the Enlightenment that encouraged ordinary people to act upon rational analysis. In antebellum America, these two strains coexisted, often intertwined, and ultimately kept populism from splitting into left- and right-wing interpretations as it did in the twentieth century.[29]

Two decades before the formation of the People's Party, American insurgents were already nurturing a language of bitterness and betrayal while waxing sentimental about the mythic lost world of smallholders and artisans. Often, they railed against "elite" financial manipulation and political corruption.[30] Stock traces American rural radicalism and antielite sentiment (elite here interpreted as proprietors) back to white settlement along the eastern seaboard. She notes that many colonists were prepared for radicalism because "they carried with them collective memories of crowd action and agrarian insurgency from their homes in premodern Europe."[31]

Eventually, Enlightenment ideas seeped into earlier conventions and "republicanism"—ideas about human equality and the ability of citizens to form governments by consent—which eroded traditional monarchial society. These republican ideals and experiences served to strengthen American tenants' resolve not to become a permanent peasant class. Stock argues that burgeoning republicanism amid a hierarchical society, a personal stake in independence, population growth, scarcity of land, and improved material circumstances sparked rebellions against landlords in the eighteenth century. Although the elite classes often quelled such insurrections, other uprisings brought about new laws that favored land tenants and small producers.[32]

Like these earlier protests, a major element of populist rhetoric (whether capitalized or not) is an emphasis on "elites" who exploit "the people."[33] Indeed, in Populist rhetoric from the 1890s, a sense of righteousness against elite financiers and bankers, railroad owners, grain elevator middlemen, mine owners, and monied corporate strangleholds served to galvanize "the people" in an attempt to save the ideals of the nation and fix good institutions (e.g. Congress, the presidency, local government) that these elites had damaged.[34]

Prior to the twentieth century, the Enlightenment strain of populist ideology stressed economic grievances (against "the elite") and reaffirmed a producer ethic, while inheritors of evangelicalism emphasized ethical beliefs and called upon the nation to return to Christ. These differences hardened in the twentieth century and resulted in *two* populist heirs, one of which was the rightist strain that appeared in, for example, the 1920s Ku Klux Klan (exemplified by Tom Watson, who cut his political teeth as an antiracist in the early days of the Populist Party) and later in the 1980s Populist Party and the other of which was the more moderate strain that appeared among Progressives in the early part of the twentieth century and later during the 1980s Farm Crisis.[35]

To understand, however, who "the elite" have been at any given time, we must place the members of that class in opposition to something or someone. In populist rhetoric, that "someone" was "the people" and that "something" was made up of the core principles of the republic, in which "all men are created equal." Who, though, is "the people"? Kazin argued that the rising of "'the people' was an avowedly white affair; the democratic vision rarely extended across the color line."[36] He noted that even the most tolerant of populist speakers tried to minimize the profound meaning of America's race-divided history and thus treat African Americans as just one section of a cultural amalgam; dominant images of "worker," "labor," and "producer" were, he continues, always white.[37]

Elizabeth Jameson notes that, in mining areas of the West, miners placed themselves in opposition to mine owners, but white male mine workers excluded men of color from their ranks, claiming a common racial heritage as "white."[38] Local workforces were often segregated by race and gender, as workers with similar ethnic and racial heritage built communities with each other and not across race or class lines.[39] Jameson notes that "the corrosive significance of working-class racism underlay the impressive solidarity white workers achieved."[40] Like Kazin, she finds that race in the West served as a boundary between male workers. So, though on the surface the Populist Party of the 1890s sought to build coalitions and elevate workers, racial tensions did underlie various factions within, even though most were of the same working and/or lower socioeconomic class. "The people" was not a term that proved as inclusive as it should have.

In terms of rural radicalism, "the people" are the producers—farmers and ranchers. But "the people" can also include industrial laborers—the "average Joe" who keeps American machinery and factories humming. In essence, "the people" are those Americans who work hard (generally in what we might call blue-collar professions), who are ultimately contributing to the American economy through the products they produce or help build, who are God-fearing, honest, rugged, and generally perceived as white.

In American cultural mythology, workers and farmers are overwhelmingly white and overwhelmingly male, regardless of historical fact. Consequently, though populist sentiment and rhetoric makes pleas for the underdog and for the forgotten whose labor and products are exploited by a merciless, greedy elite, the message gears its appeal to white male Protestants—"Americans" who need to wrest the country from the control of a corrupt few. Perhaps it is better to suggest that populism, as a product of the Enlightenment and Protestant evangelicalism, simply could not grow far from its vine. White farmers and laborers who involved themselves in rural radicalism and the People's Party and later in populist movements throughout the twentieth century both knowingly and unwittingly created this framework for their message. As a result, rightist sympathizers infused populist ideology with conspiracy-laden, exclusionist rhetoric at the end of the twentieth century that ultimately damaged both those who espoused it and those who were victims of it.

Late-twentieth-century rightist (and extreme rightist) populism has roots in not only its leftist predecessors like the farmers' movements, but also earlier conservative coalescence during the early 1960s. According to Chip Berlet and Matthew Lyons, "Right-wing populism experienced a dramatic resurgence in the 1970s and 1980s." Building on earlier ultraconservative themes, a loose coalition of political strategists, grassroots supporters, and corporate backers forged a "New Right" identity that helped put Ronald Reagan into the White House.[41]

Jean Hardisty notes that several different historical factors converged during the 1970s and 1980s, creating a climate in which a conservative movement that included people further to the right could flourish. These factors included a conservative religious revitalization, the approach of the year 2000 (with its attendant apocalypticism), economic difficulties and subsequent restructuring, social stresses and backlash, and a network of well-funded right-wing (though not necessarily extreme right) organizations.[42]

The years after the Vietnam War were socially and economically turbulent. The so-called New Right became popular because it spoke to the sense of crisis many Americans felt. The organization network of the "New Right" was also very good at framing issues and debates in ways that helped further a decidedly conservative and occasionally extremist sensibility among disaffected Americans. In that regard, the late-twentieth-century evolution of the right is a reactionary response to perceived social, political, and economic turbulence.[43]

Berlet and Lyons note further that the "New Right" coalition of the 1970s and 1980s represented a reassertion of older ideas: a blend of anticommunism, traditionalism, and libertarianism. Furthermore, the rise of a fundamentalist Christian movement injected an emphasis on "morality" into the movement that had not existed in the 1950s. Corporate-backed conservative think tanks, Republican political strategists, and a large base of mobilized conservative evangelical Christians formed the backbone of this emergent rightist movement.[44]

This new conservative and rightist movement had a two-pronged backlash, according to Berlet and Lyons. First, it incorporated the longstanding effort of the "Old Right" to do away with the welfare programs and regulation of corporate prerogatives brought about by the New Deal. Second, the "New Right" jumped aboard the broader and more recent backlash against social liberation movements and government reforms of the 1960s and 1970s. The focus on social and cultural issues may have reflected an effort to preserve traditional hierarchies while partially masking the anti–New Deal approach.[45] One of the more effective tactics the "New Right" has employed is overt and implicit scapegoating of groups traditionally ascribed minority status, but also of non-Christians and environmentalists. The "New Right" would combine these attacks with distorted antielitism while attempting to further its calls for "reform."[46]

In the midst of all this foment, another Populist Party would appear. Founded in 1982 by Willis Carto, a long-time advocate and tireless organizer of rightist and extreme rightist organizations and publications, the new Populist Party attempted to mask its founder's views in its platform.[47] Carto deliberately made comparisons between his Populists and the 1890s Populists. He also attempted to hide his more extreme anti-Semitism in the party's platform by calling for "respect for racial and cultural diversity." However, that same platform went on to state that "the Populist Party will not permit any racial minority, through control of the media, culture distortion or revolutionary activity, to divide or factionalize the majority of the society-nation in which the minority lives." The platform also included planks for abolishing the income tax and immigration, opposing the Equal Rights Amendment, and abolishing the Federal Reserve.[48]

Carto was attempting to unite a variety of extreme right groups under the party's aegis. It included members of the American Independence Party, the American Party of Indiana, the Constitution Party (all three right-wing parties), various Klan groups, and others from Christian Identity organizations. The party touted "constitutional fundamentalism," rejecting all government institutions that were not mandated in the original Constitution.[49] Using the Constitution as a rallying point of sorts, the modern Populist Party may have attracted people with conservative, but not necessarily extremist, leanings.

The party ran a candidate in the 1984 presidential election—former Olympian Bob Richards—who ended up withdrawing because of a political fight with Carto over the latter's blatant anti-Semitism. By 1988, Carto was warring with another party leader and the Populists split. Carto's Populist Party ran David Duke, who had garnered 22,000 votes in the Louisiana primary as the Democratic presidential candidate in an unsuccessful bid for president. Duke has a long association with Klan and neo-Nazi organizations (and politics) throughout his lifetime. In 1990, he campaigned as a Republican for a U.S. Senate seat. Although he lost, he collected more than 60 percent of the white vote in the state of Louisiana.[50]

Even with such high-profile extreme rightists as Carto and Duke, the twentieth-century version of the Populist Party did not enjoy the successes of its nominal predecessor. From the outset, it experienced dissent within its ranks as people jockeyed for leadership with Carto, causing splinter parties to leave the fold and claim the mantle of the Populist Party. By 2000, the party was defunct.[51]

Unlike the nineteenth-century Populists, Carto's group targeted a rightist base. In so doing, members may have hamstrung its effectiveness. The earlier Populist Party attempted to build larger coalitions than Carto and colleagues did, across rightist and leftist spectrums to further an agenda that worked to help the greatest number of people. As a result, the earlier Populists, though not long-lasting as an organized political force, still managed to change the face of government and reform in the United States. Carto's efforts, preaching exclusion rather than inclusion, may have doomed the twentieth-century party from the start.

Fertile Ground

Henry Nash Smith wrote in 1950 that with each "surge of westward movement a new community came into being." The communities did not continue marching ever west, but rather "devoted themselves to ... cultivating the earth." Smith claimed that the growing agricultural society in the interior of the continent became "one of the dominant symbols of nineteenth-century American society ... that defined the promise of American life."[52]

Transformed more and more by commerce, industry, and technology, the image of an agricultural Eden out West continues to stir comfortable longings for a "real America." In the imaginations of many Americans, an earlier, simpler, and somehow happier time existed in the farm communities of the West and midwest. Smith argued that this image was a potent force in American politics and society, surviving to the end of the nineteenth century.[53]

I will argue here that rural nostalgia—the longing for these "simpler, kinder" times—has in fact survived into the twentieth century, and, as the millennium closed, it still had widespread appeal among rural radicals and other right-wing groups who sought a "return" to "the way things used to be." First, though, I will explore how the agrarian myth has flavored populist sentiment and especially how it has informed right-wing groups such as the Posse Comitatus. Other groups with neo-Nazi leanings have also employed the agrarian myth in their literature. Matt Koehl, leader of the National Socialist White People's Party (NSWPP) during the 1970s and 1980s, for example, demanded protection for the family farm, because of the "supreme importance of a healthy farming community" in a "sound society." [54] Koehl also claimed that "the health and well-being of any nation can be judged by the condition of its farmers." In the early days of the American republic, he continued, "when we had a sound and sturdy rural population, we were a strong and vigorous nation." However, "among all our racial brothers and sisters, perhaps none have fared worse in recent decades than those who have tried to make an honest living on the land." [55] Richard Butler and Robert Mathews also expounded the virtues of an agrarian society, calling it the touchstone of the White American Bastion.

To develop agriculture, however, it is first necessary to have land. As Americans pushed west into vast stretches of land untouched by European-style plows, they first confronted "wilderness" that demanded "taming." That process—the way in which Americans "tamed" wilderness—has also become a part of American cultural mythology. Ever pragmatic, cheerful, and hopeful, Americans carved farms from primeval forest and in so doing, helped contribute to what Smith called a growing symbolism of American society and life.

Wilderness as a place and as a concept in American nationalism has its own baggage. Puritans were on an "errand into the wilderness," trappers and traders forged paths through the wilderness, Jefferson sent explorers to map the wilderness, and Manifest Destiny implored Americans to settle and "tame" the wilderness. By the middle decades of the nineteenth century, wilderness was recognized in the popular mind as a cultural and moral resource and a basis for national self-esteem. [56]

Much of the untamed wilderness in the United States during the nineteenth and early twentieth centuries was in that part of the country deemed "the West." Brian Dippie notes rather poetically that "[m]ore than a direction or a place, the West was a cultural ideal signifying quest and the prospect of fulfillment in some elusive Elysium. To the West, then, myths ran their course, and America was simply a new stage for an old dream." [57] From American wilderness would come the American pastoral Eden and visions of proud yeoman farmers taming and shaping the wild for noble agricultural pursuits. From this Eden would emerge the foundations of an American agrarian mythology.

Annette Kolodny has delved into the development of this mythology. She notes that the mythology itself is gendered, a crucial point because the archetype of the farmer is invariably male. Men were to master and possess the vast new continent. Women, by contrast, were to re-create domestic spaces and maintain their roles therein. Thus, while men sought new Edens and created new Arcadias for themselves, working and altering the landscape to make it comply with their dreams of receptive and bountiful realms, women patched quilts, darned socks, cooked, and swept those soddies clean.[58]

Myths, Reginald Dyck tells us, "are produced or adapted within particular sociohistorical contexts in order to meet the specific needs of a culture."[59] The needs of many Americans during the eighteenth and nineteenth centuries rested on expanding industry and agriculture westward. Whether small landholdings or corporate pursuits, the vast lands west of the Mississippi seemed to offer opportunities to all expansionist interests.

Within this maelstrom of expansion, Americans constructed a myth to relate democracy to agriculture via the acquisition of land. An agrarian myth sprang from the need to believe in a Garden of Eden beyond the Appalachians even when faced with harsh environmental realities. Anne Hyde theorizes that white Americans heading west chose two strategies to deal with the geography of the region and both reflected the power of the cultural filters through which they viewed it. One method denied the facts of the landscape (e.g., arid, rocky, mountainous) and instead insisted that the region could and would support traditional agricultural patterns. Semiarid plains could become agricultural bonanzas and deserts and mountains could be irrigated and mined. Manifest Destiny, a white Protestant construction, made geographical barriers impossible.[60]

The other method westward-wanting Americans used to deal with harsh geographic realities was to search for areas that *did* fit public perceptions of what the West should be and then pretend that nothing else existed.[61] Hyde goes on to state that "most white male Americans perceived the West through a cultural filter of optimism, Manifest Destiny, and pure stubbornness" though how one traveled west also influenced how one viewed it. Going west in a covered wagon or on horseback was a very different experience than watching the landscape rush by from the comfort of a parlor car. Surely if men could build railroads to cover the vast expanses of the western plains, they could also cultivate those plains.[62]

Robert Athearn points out that the agrarian onslaught onto the nation's plains was part of a powerful agricultural impulse that had been a part of American history since Jamestown. At no time in the past, he noted, had the farming frontier changed the country more than during the years when cattle ranchers moved onto the Great Plains. Farmers soon followed. From 1607 until 1870, American farmers occupied 407 million acres. Between 1870 and 1900—a mere thirty years—farmers occupied an additional 430 million acres.[63]

Parts of the agrarian myth are older than the nineteenth-century push for Manifest Destiny. They derive from Thomas Jefferson's well-known statements about farming, in which the third president stated that "cultivators of the earth are the most valuable citizens." To Jefferson, farmers were "the most vigorous, the most independent, [and] the most virtuous." They were tied to their country and to their liberty, Jefferson wrote, "by the most lasting bonds."[64]

Even older aspects of the myth arrived in the New World via Protestant sects hoping to escape persecution abroad or looking for a good business venture. This country, therefore, has deep agricultural roots, so it makes sense that an "agrarian myth" swirls through other ideas about democracy and American identity. Jefferson's arguments about agriculture also suggested that farming would induce longstanding patterns of conduct that would broadly characterize American society.[65]

By the nineteenth century, the role of the American citizen-farmer had become even richer and more romantic than in Jefferson's time. The romantic aspect suggests two major themes: first, nature is a formative element in the American national character, and second, hard physical labor is a prerequisite for achieving the virtues necessary for self-realization.[66] The pastoral ideal— a place of safety between the corruptions of urban civilization and untamed wilderness—has remained a symbol, a dream, and a definition for America since the age of discovery. "The pastoral ideal," Leo Marx states, "has been used to define the meaning of America ever since the age of discovery, and it has not yet lost its hold upon the native imagination."[67] In the nineteenth century, though pastoral ideals clung stubbornly to many American psyches, intruding realities such as increased industrialization in the Northeast hinted of things to come.[68] By the twentieth century, the myth lingered, but greater industrialization and expansion of corporate enterprises altered both American agriculture and American society in general.

Athearn notes that after the turn of the twentieth century, starting in the teen years, American farming began to change. No longer solely made up of small patches of family-homesteaded land, the advent and expansion of business slowly "corporatized" farming. Individual farms grew in size, and absentee ownership flourished since 1910. With World War I, large-scale farming and early agribusiness accelerated, perhaps foreshadowing twentieth-century crises that include the Great Depression during the 1930s and the terrible slump in agriculture during the 1980s.[69]

Other factors that created a backdrop for the yeoman farmer myth include the influx of more peoples from eastern and southern Europe and from Asia around the turn of the nineteenth century. Rumblings of national decline accompanied this wave of immigration, though nativist sentiment is nothing new in American culture and history. Athearn points out that in periodicals from the era, "decline" came to be associated with all the newcomers, whereas "Americanism" and "individualism" became equated with the values of old-stock Protestants. In addition, these periodicals suggested, the West was a haven for these besieged virtues.[70]

Not that this was a new notion. Somewhere out West, those of Anglo-Saxon descent had dreamed since the seventeenth century about the hill on which they would build their city, as God had promised them. In the twentieth century, however, with the rise of urban centers and technological advancements, it seemed more imperative to claim the West of imagination and reality for exclusive use, and these ideas were best expressed in the popular fiction and media of the day.[71]

Between 1880 and 1920, hostility toward immigrants, coupled with "scientific" justification for racism, culminated in the Restriction Acts (anti-immigration) of 1921 and 1924. Also during this period, interest in the West and pride in a "western" heritage grew and found expression in popular American literature. In the United States, these emphases on Anglo-Saxons as the noblest branch of the Teutonic family magnified with the passage of time. This, along with images of the West and of brave Anglo-Saxon missions into it, only exacerbated anti-immigration sentiment at the turn of the twentieth century.[72]

One overriding impression many white Americans formed was that the West served as an Anglo-Saxon theater, an empire of sorts in which only "old-stock" Americans developed and in which new immigrants (and people of color) played no part. Two themes emerged and pervaded popular literature of the time: one concerned the westward movement of a great people to the Pacific and the other involved looking at the West as a process of development—an evolution of civilization and all the benefits that civilization conferred on those who were not white or not Protestant.[73]

Perceptions of the West that formed in the nineteenth century have continued to shape ideas and behavior. Many of us still view the West as "original, distinctive, and quintessentially American," but the irony is that much of the region that is so important to American self-perception either never existed or has disappeared beneath the onslaught of settlement, industry, and resource extraction.[74] Earl Pomeroy writes that, at least into the twentieth century, Americans felt that "in much of the West they returned to the ways of their ancestors, retreating from urban complexity to rural simplicity."[75]

The reality, however—especially in the twentieth century—of American farming is actually one of agricultural dependence on the federal government. This is ironic, in view of the American mythology that paints farmers as noble independent yeomen. Federal intervention and regulation of American agriculture has occurred persistently and in many forms since the turn of the twentieth century.[76] Concurrently, government farm policy has historically been geared to meet the credit needs of an affluent class of commercial farmers and landowners.[77]

By 1920, American farm men and women had managed to develop the most productive, diverse, and profitable agriculture in the world (with the exception of the South), but the net result was the creation of reasons and opportunities for farming folk to buy more on credit. As long as prices remained high, these debts could be paid. The history of American farming, however, is one of boom and bust, which means that if a farm family has not paid off its debt by the time a bust cycle rolls around, chances are they will end up in a tragic economic bind.[78]

Booms and Busts

Although the Populist Party lost its prominence after the 1896 presidential election, it lingered—Tom Watson ran for president two more times—and some of its reform planks were picked up by the Progressive movement. American agriculture benefited substantially from Populism and earlier agrarian reform movements, entering one of its most productive eras during the first twenty years of the twentieth century.

One of the primary goals achieved by the farm lobby after 1896 was to establish "parity" as a national policy goal. In parity, the federal government agreed to establish a price level for farm products, yielding a purchasing power for farmers equal to what they had during the industry's most prosperous years (1909–1919).[79] Parity is designed to benefit farmers and keep them solvent during lean years. However, domestic and foreign fluctuations in demand and overproduction in farming sectors have strained the ability of the government to guarantee parity all the time. As a result, though farming boomed after the Populist era of the 1890s, it would still be subject to the vagaries of foreign and domestic markets, just like most industries in a rapidly expanding global economy.

The number of American farms rose between 1900 and 1920, when optimism about farming as a business opportunity prevailed. Other industrial sectors in the country were expanding as well; this, coupled with increased urbanization, created a demand for farm products. Urban residents needed food and fuel to maintain and continue expansion.[80] World War I (1914–1918) also spurred tremendous growth in the agricultural sector of this country as farms worked to produce food for the Allied powers. Prior to the war, industrial output in the United States expanded at three times the agricultural rate, which set up favorable terms of exchange between industry and agriculture. Profitable prices and rising land values just after the war meant unmatched prosperity for American farmers.[81]

There was, however, a downside. A speculative land boom put hundreds of thousands of farmers into debt to buy more land and livestock in the boom years, on the assumption that the high prices for their products would continue. As is the case in many postwar years, the business sector contracted as American and European economies adjusted to a postwar slump in output and demand. A half million farmers would go bankrupt in the early 1920s.[82]

After World War I, the agricultural recession marked the beginning of a new age in relationships between farmers and the federal government—one in which many farmers actually came to prefer federal regulation of farm prices. In the years 1923–1929, American farming enjoyed a sluggish recovery but farmers faced rapid changes. European farmers, recovering from the war years, were in direct competition with American farmers for European markets. A weaker domestic market, a population that was growing slowly, and lower immigration rates added to the troubles in American agriculture. Ironically, better technology in American farming during these years was enabling farmers to produce much more at a faster rate, but decreased demand from foreign markets drove prices down. America's status as a creditor nation during these postwar years also hindered exports from the United States.[83]

Technology may have allowed agriculture to produce more, but it also forced farmers to be dependent on a nonfarm economy to purchase the innovations necessary to remain competitive with other farmers. Many people left agriculture during the latter years of the 1920s, and the stock market crash in 1929 would only cause further difficulties. Between 1929 and 1932, the prices of crops and livestock fell 75 percent.[84] Those farmers who stayed during the dirty thirties would face a constant struggle.

The Depression years coupled with the Dust Bowl hit agriculture hard in this country. For obvious reasons, farming declined during the 1930s, as did the number of farms. Most industries struggled during the 1930s; farming was just part of the larger picture. The first few years of the 1930s saw a new type of protest among farmers who attempted to organize and resist foreclosure. "Penny auctions" were popular especially from 1930 to 1932. When a bank foreclosed on a farm, personnel would auction off the farm and farming implements to pay off the farmer's loan. In a penny auction, on the day of the event, attendees (often friends and neighbors of the foreclosed farmer) would bid pennies for items, often forcibly encouraging noncompliers to do the same. At the end of a frustrating day, the bank might have only five or ten dollars to show for its efforts when hopes had been for hundreds or thousands. Those who bought the items for pennies would generally return them to the foreclosed farmer. Some auctioneers would receive no bids at all as farmers in attendance hoped to help their foreclosed neighbor by not supporting the auction.[85] As banks figured out ways around these auctions, farmers took their fight to the political arena, winning moratoriums on foreclosures passed in several midwestern states. The moratoriums were designed to last a year because popular wisdom suggested that the Depression could not last much longer. Unfortunately, it did, and foreclosures continued after the temporary reprieve.[86]

When Franklin Delano Roosevelt was elected president, he addressed as many problems as he could through New Deal legislation. Some of it provided direct monetary support to improve farm income through various production, credit, and loan programs and also ensured a minimum income to participating farmers. By World War II, which finally broke the Depression, many American farmers had come to depend on the federal government for acreage-reduction payments, low-interest credit, price supports, conservation aid, and rural electrification.[87]

The years between 1940 and 1960, though marked by greater involvement of the federal government to support American farming, were also marred by continued declines in farm population and numbers of farms. The fifty years between 1940 and 1990 witnessed a drop in farm population from 30 million to 4.5 million. A substantial decrease occurred among nonwhite farmers as well. In 1920, 15 percent of farmers were nonwhite; in 1950, 10 percent were. But in 1997, only 1 percent of total farmers in the United States were nonwhite.[88]

The years 1950–1970 saw the United States lose half its farms.[89] Successful farms were much larger than in the past, gobbling up surrounding land and mechanizing to produce as much as possible. Smaller farmers simply could not compete, as agriculture became more corporate and more tied to science and industry. The decade of the 1970s, however, was another boom period, comparable to the post–World War I era.

Record productivity through the 1970s created the boondoggle that had plagued American farming almost since its inception.[90] More farmers were able to buy more on credit, but when a bust cycle developed in the early 1980s and the federal government's policies didn't alleviate the economic downturn, farmers simply could not pay back what they owed, just like in the early 1920s. Nor could they produce enough to help pay off their debts because prices remained internationally low. The results were hundreds of farm foreclosures and economic depressions throughout American farming communities, many of which have not recovered.[91] It is in this wreckage—generated by financial ruin and deep frustration at ineffectual government policies—that extremist rhetoric took hold in some pockets of the farming West and Midwest.

American agriculture had boomed during the 1970s. In May 1973, President Richard Nixon negotiated the Smithsonian Agreement, which replaced Breton Woods and subsequently allowed currency values to fluctuate. Its effect was to devalue the American dollar. The price of imports increased, which ensured that American exports become more competitive in a global market. For American rural areas, floating exchange rates and the increased purchasing power of oil-producing nations created a demand for American agricultural products.[92]

From 1973 to 1979, worldwide inflation had dramatic effects in American rural areas. High commodity prices and inexpensive land abounded; many farmers took out more loans to purchase more land so that they could grow more products. Agriculture was booming. But in 1979, Paul Volcker was appointed head of the Federal Reserve. He decided to reduce inflation by controlling the money supply. In so doing, he triggered a recession that had worldwide repercussions during 1980–1982. The price of commodities dropped because the purchasing power of those nations that had previously borrowed to buy food, build more factories, and buy oil declined. The dollar gained in value as it became scarcer because of Volcker's policy.

In 1981, the Reagan administration passed the Economic Recovery Tax Act, designed to reduce federal income through tax cuts. Federal spending increased as did the deficit. As a short-term solution to a flagging economy, the act may have staunched some of the bleeding, but, in the long run, it ended up hurting agriculture and the American economy as a whole.[93] The United States government increasingly borrowed to cover the deficit; consequently, interest rates rose. In response, the value of the dollar went up even more.[94]

Because of the high-value dollar, demands for American exports decreased. Inflation did slow, but real interest rates (low or even negative during the 1970s) jumped to unprecedented levels of 8–10 percent during the 1980s. Farm commodities in foreign and domestic markets were simply too plentiful to sustain 1970s prices. Farmers' incomes subsequently dropped and land values, dependent on current farm income and prospects for income growth, declined. The debt levels of the 1970s could not be sustained in the 1980s. Farmers whose solvency depended on rising land values or who had pursued an aggressive expansion strategy during the 1970s could not pay on their loans and faced foreclosure. Even the farmers who had been more cautious during the 1970s suffered, when droughts gripped the farm belt in 1980 and 1983.[95]

By 1985, one-third of all family farms owed almost 50 percent of *all* farm debt and consequently suffered some kind of financial difficulty. Farms that had sales of $50,000 to $500,000 yearly were the mainstream of these family-sized farms. As a result of the Farm Crisis, and by 1985, more than a quarter of all family farms had some kind of financial stress, whether it involved stretching out loans or technical insolvency. These farms owed 36 percent of all farm debt. An estimated 30,000 farms were insolvent, having debt-to-asset ratios in excess of 100 percent. They owed 6.5 percent of all farm debt. Another 34,000 farms (roughly 7.5 percent) had debt-to-asset ratios of 70–100 percent. They were headed for insolvency. Some 114,000 farms were highly leveraged, meaning their debt-to-asset ratios were 40–70 percent. They faced serious financial problems and owed 22 percent of all farm debt. The larger farms—those with annual sales of more than $500,000—tended to be highly industrialized and specialized. Most of these farms maintained a positive cash flow throughout the crisis, but they were not the mainstay of rural America during the 1980s.[96]

The boom and bust cycles of farming in America are tied to larger currents. Usually, there is no one reason for a bust. Instead, a number of factors come together and create the situations that work against farming. In the Farm Crisis of the 1980s, three federal policies operating two decades in advance helped create the crash. Five successive presidential administrations had treated inflation as a "normal" part of economic life. High inflation had resulted from American involvement in Vietnam without a tax increase to help offset the costs of the war. This, compounded with rapid increases in oil costs after 1972 because of an oil embargo, contributed to high inflation. In 1979, a decision of the Federal Reserve Board limited the supply of credit in the American economy, which created high nominal interest rates and sent inflation even higher. Finally, the 1981 tax cuts and ballooning federal deficit completed the circuit that created the most recent crisis in American farming.[97]

Popular opinion and an American agrarian myth tell us that somewhere out West we can find our own homesteads; we can find clean air, good health, unpopulated areas, and big skies. Even in the late 1990s, there are people who have fled urban areas in search of their own agrarian myths. They have gone in search of "America"—the America that once was. In reality, though, this Garden of Eden never existed. We cannot go back to something that never was. Nevertheless, many Americans have tried and are still attempting to re-create fields of dreams. The encounter of innocence with complexity is a recurrent theme in American culture and the West, and its history provides the most dramatic backdrop and longest sustained case of high expectations that invariably slam into the reality of western environments and the hardships they hold.[98]

However one traces its development, the agrarian myth has pervaded American history, latched onto and oftentimes inextricably intertwined with ideas about American "character." Frequently combining with white nativism, sexism, and racism, the myth can create a discourse of "Americanism" that is exclusive, xenophobic, and, in some cases, deadly.

The Posse Comitatus and the Common-Law Movement

Farmer Gordon Kahl died 3 June 1983 in a tear-gas-filled and burning Ozark Mountain farmhouse. Charged with both tax evasion and the murders of two federal agents in Medina, North Dakota, a few months prior to his own death, Kahl had been hiding in Arkansas when federal agents surrounded the house and opened fire. Throughout his days as a fugitive and since his death, Kahl has served the extreme right as a martyr for his "resistance" to the American government.[99]

How does a sixty-three-year-old father of six who served in the Army Air Corps during World War II end up dead at the hands of American law enforcement agents? How does a man born on a North Dakota farm who willingly served this country as a military man and who was awarded the Purple Heart come to denounce the very government for which he had fought? Come to kill two other Americans in defense of his radical beliefs? Come to die himself for his beliefs? How, indeed.

Kahl had been a member of the Posse Comitatus, a group originally founded by William Potter Gale in 1971. Gale, who was based in southern California, was one of the early leaders in the Identity movement and was familiar with paramilitary organizations. He founded his own in 1960; the California Rangers were put on that state's attorney general's list as a threat to peace and security. By the early 1980s, Gale was making the rounds in various rightist paramilitary training seminars, including a 1982 Posse session in Weskan, Kansas.[100] Gale followers no doubt ended up in the Posse touting Identity, its accompanying apocalypticism, and strictly regimented gender roles, which distinguish the group today.

Gale continued his antigovernment activism throughout the 1980s by helping launch the so-called Christian Patriot movement. Before the term "militia" entered the public lexicon in the 1990s, Gale had already introduced the concept of private armies and "unorganized militia" groups prior. Since leaving the army in 1950, Gale was one of the most influential rightist figures in the country until his death in 1988.[101]

Because the term "posse comitatus" literally means "power of the county," extreme rightists believe that all politics and legal jurisdiction are inherently local; the federal government thus has no business interfering with local American communities. The genius of Gale's creation lay in how he embellished the anti-Semitic, racist, and antigovernment rhetoric with elaborate legalistic jargon drawn from the Constitution, the Magna Carta, and other principles of British law to legitimize his calls to violence.[102] Gale claimed that all healthy men between the ages of eighteen and forty-five who were not in the military could be mobilized into a posse comitatus to redress their grievances.[103]

Although Gale initially relied on a network of Christian Identity believers and military veterans to spread the Posse doctrine, he soon began attracting rightist tax protestors and unrestricted gun rights advocates, the latter concerned with the perceived rise of communism in the United States in the 1960s. During the early 1970s, Posse chapters spread from California up the West Coast and then into the Midwest. In Oregon, Henry Lamont "Mike" Beach, a retired laundry-equipment mechanic and salesman, plagiarized Gale's writings and declared himself the national leader of the "Sheriff's Posse Comitatus." What he lacked in charisma he made up in effort—Beach worked tirelessly to spread Posse rhetoric across the nation.[104]

Beach wrote the text for most of the pamphlets, brochures, and leaflets during the early years and spent most of his time networking and putting together mailing lists. Gale, for his part, was extremely vocal about his involvement with the Posse but did not seem to contribute much to the mechanics of the group. He did, however, probably serve as a great encouragement for rightists to join Beach's Posse during the 1970s and 1980s.

There is some confusion on this point. Some sources claim Beach was the founder of the Posse. Beach set himself up as the founder, but, though his work was instrumental in spreading Posse ideology, Gale was the founder. James Coates claims that the U.S. Department of the Treasury traced the Posse's formation to Beach. What probably happened was that Beach's constant self-publicizing led the department to that conclusion.[105] There is no doubt that Beach worked hard on the Posse; he did not, however, found it, though he did not dissuade observers from thinking such.

Beach coined the name Citizens Law Enforcement Research Committee (C.L.E.R.C.) and based it in Portland, Oregon, from where he disseminated thousands of copies of his version of Gale's Posse manifesto, dubbed the Posse

The logo of the Posse Comitatus, old and new. The original logo is a sheriff's star with a circle but no other designs. The modern version retained that shape but added a bible, a noose, and a sword in the center. Original from a Posse pamphlet probably from the late 1960s or early 1970s. Courtesy of the Wilcox Collection at the University of Kansas Libraries, Lawrence, RH WL Eph uncat. The modern version is from the now-defunct Posse Comitatus website, which was located at www.posse-comitatus.org. The image here is from 1999.

Blue Book, probably after the John Birch Society's *Blue Book.* He also sold hundreds of so-called Posse charters to activists interested in launching a local chapter—among the guidelines is the necessity of assembling a core of seven white Christian men.[106] Early Posse literature that Beach put together called for a "Citizens [*sic*] Posse in every county in the United States, with every able-bodied patriotic *male* of good character, who is interested in the preservation of law and order, becoming a member" (emphasis mine).[107]

It is also no accident that the Posse models itself after old-style "western" vigilantism. The first members were white western men who approved of organizing posses and meting out justice on those they deemed in need of such treatment. An early Posse tract evoked memories of a heroic western past with such statements as "vigilantes brought law and order" to western territories like Montana and "what our forefathers did over one hundred years ago we can and must do today to restore law, order, and freedom" to Americans.[108] Another Posse information sheet states that "[t]his Posse is the entire body of those inhabitants who may be summoned by the Sheriff, or who may volunteer, to preserve the public peace or execute any lawful precept that is opposed."[109]

The Posse preaches that the federal government has exceeded the limits originally prescribed in the Constitution and that, by means of a coalition of lawyers and judges, the government has violated the basic terms on which this country was founded. The first page of a five-page Posse handbook I discovered during my research has one of the Posse symbols displayed prominently—a sheriff's star—and includes the statements, "It is the duty of government to prevent injustice—not to promote it" and "[t]he United States of America was founded as a protest against taxation."[110]

In the first Posse manual, Beach insisted that government officials who "commit criminal acts or who violate their oath of office" will be removed by the posse "to the most populated intersection of streets in the township and, at high noon, be hung by the neck," with the body remaining until sundown to serve as an example to those who would "subvert the law."[111]

Beach, Kahl, and other Posse members and advocates based much of their ideology on an interpretation of the legal doctrine surrounding the congressional Posse Comitatus Act passed in the wake of the Civil War. Specifically used to bar the federal military from intervening in local police matters, the act was a response to President Ulysses S. Grant's post–Civil War efforts to use troops to guard ballot boxes and prevent election fraud. Congress ordered that such police powers could reside only at the county level. Federal troops, therefore, were effectively barred from enforcing domestic laws. The legal doctrine established by the Posse Comitatus Act has become to some a hallmark of American democracy because it prevents presidents from sending federal soldiers to implement policy or enforce domestic laws in any state.

Although the Posse Comitatus Act established that presidents cannot send federal soldiers to implement policy or enforce domestic law within a state, there have been situations in which this happened. For example, the 1899 Coeur d'Alene, Idaho, strike involved federal troops sent in to handle a chaotic situation, and in Arkansas, in 1954, federal troops enforced school desegregation following the *Brown v. Board of Education* decision. In light of the potential for violence in both situations, the Posse Comitatus Act was suspended so the federal government could restore order.[112] These incidents are few and far between, but they serve as a reminder to Posse members that the federal government can and does interfere in what they consider "local matters."

Furthermore, modern-day Posse adherents, distinguished by their zeal for amateur lawyering, connected the Posse Comitatus doctrine to their religious (Christian Identity) faith. No citizen is bound to obey any authority higher than that of county sheriff, they will tell observers. Paying income taxes, making Social Security payments, and even purchasing license plates and acquiring a driver's license violate this Posse principle. Many—though not all—followers take matters further and claim that God divinely revealed Posse doctrine. Therefore, paying taxes is not only illegal, it is sinful.[113]

Common law is another Posse hallmark; the group's rhetoric has been laced with quotes from the Declaration of Independence, the Magna Carta, *Black's Law Dictionary,* and the Bible, generally with no coherent context and often lumped together. Posse adherents also claim that the Federal Reserve System is fraudulent and therefore illegal because it is not backed by gold and silver. In Posse doctrine, Jews control government, media, and all monetary aspects of the country while conspiring with international bankers and socialists to form a global monopoly.[114]

These are not new ideas in the labyrinth of rightist ideology and history; their roots extend to the anti-Semitic rhetoric espoused by the 1920s Ku Klux Klan and to the neo-Nazi groups that evolved with the advent of Hitler. What the Posse did that *was* relatively new was to actually use the court systems to *subvert* those systems. Posse members were some of the earliest extreme rightists who began clogging courts with bogus property liens and multimillion-dollar common law liens, most against public officials.

More recently, in 1996 and 1997, the Montana Freemen and the Republic of Texas gained nationwide attention in their members' separate standoffs with federal agents. Both the Freemen and the Republic of Texas engaged in what has become known as the "common law" movement in which rightists file bogus liens and lawsuits against judges and local officials. The courts must subsequently expend time and money to have the cases dismissed. Once they do, however, rightists simply file more.[115]

The common law movement has become an effective weapon in the arsenal of 1990s rightist groups. Using a plethora of sources, those who engage in the practice construct pseudo-legal documents so jargon-filled as to be nearly incomprehensible to those who have to deal with them:

> *COMES NOW, John Doe*[116], *a People for the Freely Associated Compact States of America, that has pledged his life, fortune and sacred honor, to forcing the De Facto government agents of the New Deal Socialist Communist Democracy to recognize and respect John Doe's free character and to stop violating their oath of office. … It is a matter of fact that their [sic] is [sic] Two Jurisdictions, that of Nature and Natures [sic] God, and that of Satan, the evil ones. This case was filed in Our Constitutional Common Law and can not [sic] be deviated into an Administrative tribunal that operates in Admirality Jurisdiction under the Commander and Chief of the Corporate New Deal United States of the District of Columbia.*[117]

The idea of "common law" derives from the legal precepts laid down in the Bible and the Magna Carta; consequently, common law is a "higher law" than what exists in the country. To common law adherents, individuals are blessed with natural and inalienable rights; only laws based on local custom and precedent (i.e., common law) are legitimate, and only a local sheriff has the authority to enforce them. Since 1995, common law courts have been multiplying so fast that law enforcement officials and watchdog groups cannot effectively track them all. The Southern Poverty Law Center, in Montgomery, Alabama, claims that the courts have operated in at least forty of the fifty states.[118]

Common law tactics thus far have involved "quiet titles"—a proceeding by which practitioners declare themselves "sovereigns" or "freemen" and instantly become immune (in their eyes) from income taxes and other laws perceived as intrusive. Common law courts also "try" public officials in absentia for treason. Common law adherents threaten and harass judges, sheriffs, and county prosecutors. Some of the liens explicitly state that the penalty for the alleged crime is death. Though no follower has gone this far, the threat of the possibility leaves many legitimate state court and law enforcement officials uneasy.[119]

How did a group founded in 1971 by a retired military veteran find its way into agricultural pockets of the West and Midwest, and why would it become so attractive to disaffected Americans in rural areas? The Posse operated in relative obscurity until 1975. That year, the Little Rock, Arkansas, FBI office was alerted to a possible assassination attempt against Vice President Nelson Rockefeller. The Posse viewed Rockefeller as a major "money czar" in their alleged global conspiracy; a subsequent FBI probe revealed seventy-eight Posse chapters in twenty-three states, including California, Texas, Colorado, Kansas, Wisconsin, North and South Dakota, Nebraska, Minnesota, and Virginia. The groups generally included two or three dozen members who met regularly to discuss the evils of the Federal Reserve System and the income tax and who wished to organize a Posse-style government.[120]

It was following this 1975 incident that media became interested in the ideology and origins of the Posse and some of the group's members began to appear in a variety of newspapers. Perhaps the most visible and virulently racist chapter was that of Identity adherent James Wickstrom, in Tigerton, Wisconsin. Wickstrom, who remained active in the late 1990s (and past 2000), tied Identity racism and apocalyptic beliefs to Gale's common law tenets. The combination, already blossoming through Gale's and Beach's influence, fueled Posse chapters and their survivalist ideas throughout the 1980s and 1990s.

Something else Wickstrom ensured when he formed his chapter in the early 1970s was that it was understood that women could not serve as Posse members. Only men age fifteen and older could join. "The Bible states man is over woman," Wickstrom has explained. Women should not be drafted for combat, though Wickstrom has encouraged women to be trained in combat; "we think it's their right to be able to defend themselves when no one's around." [121] Women could also use .22 caliber rifles. The heavy armaments that the Posse stockpiled remained a male prerogative.[122]

Wickstrom uses biblical interpretation to justify the roles men and women are to play in the Posse. Beach may have had similar thoughts, but from the literature I have seen, he was more concerned with the constitutional right for the Posse to exist. He did state in one of his information packets, however, that "[t]he Sheriff can mobolize [sic] all men between the ages of 18 and 45 who are in good health and not in the federal military service. OTHERS CAN VOLUNTEER! This body of citizens is the Sheriff's Posse. Each must serve when called by the Sheriff. The title of this body is the Posse Comitatus."[123]

During the 1990s, Wickstrom modified his beliefs about women participants. Although he still seemed to feel that only men should be on the front lines defending their homes and families, women were allowed to operate as support troops if necessary, but only as a last resort. The white race could be better served, after all, if women stayed home and provided good homes for their men and children.[124]

Wickstrom also exemplified the ties the Posse has to rural America and its agrarian roots, stating in one instance that "the land is the birthplace of our freedom. If someone comes and threatens a man's sweat and toil for 30 years, he's gonna say, 'Get the hell off the land,' and he's gonna go inside and get a shotgun and blow their heads off." To Wickstrom, "the family farm is the backbone of the nation" and it is in danger from "corrupt forces." Wickstrom's apocalyptic views are further evident in his prediction of "a coming revolution" in the same statement, saying that city dwellers would flee into the countryside for food and shelter in a massive "bloodbath." [125] In other words, the safest place to be was rural America.

As a movement that not only advocates local county control and the right to bear arms, but also invokes references to western-style vigilantism and "traditional" American ties to land and farming, the Posse has managed to construct the groundwork that would provide essential leverage for another rural American uprising. The Farm Crisis—barely an apprehensive whisper in the late 1970s—would send hundreds of farmers searching for answers to their plight. Some would find those answers in the shadowy, paranoid world of the Posse Comitatus.

The Seeds of Discontent

In 1987, Methodist minister Tom Mason of Claxton, Georgia, appeared before the Senate Committee on Agriculture, Nutrition, and Forestry and pleaded for "a concerted effort to preserve deep values which anchor our country because it is stability which our urban and suburban areas do not have and cannot provide." Farmers, Mason stated, "have always been different" and "independent." They've always "done what they could with what they had to feed as many people as possible." [126]

Mason's statement spoke to the deepening crisis in farming that was putting a terrible strain—psychologically, economically, and politically—on rural America. The minister spoke of the "sense of betrayal" by the government that had encouraged farmers to plant as much as possible and by lenders who had not provided financial counseling. As a result, the values on which America rests were at risk. To Mason, who dealt with a rural Southern area, he could see only too well what the Farm Crisis was doing to rural pockets in the United States. Out West, the situation was echoed on the grain- and soybean-producing plains of Colorado and Kansas.

Springfield, Colorado, is the seat of Baca County, which sits in the southeastern corner of the state. Thirty miles north of the Oklahoma border, this plains town of roughly 2,000 has relied on agriculture for its primary livelihood since its founding in the late nineteenth century. Even by 2003, farming and ranching were predominant industries in Baca County, but the town that used to host a thriving main street of bustling storefronts and family businesses is a shadow of its former self.

Many of the storefronts stand empty, as worn and faded as the "For Rent" signs posted in their windows. An Alco store survives along Highway 287 as you drive into town. As of August 2004, a nascent arts movement has begun in the downtown district in an attempt to attract tourism. Folks still farm around Springfield, but the industry that was able to provide sole support for families just after World War II can no longer do that, and many who continue to farm and ranch have had to subsidize their incomes by taking outside jobs.

The sons and daughters of Springfield's predominantly white, Protestant families started new traditions in the 1980s: many started leaving home after high school and rarely returned or they took jobs in the area off the farm, breaking from agriculture because it no longer paid the bills. In the late 1970s, the Posse Comitatus found a welcoming audience among some Springfield residents.

This small Colorado town could be Anywhere, rural America. The agricultural boom-and-bust that began in the early 1970s and devastated Springfield was mirrored throughout American agricultural regions. Not only did the industry itself suffer, but the towns it once supported virtually died as Main Street businesses folded and more and more people moved to take employment in larger towns or cities. Locally owned businesses have been supplanted by chain stores such as Wal-Mart and chain restaurants such as Denny's in more populated areas since the early 1980s. These stores are generally built on a town's outskirts near a large freeway or highway. No one passing through has reason to go downtown because they can stop at the chains and then travel on without ever going directly through a town's heart.

Few Americans born after 1980 know much about the Farm Crisis. Those of us born during the 1960s and early 1970s remember reading about it in newspapers or seeing farm auctions on television news during the 1980s. Unless you are directly involved in agriculture, however, it is difficult to comprehend its devastating effects on farming families and the local communities they helped support through agriculture. Hundreds of farmers lost their land, their livelihoods, and their history. Others committed suicide rather than face what they considered to be the humiliation of the auction block. Even years later, many still battle depression and anxiety, literally suffering from post-traumatic stress disorder because they lost what had been in their families for generations.[127]

As Oklahoma farmer Maureen Wade wrote, "I wish I could tell you that we haven't had a suicide in our part of Okla., but I can't tell you that because we've had several."[128] Another speaker at an Oklahoma town meeting said that her husband became "completely consumed by our circumstances caused by the Farm Crisis." He left her. The couple had been through all matter of natural disasters and had weathered them. But "when the threat of losing everything comes to your doorstep because of the bad economy, low commodity prices and high interest on your base notes has left you hopelessly in debt, your faith is sometimes shaken."[129]

It is difficult for many who have not been farmers or who have not grown up in farming areas to understand why "losing the farm" would cause such despair and, in many cases, rage. It is difficult because many of us who live in cities or who have left the small towns in which we were raised have created our livelihoods and family bases elsewhere. We do not have the sense of allegiance to the land on which we were raised (many of us weren't raised as farmers or ranchers) or the sense of obligation to "take over the farm" once our parents are gone. We do not have a connection to "the land" that many farmers have had because they inherited land from their parents and grandparents. And we do not base our identities on that land or that industry.[130]

As Abby Ferber and Michael Kimmel argue, the agricultural crises of the 1980s (and the continued economic downturns in rural America) struck a particular chord with white men who lived and worked in the area.[131] Many who farmed and ranched and who faced foreclosure had to deal with the fact that they were losing the family land. That is, the land that perhaps had been in their families for generations, passed from father to son, was slipping through their hands. The guilt and shame of being the man to lose the land created all manner of reactions, whether depression, suicide, or rage that some channeled through extreme rightist groups.

Henry Nash Smith notes that the failure of the Homestead Act (1862) in the late nineteenth century was linked to the monopolization of available western lands by railroad companies. In fact, the public land system actually encouraged monopolies. After the Civil War, the myth of the independent yeoman farmer and his self-sufficient homestead collided with reality. Instead of independence, the yeoman farmer was at the mercy of urban centers like Chicago and transportation to and from market centers.[132]

Since the turn of the twentieth century, agriculture has depended on market forces beyond the boundaries delineated by individual farms. Nevertheless, the idea that farming enables one to be self-sufficient continued throughout the twentieth century, which may explain why such disillusionment and grief spread throughout farming areas in the West and Midwest during the Farm Crisis.[133]

Farmers, though they are essentially their own bosses and operate, to a degree, their own businesses, are still tied into national and world markets. The Farm Crisis that hit this country in the late 1970s and continued throughout the 1980s and even into the 1990s was the result of these market forces. And no matter how rugged or independent a farmer is, if one is not getting a good price for one's product, there are bound to be repercussions. This is what happened to American family farming during the Farm Crisis. Many farmers and ranchers lost their land and homes to foreclosure. Others managed to survive because they took jobs off the farm. A few killed themselves and, in some cases, their families as well.[134] And still others decided to fight what they perceived was a Jewish conspiracy designed to undermine them and, by extension, "true" American values and institutions.

Groups like the Posse Comitatus found some welcoming audiences in rural western and midwestern America during the Farm Crisis. Looking for scapegoats, some farmers and ranchers were receptive to the anti-Semitic and racist rhetoric the Posse supplied. To be involved in a group that was sympathetic to their plight and that even offered solutions through tax protest and antigovernment sentiment provided some farmers and ranchers a modicum of comfort and the sense that they were doing *something,* however inappropriate it might seem, to deal with the situation.

Roughly 200,000 family farm operations suffered some kind of financial loss during the first part of the 1980s. By 1989, rural America had lost between 700,000 and a million small- to medium-sized family farms.[135] But the economic problems did not end where farm driveways met main roads. Because most rural communities depended on agriculture to some extent to maintain local businesses and banks, they, too, suffered when farm prices dropped. Factories moved overseas for cheaper labor, local merchants closed up, and chain stores and restaurants moved in, but the money they generated did not go back into the local economy. Consequently, many rural Americans left to find work elsewhere, whether in a neighboring town or city.[136] Caught up in the economic stress and despair of foreclosure, what was a farmer to do?

On 4 January 1983, 300 farmers and sympathizers from seven states gathered in Springfield, Colorado, to protest a court-ordered farm auction. The protest led to arrests, injuries, and tear gas on the steps of the Baca County Courthouse. Farmers had attempted to force their way into the building after their shouts and chants halted the auction that was taking place on the courthouse steps. A twenty-minute melee ensued in which deputies in riot gear employed tear gas and Mace to disperse the farmers.[137]

Farmer Jerry Wright owned the wheat and milo farm that was scheduled for auction that day in 1983. In 1977, he was a founder of the American Agriculture Movement (AAM), a militant farmers' group best-known for tractorcades and protests at state capitols and in Washington. The organization was founded at A. J.'s 66 Station in Campo, Colorado, a tiny town located about thirty miles south of Springfield. Wright and other supporters of the AAM argued that high interest rates set by the government on farm loans and embargoes on grain sales overseas made it impossible for farmers to make profits on crops.[138]

In imitation of unemployed farmers during the 1930s, members of AAM used radical protest techniques like tractorcades and penny auctions. If the bank was unwilling to accept the pennies offered at the foreclosure auction, the sale would

Georgia farmers protest low farm prices in a tractorcade, 25 November 1977.
Thousands are parked in a field in Plains, Georgia, the hometown of President
Jimmy Carter. Copyright © Associated Press.

be postponed only to turn into another penny auction. If the bank accepted the
penny bids, those who bid them turned the farm and equipment back over to their
owners debt-free. It was not uncommon for those engaging in a penny auction to
strong-arm people who attended the auction with the interest of purchasing
something into keeping quiet or also bidding pennies.[139] Three thousand farmers
descended on Washington, D.C., on 18 January 1978 on tractors and in pickup
trucks to showcase the plight of farmers. The second tractorcade on Washington
occurred on 5 February 1979. A line of tractors twenty-five miles long came into
the city, wreaking havoc with traffic. Police managed to corral the tractors in the
Washington Mall, but a few farmers drove their tractors up the steps of the Capi-
tol, released chickens and goats onto the grass, and threw tomatoes at Secretary of
Agriculture Robert Bergland. Others set three tractors on fire.[140]

By 1983, because of its militancy and aggressive tactics, AAM had lost appeal
with some farmers who worried about repercussions and public image. In 1979,
it was already losing its appeal with some farmers mistrustful of government because it had become too organized—it sported a Washington office and a full-
time director to lobby Congress. Those farmers felt that this indicated the possibility that the group was in danger of becoming a government shill. A split in

the movement during the 1980s pitted moderates against radicals; moderates wished to bring about change by lobbying Congress, whereas radicals preferred radical protests and were not averse to violence.[141]

The more militant AAM members were those in the Springfield area. Leaders of the group held bomb-making seminars during the early 1980s and encouraged members to attend a "training school" in Weskan, Kansas, that encouraged paramilitarism and antigovernment protest. Weskan sits very close to the Colorado border. One of the instructors involved in the Weskan training sessions was James Wickstrom, the Identity adherent and Posse organizer who billed himself at the time as the national director of Counterinsurgency for Posses of America. Other instructors included unnamed Vietnam veterans. The training school was euphemistically labeled as an "ecological seminar to clean up this land of ours."[142]

Campo, Coloradan Eugene (Gene) Schroder taught bomb-making seminars on his father's farm that were sponsored under the auspices of the AAM. Farmers from Colorado, New Mexico, Kansas, Oklahoma, and Texas attended to learn how to make simple bombs and booby traps to ward off any government officials who sought to evict farmers from their land.[143] Although Schroder has denied his involvement in these activities, his presence was documented and the existence of the seminars was well known in his community.

He was quoted in 1983 in the *Wichita Eagle-Beacon* as saying, "We went to Washington and got nothing from the government ... now the government has come to us, trying to take our farms. If we've got to take them on, let's do it here, on our home ground." Schroder continued his antigovernment activism throughout the 1980s and into the 1990s. One of his books, cowritten with Micki Nellis, *Constitution: Fact or Fiction* (1995), is still a major rightist information source about monetary conspiracy in the United States.[144]

By 1983, Posse Comitatus members and sympathizers had found a foothold in the antigovernment militancy of the more radical edge of the AAM. Though never officially merging, the two organizations shared members and paramilitary training sessions. Part of the reason many moderates left the Springfield AAM was because of the Identity-laden and virulently antigovernment views some members and leaders such as Alvin Jenkins and even Gene Schroder were expressing.[145]

It didn't take an organization already in place, however, for the Posse to find adherents in farm country. Severe economic stress and social unrest displayed at auction protests provided more than enough fertilizer for the kind of scapegoating Posse members advocated. And, although some farmers may have avoided Identity, the Posse provided other rightist ideologies such as tax protest

and common law to which these members could subscribe. Some chapters often used names such as "America First" in Wichita, Kansas, or the "Educated
Citizens of Iowa" to help cloak their activities from investigators and perhaps to
attract more moderate members.[146]

Cairo, Nebraska, farmer Arthur Kirk may have once been politically moderate. He spent his last few years as a Posse adherent. During the mid-1980s, he
borrowed a large amount of money against his farm, not unlike many other
farmers. By 1984, it was apparent that he would not be able to pay the $300,000
debt and foreclosure was imminent. Hoping to stave it off, Kirk sold about fifty
head of cattle to raise money for a loan payment, but the animals had already
been pledged as collateral for the loan's principal. The bank complained to the
county sheriff, and officers notified Kirk that they would have to seize his
remaining cattle as collateral for the bank. Kirk warned them not to try.[147]

On 23 October 1984, two sheriff's deputies arrived at Kirk's farmhouse to serve
him papers concerning his dispute with the bank. Kirk pulled a revolver and the
deputies hurriedly left, not wishing to get involved in a gunfight at close range.
They instead called in a Nebraska SWAT team and a standoff ensued in which Kirk
refused to compromise his position. He would die before he gave up his farm. In
a taped phone conversation with police during the standoff, Kirk expressed his
anti-Semitic views. "God damn fuckin' Jews, they destroyed everything I ever
worked for." He said that he wasn't "putting up with their bullshit now." He continued belligerently that "farmers fought the Revolutionary War and we'll fight
this son of a bitch. We were hoping to do it in court but if you're going to make it
impossible, then damn you, we'll take you on your own terms."[148]

After several hours, Kirk made a run for his barn, out the back door of his
house, armed with a gas mask and a machine gun and wearing a motorcycle hel-
met. He died in a hail of SWAT team bullets. A later search of the farm revealed
twenty-seven weapons and piles of Posse brochures and literature on Kirk's
kitchen table, including a copy of the *Protocols of the Learned Elders of Zion*. At
a farm auction a few days after his death, hundreds of people showed up wearing black armbands in his memory. Kirk had picked up the Posse credo after he
joined Roderick Elliott's National Agricultural Press Association (NAPA). Elliott
hailed from Fort Lupton, Colorado, and was largely responsible for a newspaper
called the *Primrose and Cattlemen's Gazette,* known for its odd mixture of conventional ranch news and Identity rantings.[149]

Kirk was born and raised where he died—on his family's 240 acres near
Cairo. His mother had been raised on the same farm. Her forebears were among
the Germans who had arrived in the late nineteenth century and who, by sheer

numbers, came to dominate the Platte Valley farmland nearby. Kirk's family, for all their work ethics, were not prosperous farmers. Kirk himself ended up moving into nearby Grand Island during his twenties because he and his father had differing ideas about farming. Kirk spent about twenty years working first as a meter repairman and then a service driver for the gas company.[150]

In 1979, Kirk, his wife Dee, and their children moved into his old family home because his father had died. Finally, Kirk could be the farmer he had always wanted to be. Unfortunately, the changes in the economy precluded the success he wanted to enjoy, though he seemingly worked night and day to make it happen. By May of 1984, he had become involved in the Posse, but he may have been even more vulnerable to its conspiracy-laden and paranoid message because of personal tragedies. One of Kirk's sisters had killed herself some years before, and his teen-age son had so lost control that Dee had tried to convince the county sheriff's department to put him in jail. In 1982, one of Kirk's married daughters committed suicide in her parents' home. These events, in combination with the deepening Farm Crisis and its effects on Cairo, Nebraska, may have contributed to his association with the Posse.[151]

Rather than turning the gun on himself, Kirk turned it on the "outside world," particularly on the government officials he believed were ruled by a Jewish conspiracy that was going to take his land and, with it, everything for which he had worked all his life. The events leading up to his standoff with the SWAT team were common in the farming and ranching regions of the American landscape. The standoff itself was not common, but after Kirk's death dozens of angry letters in support of the dead farmer peppered local papers. Kirk's pastor wanted to know why someone from a church hadn't been called in to help negotiate terms. Kirk's wife wanted to know why she hadn't been allowed to go to her husband. Others wanted to know why it was imperative for Kirk, a man who held no hostages and didn't seem to pose an immediate threat to the community, had been confronted with such a force of arms.[152]

To many struggling farmers, Kirk's "I-can't-take-it-anymore" last stand struck an empathetic chord, regardless of the fact that he had been subscribing to racist and conspiratorial beliefs prior to his death. To many farmers and ranchers, he represented agricultural America and his plight was their plight. Caught up in the boom of the 1970s only to have prices pulled out from under their feet, struggling with loan payments, facing foreclosure—Kirk was Everyfarmer and his death was the result of pressures many farmers felt. They couldn't, perhaps, condone a police standoff, but they could understand how he had gotten there.

The Posse played on these rising fears and pressures, especially in midwestern and western America. When a death such as Kirk's occurred, the event served to drive more people into radical movements like the Posse, especially when the death involved law enforcement officials. The rhetoric the Posse espoused, after all, claimed an anti-American conspiracy in government and traditional law enforcement institutions. Kirk—a lone man—was shot down outside his Nebraska farmhouse, surrounded by perhaps thirty local police and SWAT team members. Like his predecessor in death Gordon Kahl, Kirk became a banner not only for the Posse, but also for other radical rightists in this country.

Harvesting Despair

Continuing economic crisis for farmers and workers will spur others to take the white pride promises of the far right seriously.

—Lynora Williams, Center for Democratic Renewal, analyzing former Klansman David Duke's 1989 successful run for state senate in Louisiana[153]

On 13 February 1983, Gordon Kahl and his adult son, Yorie, shot two U.S. marshals to death just outside Medina, North Dakota, some 125 miles west of Fargo. Yorie was later convicted of murder in the shootings; the police officers contend that it was Yorie who opened fire first, killing Officer Kenneth Muir. Gordon Kahl shot and killed Robert Cheshire, who had already taken a hit. Kahl would later shoot and kill Sheriff Gene Matthews in Arkansas during his last standoff with police.[154]

Wanted for tax evasion and faced with $397,000 in farm debt, Kahl had had enough, too. Steeped in Posse rhetoric and a strong believer in Christian Identity, Kahl had spent much of his time trying to organize a larger movement to resist what he believed was the Jewish-controlled government closing in on white people. As a white man, Kahl felt it was his duty to protect his family and Posse brethren from the "conspiracy" that would ultimately kill him.[155]

Immediately after the deaths of Marshals Muir and Cheshire, Kahl headed south and took refuge with Arkansas farmer and carpenter Leonard Ginter, a member of the Association for Constitutional Enforcement, a Posse-like group that touted Identity and encouraged tax protest. Meanwhile, the investigation of the Medina shootout, much to detectives' chagrin, revealed deep roots of sympathy for Kahl and his beliefs. Rodney Webb, a lifelong resident of North Dakota who had returned to his hometown after college to practice law, stated, "I don't think Gordon Kahl is carrying the flag for the woes of the farm community, but there is a lot of sympathy among many, many people who feel the government isn't protecting them in the farm field." Webb continued that many people felt "ill will toward their government because of the Farm Crisis."[156]

Among local entrepreneurs who sold hats bearing "Go, Gordie, Go" slogans and tee-shirts with "Gordon Kahl Is My Tax Protestor" emblazoned on them, investigators not only confronted people whose beliefs were close to Kahl's, but also uncovered other rightist antigovernment groups that had sprouted in America's heartland during the previous decade.[157]

Groups started making the news, like Idaho's Aryan Nations and Arkansas' Covenant, Sword, and Arm of the Lord (CSA), which built survivalist compounds and preached Identity while they stockpiled arms and food for the coming "bad times." Investigators also discovered that many of these groups kept in touch with each other and that fugitives from the law could find refuge among group members or sympathizers across the country. It was perhaps a sobering and frightening realization for those who wanted to believe that Kahl and Kirk were anomalies—American "crazies" who took the law into their own hands and paid the ultimate price.

On the evening of 1 June 1983, Ginter's eldest daughter met with FBI agent Jack Knox and told him where he could find Kahl. On 3 June, various law enforcement officials surrounded Ginter's farmhouse. Ginter and his wife immediately emerged, but Kahl remained inside and began shooting at the men gathered outside. Lawrence County Sheriff Gene Marshall returned fire but was hit and later died. He was convinced he had killed Kahl, but only after the house had been filled with tear gas and burned nearly to the ground was his belief confirmed. Kahl's body was found near a chair, lying on top of a mini-14 rifle, a bullet wound in his head.[158] In fact, Kahl may have died after he shot Sheriff Gene Marshall not because of a single bullet wound to the head, but rather because another law enforcement officer lobbed a smoke grenade into a stove flue and the device set off several boxes of ammunition, killing Kahl instantly.[159]

Regardless of whether the bullet or the grenade killed him, Kahl's death galvanized the Posse and other rightist groups. He, more than Kirk, became a martyr for the cause because of his visibility, involvement, and leadership within the right. Louis R. Beam, Jr., former Klansman, and longtime Identity adherent, wrote an ode to Kahl in which he stated that "it's over. It's done. Gordon Kahl has died this night in a heroic struggle for freedom and liberty." He compared Kahl to Davy Crockett and William Travis as he "hurl[ed] his defiance at the government which has now become the enemy of the people." Using Nordic imagery, Beam declared that "a soldier of our Race has died. Visions of vikings [sic] standing at the gate to Valhalla—arms outstretched in salute to another brave warrior [sic].[160]

Kahl's reputation as a farmer and a religious family man also brought sympathy for his cause from more moderate people in rural America, as investigators soon discovered. What was surprising to them, however, was old hat to those struggling through the Farm Crisis. These were people who had endured personal tragedies, natural disasters, and hard times, but nothing like the hard times of the 1970s and 1980s. When banks foreclosed and local law enforcement officials came to the front door to evict Americans from their homes, from the land they had worked for years—perhaps generations—the sense of betrayal and loss was so profound and so complete that some farmers preferred death to this, the ultimate humiliation.

So entrenched has the agrarian myth become in perceptions about rural western and midwestern America that it is difficult to reconcile failure with the promise of success. "The West" has always tantalized Americans with visions of a patch of land and self-sufficiency, so when that dream fails due to environmental realities or corporate monopolies, a sense of profound disillusionment can develop in those who do not succeed. Wallace Stegner writes that a discrepancy exists between the real condition of the West, which enforced cooperation and group effort, "even among outlaws," and the folklore of the West, which "celebrated the dissidence of dissent."[161] Stegner further notes that the white West opened during a time of rapid advances in communication and transportation. The expansion of these industries ensured that the West would fill up with corporate monopolies that, in turn, would stir up protest.[162]

The perceptions that the West was a land of never-ending resources and always-available land set many homesteaders up for extreme disappointment, simply because the environmental realities of many parts of the western United States were never conducive to successful agrarianism.[163] Contrary to the agrarian myth, agriculture was "one of the first areas where ... dependency on the global industrial economy appeared."[164] Walter Prescott Webb writes that capitalism and democracy existed side by side in the West and that the rise of corporate interests could be in opposition to the individualism that American folklore presented.[165]

Patricia Nelson Limerick also discusses the reality westerners faced in the fact that large tracts of western lands had been government-controlled since the nineteenth century.[166] The ire that many farmers felt during the 1980s was nothing new; the federal government had been regulating farm prices and markets since the turn of the twentieth century. The agrarian myth and ideas about American utopianism, however, continue to influence how some Americans deal with modern problems like failing farms and economic downturns. Some Americans reeling from the Farm Crisis searched for answers and found them— however misguided and tragic—among rightist groups like the Posse Comitatus. Feeding off economic pressures and white Protestant fears about social decay and a turncoat government, the Posse tapped into the American agrarian myth and ideas about western-style vigilantism and citizen righteousness in an effort to garner support for its cause. Many of the men who joined the Posse and its spinoffs during the Farm Crisis were actually socially moderate and religiously conservative family men, with years of farming and ranching behind them.

Some, like Kahl, were also military veterans who had been proud to serve their country. All who joined shared feelings of betrayal and abandonment. The government had left them to hang, they felt. But the Posse offered them the chance to fight back and they took the bait, searching for individual and community empowerment that did not come then and has not come yet, because the Posse could offer only division and secrecy, not coalescence and commonalities.

Nonetheless, the right wing, like leftist groups, offers solutions and comradeship during times of severe economic stress. Ultimately, the fruit of this tree rots from the inside out, succumbing to extreme paranoia and fear. In light of the social and economic havoc the Farm Crisis wreaked, I can't help but wonder whether perhaps the questions we should be asking about the right are not about what it's preaching, but rather about what could be so wrong that a shadowy world of half-truths, conspiracy, racism, and lies stands as a problem's solution. As right-wing groups continue to mushroom throughout the West and the potential for further violence grows with them, these are questions for which we should seek answers.

CHAPTER 5

Patriots and Protests

Showdowns at the Not-So-OK Corral

In *The Patriot* (2000), Mel Gibson stars as Benjamin Martin, a South Carolina gentleman farmer and member of the local legislature who served in the French-Indian War. The year is 1776, and Martin is the widowed father of seven, trying to steer clear of the looming conflict with the British. Martin declares his antiwar stance publicly; he's been in combat and knows that the people who suffer the most are civilians. As a parent, especially, he wishes to stay uninvolved.

This is Hollywood, though, so as an audience we know that Martin will have to participate in some way to put to rest whatever demons he carries and also to let us know how terrible war is and how sometimes we have to do odious things to achieve what is right. Martin's oldest son enlists in Washington's army (against his father's wishes, of course) and British troops capture him, bringing the Revolution right to Benjamin's southern porch. When British Colonel Tavington shoots one of Martin's sons to death, our protagonist realizes that he has no choice. He takes up arms as a father, but when he sees the atrocities the British are wreaking across his rural countryside, he realizes he is taking up arms as a soldier, as a defender of America, a patriot.

"Patriot" gets thrown around quite a bit. When we try to figure out exactly what the term means, we discover that, like the contexts in which it is used, those meanings can change. Mel Gibson's Martin was a patriot because he defended his family, home, and ultimately land and country from an oppressive, invading force. In that sense, the term "patriot" means someone who loves his community and country enough to actually take up arms and defend it from encroachment. In the movie, the enemy was clearly defined (the British) and anyone who fought them could thus be considered a "patriot."

Real life and real history are much more complicated than on screen. One does not necessarily have to take up arms, after all, to support a patriot or the ideology behind a patriot movement. During the Revolutionary War, patriots opposed certain policies that the British government enacted that stood to affect land ownership, tenure, and taxation in the American (then British) colonies. In response, some soon-to-be Americans began pushing for change. They were ready to take the law into their own hands and throw off the yoke of British oppression. This leads us to another aspect of patriotism: vigilantism.

By definition, vigilantism means "taking the law into one's own hands." It isn't necessarily bad or good, but it does imply a group of people who band together and work either against what is considered the "establishment" or against someone who is perceived as going against the "establishment."[1] The established government in the colonies prior to the Revolutionary War was the British and its appointed officials. Patriots who wished to change that were, therefore, vigilantes of a sort. They were taking the law into their own hands to bring about change.[2]

This country has a long history of vigilantism—and of citizens attempting to enforce their own rules of order if a greater order breaks down, or is perceived to be breaking down.[3] Richard Maxwell Brown notes two types of vigilante activity: the socially constructive and the destructive. In the former, organized vigilante groups deal directly with the problem and disband after the problem has been resolved. The latter is generally flawed from the outset, faces local opposition, and in some cases results in a destructive vigilante war.[4]

In American mythology, Revolutionary War patriots are always "the good guys." After all, they fought for freedom from an oppressive, distant government represented by sometimes corrupt local appointees. Consequently, the cultural baggage of the term "patriot" in this country implies a pro-America stance, historically derived from the situation in which Americans fought the British on American soil. A patriot is an implied freedom fighter, battling for American liberty against any threatening force. The trope for "patriot" in American myth, however, is generally a white man ensuring the safety of his home, family, and land.[5]

Since 1970, another type of American patriot stands ready to defend his holdings from invasion. The so-called Patriot movement involves elements from a variety of rightist leanings.[6] Patriots use Posse common-law tactics as a means to clog courtrooms. They design fraudulent checks and use them to purchase computers, fax machines, and whatever else they can. They refuse to pay taxes, and many claim not to recognize any government, so they don't register their vehicles or renew their drivers' licenses. Christian Identity lends the Patriot movement anti-Semitic overtones and ideas about white supremacy, while militia leanings cast a paramilitary cloud over some Patriot groups.[7]

What drives people—in this case, white and often Protestant men—together into paramilitary groups or the Patriot movement are combinations of perceived slights and financial crises. Since 1960, the growth of the racist right corresponds to the loss in Vietnam, the increasing visibility and influence of the civil rights movements throughout the 1960s and 1970s, and the end of the Cold War in the late 1980s. James Gibson argues that men who engage in mercenary work, contract killing, or race war were generally "deeply affected by the Vietnam War: their participation or their failure to make a personal appearance on the battlefield was a crucial event in their lives."[8]

In addition, these men, whether they fought in the Vietnam War or not, concluded that America's loss in that war meant the end of white male dominance and that "dark forces of chaos had been unleashed and dangerous times made it not only permissible but morally imperative for them to take their personal battles far beyond the law."[9] Paramilitary mythology thus offered men the possibility of escaping their lives and becoming reborn as warriors with the power to remake the world.

Susan Jeffords links "angry men" to the loss in Vietnam. She argues that Vietnam veterans are portrayed in contemporary American culture as victims of their government, the war, the Vietnamese, American protesters, and the women's movement. They thus become "emblems of unjustly discriminated [against] masculinity," and, through this image of the veteran, American manhood is regenerated by rejecting the feminine. Reborn and purified, the veteran is perhaps looked upon as an experienced leader and spokesperson for a revived morality and for social politics that will regenerate America itself.[10]

At the end of the 1970s, some white men found the kind of world they were seeking through the pages of fiction and magazines like *Soldier of Fortune* (*SOF*). Early issues of this publication carried advertisements for mercenary services and, prior to 1985, advertisements from neo-Nazi organizations like William Pierce's National Alliance. Pierce had purchased *SOF*'s mailing list in 1981 and sent literature to the magazine's subscribers hoping to recruit new members. *SOF*'s consistent support of white Rhodesians throughout the late 1970s during that country's civil war and its advertisements for World War II German uniforms, helmets, insignia, and weaponry may have led Pierce to believe that some *SOF* subscribers might be interested in the coming apocalyptic race war and the need to prepare for it.[11]

Gibson also argues that, in the late 1970s and into the 1980s, men on the racist right were reacting to the defeat in Vietnam and a perceived collapse of American political, military, and economic power at home and abroad. The racist right simply began to equate "nonwhites" (including Jews) with communists. Losing to communists, Gibson continues, symbolized that white men had been defeated by nonwhites.[12] In a newsletter published by the Christian-Patriot

Defense League (C-PDL), the anonymous author stated that "many Americans are apathetic ... our earlier retreats from victory in Korea and Vietnam and now the ten-billion dollar Panama Canal give-away have so demoralized freedom-loving Americans that they actually feel we are not only leaderless but hopelessly lost." [13]

Daniel Junas notes also that, with the end of the Cold War, conspiracy-minded Americans turned their communist-hunting inward, toward the federal government. Other factors that bring men into the Patriot movement involve economic and social concerns. Junas argues that the Patriot movement provides a pool of potential recruits for militias, and it draws its members from a large and growing number of American citizens disaffected from and alienated by "a government that seems indifferent, if not hostile, to their interests." Predominantly white, male, and middle and working class, this sector of American society "has been buffeted by global economic restructuring, with its attendant job losses, declining real wages, and social dislocations." In addition, these white male Protestants have seen their "traditional privileges and status challenged by 1960s-style social movements such as feminism, minority rights, and environmentalism." [14]

The Patriot movement is an umbrella for a variety of groups and individuals that often espouse competing ideas, including a variety of militia and Posse chapters. All have a few things in common, including opposition to gun control and antigovernment sentiment to one degree or another. Not all Patriots, however, are racist or anti-Semitic and not all are members of militias or the Posse Comitatus. Furthermore, the Patriot movement, like the militia movement, is broad-based and far-reaching and, consequently, has not coalesced behind a single leader or faction but finds resonance across the American West and Midwest, especially among people in economically depressed agricultural regions. [15]

An important part of the modern militia movement is comparisons between the latest militia/Patriot incarnations and the Minutemen militias that fought in the American Revolution. This rhetoric is common not only among militiamen, but also in the Patriot movement as a whole. Unlike modern militias, however, which assemble independently without state assent, colonial patriots were called into service by selectmen, constables, mayors, and other representatives of local government. In 1775, militia members (all men) had to sign a muster roll that bound them to the articles of war. They were also paid for their services from the public treasury and chartered by the states; they swore allegiance to the state and were ultimately part of the state's military forces. [16]

These colonial soldiers appear as a rallying cry in the modern militia movement. Like rightists before them, militia members use a past they have selectively interpreted to stir emotion in their ranks and encourage greater participation from current and future members. Participants in the latest Patriot movement glorify the efforts of the colonial Minutemen who fought an oppressive British government and won liberty for their fellow Americans. Eighteenth-century militiamen have become a testament to the resilience of the "American spirit" and its "traditional values" as propounded by rightist Patriot groups.

The Patriot movement, like other modern rightist groups, has also been remarkably effective at using technology to spread its ideas and increase membership. Most have websites with contact information and fax machines. There are e-mail lists among sympathizers, so sending news and meeting times and places across the country is a simple matter. Through rightist websites, anyone can purchase books and survival gear, find out how to acquire advanced weaponry, modify extant guns, or learn how to make bombs. Anyone can print out a membership form, fill it out, and send it in. Anyone can post commentary or news bulletins on listservs and websites across the country from any computer that provides access to the Internet. Computers have enabled geographically isolated groups or sympathizers—something especially true in western and Midwestern states—to remain topographically sequestered but ideologically tied to the movement and current developments. As a result, the most recent manifestation of the racist right may be the most dangerous and the most organized.

Although computers, fax machines, and shortwave radios have supported a burgeoning rightist movement since the 1980s, any grassroots organization capitalizes on incidents that fuel emotion and sympathy for its cause. For the right, two ineffective and tragic standoffs that involved the FBI and Bureau of Alcohol, Tobacco, and Firearms (ATF) provided grist for extremist mills during the first half of the 1990s.

The first involved Randy Weaver, a sometime follower of Christian Identity and self-proclaimed white separatist, and his family at their Idaho cabin in August 1992. The second was the April 1993 destruction of the Branch Davidian compound in Waco, Texas. Both incidents swelled the ranks of extant rightist groups and also spawned a host of new ones that modeled themselves as paramilitary "militias." [17] Like the 1960s Minutemen group and the early Posse Comitatus, militias operate in small cells, stockpile and cache guns and ammunition in secret places, hold training seminars, and work to recruit mostly white men between the ages of eighteen and forty-five into their ranks. Websites and listservs that cater to military and law enforcement personnel have proven very effective at bringing in new members who already have experience with weaponry and battle tactics and who also have access to others with similar training and opinions.[18]

Following the Weaver and Waco standoffs, conspiracy-minded rightist networks capitalized on the journalistic coverage that implied poor government handling of both incidents. As a result, some white American Protestant men (and some women) who felt that the government had forgotten or rejected them (such as Vietnam and Gulf War veterans), or that it was ineffective at dealing with rising "race" crime, turned to militia and other Patriot groups for answers. These answers, however, involve taking up arms against the government and the "conspiracy" that rightists believe runs it.

Not all militias are racist, though all are rightist. Individuals who join militias tend to be militant gun rights advocates, tax protesters, survivalists, and/or far right libertarians.[19] Militia members also tend to advocate "sovereign citizenship" (an identity in which the citizen rejects any relationship with the current American government and instead chooses to identify with his—like the militias, most members of so-called Patriot groups are male—immediate locale).[20] Other militia members associate with the confrontational wing of the antiabortion movement and some are apocalyptic millennialists, including zealous fundamentalist Christians. Still others are part of the most militant wing of the antienvironmentalist movement.[21]

James Aho's subjects identify themselves as Christians and patriots. As Christians, they are to proclaim faith in Jesus Christ as savior, adhere to the promise of salvation for all men (though, as Aho notes, there is a debate among the patriots concerning what constitutes a human being capable of faith), and work for the exclusive monopoly of Christianity over the means of eternal life. Christian patriots consider themselves duty bound to reform the world and themselves in a manner pleasing to the Lord. Christian patriots combine reformism with an abiding sense of guiltlessness and righteousness in the Lord.

They also believe themselves divinely elected to establish God's rule on earth. They distinguish between Law (biblical) and legality, between Morality (biblical) and legalese. They believe, therefore, that they have little, if any, moral obligation to obey legal statutes that are inconsistent with Law or Morality. Furthermore, state and federal regulations interfere with and even contradict biblical and constitutional law. Christian patriots thus do battle against a satanic (often construed as Jewish) cabal that has infiltrated the dominant institutions of society—especially mass media, schools, churches, and government agencies, such as the Internal Revenue Service. The goal of this cabal is to subvert God's will by promoting agendas such as equal rights for "unqualified" ethnic and racial minorities, non-Christian religions, and moral perversion (e.g., homosexuality, abortion, pornography, crime, and usury). Christian patriots wish to preserve "Christian values" and "Americanism" (as they see them), and they are not averse to using revolutionary means to achieve their goals.[22]

The militia movement could therefore be best described as a diverse right-wing populist movement whose members are unified by the belief that the American government is increasingly tyrannical. Antigovernment sentiment is the thread that holds all militias together and has held them together particularly since 1992. Some are extreme and advocate violence against their targets.[23]

Militias can also be considered part of the larger Patriot movement, which is, in essence, an American political ideology based on an ultranationalist and selective populism that seeks to return the nation to its "constitutional" roots— a system based on white Christian male rule. At its core is the belief that such a system of government will bring about a national rebirth and end years of moral and political decline and decadence brought about by a world conspiracy of satanic origins.[24]

Many western-based militias, like the Militia of Montana (with the ironic acronym MOM) feed off tensions over environmental and land-use issues, traditional points of contention in many western states. The American West, after all, is not the proverbial "garden of Eden" that Americans imagined in the eighteenth and nineteenth centuries. Much of the western half of the country, since white settlement, has dealt with a shortage of readily available water sources and arable land. Other issues that plague the modern West involve the effects of cattle ranching, logging, and industrial and military pollution on native flora and fauna. Still others concern land rights and indigenous peoples.[25]

Conflicts over land, environment, and resources are not merely a matter of things that happened a hundred years ago in the "wild, wild West." During the late 1970s and early 1980s, for example, the so-called Sagebrush Rebellion targeted federal legislation that limited development on public lands. In 1979, the Nevada state legislature passed a law that seized from the federal government 49 million acres from the public domain within the state.

Other states—Utah, Wyoming, and New Mexico—soon joined the fray. Sagebrush rebels (mostly prodevelopment business owners) argued that extensive federal landholdings put the West at a competitive disadvantage with eastern states, which contained few federal lands and enjoyed much larger tax bases and greater opportunities for growth. The only way, therefore, to stimulate western economies was for the federal government to cede public lands to the states, which could then lease and sell some and therefore promote greater development on others.[26]

In 1980, the election of President Ronald Reagan and his appointment of James Watt to serve as Secretary of the Interior—both probusiness and pro-Sagebrush Rebellion—lent some credence to the rebellion's claims. Nonetheless, a wholesale transfer of such large amounts of public land was simply unworkable. Many Sagebrush Rebels knew as much but continued to push the cause to voice growing resentment toward federal constraints on western land use and, in the case of Reagan and Watt, a shift on the federal level to trumpet an end to "big government" and a push for local control.[27] The Sagebrush Rebellion echoed old extremes in Western history—development versus preservation. At the center of the maelstrom sit public lands.

An even more recent conflict involves the "Wise Use Movement" and its environmentalist opponents. In 1990, two political entrepreneurs, Ron Arnold and Alan Gottlieb, developed Wise Use as a fundraising campaign. Gottlieb has a professional history of fundraising for a variety of right-wing groups, but Arnold was formerly employed by the Sierra Club in Washington state. The Wise Use agenda is to remove present environmental protections and prevent future environmental reforms in order to benefit the economic interests of the organization's members and funders. However, because the agenda appeals to people who oppose federal restrictions on public lands, Wise Use has a variety of supporters outside its membership who do not directly benefit economically from the movement's success with federal and state legislation.[28]

Arnold appropriated the term "Wise Use" from the moderate conservationist tradition as propounded by Gifford Pinchot, the first head of the United States Forest Service (USFS). In 1910, Pinchot called for national forestry policies based on the "wise use" of America's trees and minerals. This position triggered a feud between Sierra Club founder John Muir and his supporters and Pinchot's adherents. Muir wanted to see wilderness valued for its own sake, not for what it could contribute to economic development. Eighty years later, Arnold borrowed the term, not because he supported the Pinchot tradition, but rather because he thought it was ambiguous and fit neatly in newspaper headlines.[29]

A key theme in the Wise Use Movement is its stance on private property rights. The movement's members argue that regulations that protect environmentally sensitive areas on private property are unconstitutional ways for federal and state governments to intrude on private lives. The movement has therefore supported legislation that seeks to expand the legal definition of what a "government taking" is to include all situations in which profits from mining, development, or logging private lands are limited by environmental regulations.[30]

Because of its antigovernment position and support of private property rights, the Wise Use movement and groups that mimic it have found a great deal of support in rural areas—especially in the West, a region of the country in which more than half of the lands are government-regulated. The antigovernment ideology and cries for private property rights have struck a chord with the modern Patriot movement. Modern militias, therefore, feed off tensions in the areas in which their members live and congregate especially in parts of the country where ideological struggles over land and private property have historically simmered.[31] The West, which is littered with the carcasses of historical land battles, provides ample fuel for regional militia groups. The variety of range wars, water and land disputes, and issues over environmental stewardship have stirred passions in westerners since Americans began referring to a "West."

Those involved in the Patriot movement who are passionate about "private rights" versus "government regulation" hold their beliefs with a religious fervor. They promote a paranoid, fearful worldview that isolates them from society's mainstream. They are antagonistic to democracy, promoting instead a political agenda that would end most of the institutions and constitutional protections that effect social justice in America. Patriots want ultimately to replace the extant system with a theocratic hierarchy founded on racist and Old Testament–based beliefs. The movement's violent rhetoric and threatening demeanor open no doors for public discourse and instead provide justification for less stable followers to commit acts of extreme violence.[32]

The Patriot agenda has been around for quite a while. Kernels of modern Patriotism have existed throughout the history of the racist right in this country. Many modern Patriots have taken up residence in the West—especially the Pacific Northwest—in an attempt to isolate themselves from various apocalyptic occurrences, but also in the hope of building a white homeland in this region, a sentiment that has repeatedly emerged in the racist right since the early 1970s.

The overt racism of many Patriot groups has ensured their long-term marginalization and limited influence in the mainstream channels of American society, but the 1990s Patriot movement represents a mutation of its traditional belief system into one that disguises the racial and antidemocratic implications of its agenda and emphasizes instead a populist appeal across a broad range of issues served in American nationalism. In this movement, any national problem—unemployment, crime, drugs, abortion, natural disasters, welfare—can be blamed on the "un-American" federal government or the encroaching New World Order.[33]

Ironically, modern militiamen and members of other Patriot groups use government documents such as the United States Constitution to justify their position. They may distrust and even hate the present government, but they hold the Constitution dear. It is a sacred document that has, they claim, been ignored by recent administrations. The position of modern Patriots is that the militia, as defined by the Constitution, is the American citizenry at large. On the surface, they are correct. The militia is further divided into the organized and unorganized militia. The former consists of persons who are called into service, whereas the latter is made up of individuals held in reserve. The Founding Fathers advocated this position: Samuel Adams stated that "the militia is composed of free Citizens," and James Madison did not fear oppression by a federal army because the troops would be outnumbered by "a militia amounting to near half a million ... citizens with arms in their hands."[34]

Patriots, though they are correct in identifying the nature of the militia as set out in the Constitution and its authors, are wrong with regard to the way in which the militia is activated. The critical issue involves the means by which ordinary citizens (defined as *the* militia) may organize and participate in *a* militia. The United States Supreme Court has interpreted the Constitution to limit the right to raise a militia to *states* rather than to private citizens. In other words, only state authorities can call citizens into a militia to protect that state from foreign and domestic enemies.[35] Consequently, the various groups in the modern militia movement are actually operating outside constitutional boundaries, though all would argue against such an observation. Furthermore, many use the Second Amendment to the Constitution as a shield, claiming that, because it guarantees the right of citizens to bear arms, they are merely exercising their constitutional rights to carry guns and form militias in the face of a tyrannical government. Nonetheless, as Daniel Levitas, cofounder of the Institute for Research and Education on Human Rights, notes, the language of the Second Amendment does not authorize or justify the existence of armed, private paramilitary gangs.[36]

In a 1995 issue of *SOF,* author Wayne Ross notes that the Second Amendment reads, "A well regulated militia being necessary [for] a free State, the right of the people to keep and bear arms shall not be infringed." Ross also notes that Article 1, Section 8, of the Constitution states that Congress has the power to call forth the militia and to train its members, which consists of all able-bodied males aged seventeen to forty-five, as stipulated under Title 10, U.S. Code, Section 311, which also includes female citizens who are officers in the National Guard. Although most citizens are members of the militia (automatically) and therefore have the right to keep and bear arms to respond to a call by lawful authority, the appointment of officers and the training of militias is the responsibility of the state, as the Constitution declares.[37]

Most militia members would argue otherwise. They see themselves instead as carrying on proud American traditions that include individualism and patriotism. Militiamen try to reflect popular constructions of frontiersmen and view themselves as brave men taking a stand and preparing for a final confrontation with forces of tyranny (i.e., the federal government). Wanting to re-establish a culture that lies buried in a nostalgic past, militias and other American Patriot groups like them enact deeply rooted mythical American identities. On the one hand, militias are the colonial Minutemen who courageously battled British forces in the Revolutionary War. On the other, they are a frontier vanguard working to bring back good, old-fashioned, Christian American values.

Unlike such compound dwellers as the now-defunct Idaho Aryan Nations, militias do not have permanent fortifications. Nor do they have a tradition of elaborate meetings and ceremonies like the Ku Klux Klan. They are, instead, small cells of "soldiers" subject to a military-style hierarchy. Many train in a variety of terrains, "just in case," and most stay in communication with other chapters through computers, faxes, and phones.[38] Although militias and other Patriots are in disagreement with each other over such subjects as racism and ways in which to fight the government, all prepare for an upcoming "showdown" with government troops. Descended from right-wing paramilitary groups like the Minutemen and The Order, the latest incarnation of militias, set in motion in the early 1990s, is the best organized and best outfitted of the survivalist right. The wheels for the movement were set in motion by two specific events, neither of which involved people who attached themselves to any particular Patriot movement.

Weaver Fever

Ruby Ridge sits at the northern tip of the Idaho panhandle. At its base runs Ruby Creek, and near the creek runs a one-lane rough road that leaves the old highway to mark dirt driveways that disappear into thick forest, delineated by "No Trespassing" signs. Once the road crosses the creek, it becomes barely a path, climbing for two miles until it fades into two tracks that pass through woods so dense that a driver is enveloped in perpetual twilight. The road forks to the right;

take this direction and you will eventually end up in a steep, wooded field that spills out onto a rock-strewn geological knob with a panoramic view. On this point sits an empty cabin built of plywood, sawmill waste, and two-by-fours wedged into the hillside in a bouldered outcrop.[39]

Ruby Ridge could be a poster child for the American West, for reasons people came west in the first place. Clean air, impossibly blue skies, clear water, incredible vistas, hardy pioneer neighbors who mind their own business. Boundary County in northern Idaho is a rugged individualist's dream. Or, in some cases, a rugged family's dream.

In 1992, the cabin was inhabited by just such a family that came west to escape urban blight, the alleged Jewish-controlled government, secular influence in schools, and the crumbling of American civilization as the millennium approached. Like hundreds of travelers before them, the Weavers came west to find a new beginning and to be left alone.

Randy and Vicki Weaver moved to Idaho in 1983. Both had come from working farm families in Iowa. Randy spent time in the army; he signed up in 1968 to go to Vietnam but spent most of his service at Fort Bragg, in North Carolina. He trained as a combat engineer and later claimed to have passed the requirements for Special Forces, though some dispute that. Weaver supposedly learned survival and explosives skills, and he worked in preparing fortifications. He was promoted to sergeant and qualified as an expert with the M-14 rifle and as a sharpshooter with the M-16 and the .45-caliber handgun. His military record was spotless, and he earned a National Defense Service Medal and a parachute badge.[40]

In 1970, Randy returned home to Fort Dodge, Iowa, where he began dating Vicki Jordison. The two married in November 1971. They moved to Cedar Falls, Iowa, where Randy planned to attend Northern Iowa University on the G.I. Bill. He hoped to go into federal law enforcement. Vicki planned to work as a secretary until they had children. After two quarters, Weaver dropped out and began working at a John Deere tractor factory in neighboring Waterloo. Vicki continued to work as a secretary.[41]

Throughout the 1970s, the Weavers explored various ideologies; by the late 1970s, Randy was investing heavily in silver because he believed that paper currency would soon be devalued. The price of silver collapsed just before the 1980s, but the Weavers had moved on to something else that interested them—apocalypticism infused with a blend of Christian fundamentalism and whatever else they came across that fit with their burgeoning separatist and racist ideology. Both read prolifically and shared literature with each other before they moved to Idaho. Weaver began a Bible study group at a local restaurant in Waterloo; he encouraged the other men in the group to purchase and stockpile weaponry. When the Weavers left for Idaho, both were convinced that the world was scheduled to end in three-and-a-half years, based on their interpretations of the Book of Revelations.[42]

By the early 1980s, the Weavers had two daughters, one son, and a growing interest in government conspiracy. They came across rightist literature that had been around for decades but had lurked on the edges of the mainstream, which lent credence to the conspiracy theories the tracts contained. Through these rightist publications, the Weavers were introduced to the Illuminati, the idea of a Jewish world conspiracy, and the threat of a New World Order government that would oppress white people with the advent of the bad times. In the spring of 1983, the Weavers sold their house in Iowa, packed up their children, and headed west to Montana, seeking a refuge from the future.[43]

Finding nothing in their price range in Big Sky country, the family headed west again and eventually ended up in Bonners Ferry, Idaho, in September 1983. They met another young family that shared their apocalyptic beliefs and helped them find the Ruby Ridge land just south of town, overlooking Naples, another small town. The town of Sandpoint and the Aryan Nations compound lay thirty miles further south, and the Canadian border was twenty miles north. God, the Weavers rejoiced, had indeed delivered them.[44]

During the 1980s, Boundary County, Idaho, attracted many people whose beliefs resembled the Weavers'. Richard Butler established Aryan Nations, while other Christian Patriots (whether racist or not) who believed in a fast-approaching end of the world sought havens from the outside world in this isolated corner of the West. In the rightist publication *Instauration,* one anonymous letter-writer noted, "I am astounded by the number of West Coast WASPs moving north," including young people in vans with a child or two and perhaps a dog. The writer continued that elderly and middle-aged people moved as well, "mainly concerned about escaping the rising crime wave." Their destinations, the writer claimed, were "Oregon, Washington, Idaho. They are looking for survival camps where they can wheel in a trailer or buy a spot of land. Many of these Anglo refugees are armed."[45] Ironically, the Weavers, in seeking to separate themselves from the world, found instead a community of like-minded believers, all preparing for the end of the world at the hands of a government gone far astray.

The world, however, did not end in 1987 as Vicki Weaver had predicted. Instead, rightist activity increased in Idaho and neighboring Washington. Robert Mathews' Order had been active in the early 1980s, and the FBI began to investigate the Aryan Nations compound. In August and September 1986, five small bombings occurred in Coeur d'Alene. One damaged the home of a leader of the Kootenai County Human Rights Task Force. The four other bombs slightly damaged the federal courthouse and three businesses. Members of a group billing itself as The Order II were arrested. The group's members may have been inspired by the 1986 summer Aryan World Congress, held at the Aryan Nations compound. Among those in attendance at the time was Randy Weaver.[46]

Weaver found sympathizers at the congress, so he attended a few more. In 1989, the Weaver family made plans to attend again. Through their tenuous association with this group, they had begun drifting toward Christian Identity. In 1989, Randy also began working with a gun dealer who specialized in illegal shotguns. Unbeknownst to Weaver at the time, the gun dealer was an FBI informant who used gun running as an entrapment scheme to arrest white supremacists or, ideally, blackmail them into spying on known groups in the area. Weaver, constantly struggling for money to support his family, was out of construction jobs at the time, so the chance to earn some cash before the winter set in—acquiring a few shotguns and sawing the barrels—was a relief.[47]

In 1990, the informant's cover was blown, but his FBI/ATF associates approached Weaver and offered him a deal. If he would continue attending Aryan Nations meetings and keeping details to report back to them, they would forget about the weapons violations. If he refused, they would have to prosecute him.[48] Weaver refused. In December 1990, an indictment was handed down for Weaver's arrest on the gun charge and a letter went to the Weavers' attorney. Weaver did not turn himself in and nothing happened immediately, so he and his family, along with friend Kevin Harris, settled in for the long Idaho winter.

The standoff at Ruby Ridge has been told and retold by a variety of sources. According to my own research, when Weaver was ordered to appear in court, the letter apparently stipulated a March 1991 court date, not February as law enforcement officials claimed. Court documents also listed a March 1991 trial date. Nevertheless, when the February date passed, law enforcement authorities mistakenly began making plans to bring Weaver in. As a result of compounded misunderstandings, on 21 August, law enforcement surrounded the cabin. In the ensuing confusion and mishandled directives over the next few days, Weaver's son and his wife, as well as his son's dog, were shot to death. Both Weaver and friend Harris were wounded by gunfire.[49]

On 27 August, Colonel James "Bo" Gritz (rhymes with "fights") arrived on the scene after Weaver asked to talk with him. FBI officials at Ruby Ridge agreed to let him try to talk the Weavers out of their cabin. Gritz, a former Green Beret

Members of the media and federal agents tour outside Randy Weaver's cabin, located near Naples, Idaho, after the eleven-day standoff in which Weaver's son and wife were shot and killed. Confiscated guns and ammunition are displayed in the foreground. Weaver had already surrendered to federal authorities. This photo is dated 1 September 1992. Copyright © Associated Press.

and Vietnam veteran, had long been a rightist sympathizer and in 1992 was well known in burgeoning militia circles. At the time of the Ruby Ridge standoff, Gritz was running for president on the right-wing Populist Party platform. It was Gritz with whom Randy really started negotiating, and it was Gritz who was able to relay the news to the FBI and to the world that Sammy and Vicki were dead and that Randy and Harris were wounded.[50]

On 31 August, Randy agreed to let Harris leave the cabin with Gritz and Jack McLamb, a rightist former policeman, for medical treatment. He also consented to having Vicki's body removed, but Sara, the Weavers' eldest daughter, talked her father out of surrendering because she was certain they were all going to be killed anyway. Finally, on the same day, the remaining Weavers left the cabin and were taken into custody.

Meanwhile, at the base of the Weavers' driveway, a crowd of more than a hundred supporters had been gathered since the first day of the standoff, protesting the way the government agents were handling the situation. The protesters included neo-Nazi skinheads from Nevada and Colorado, wives of jailed Order members, and Aryan Nations members. Other protestors were friends and neighbors of the Weavers, many of whom did not adhere to racist beliefs but who were prickly about government interference in local and personal affairs. When the crowd heard that Vicki and Sammy were dead, the word quickly spread through rightist networks. Although the standoff itself had created a stir among rightists, the deaths of the two Weavers provided a rallying cry for the right wing in general and militias in particular.[51]

What happened during the Ruby Ridge standoff is as much a matter of opinion as it is of public record. With the exception of the charge of missing his first trial date, Randy Weaver was ultimately acquitted of all counts—which included murder, conspiracy to commit murder, and owning and selling illegal firearms. During his and Harris' trial, it was revealed that the summons he had received notified him that his court date had been changed from 20 February 1991 to 20 March. The mistake was the court's. Harris was also acquitted of murder (shooting and killing U.S. Marshal William Degan) and harboring a fugitive. During the trial, the defense found that the government agents' reports contained discrepancies, evidence had been mishandled, and the rules of engagement instructed the agents on Ruby Ridge to shoot and kill any armed male at the cabin. At the end of the trial, the judge in the case fined the FBI and the ATF for deliberately delaying evidence shipments. Randy sued the government for the wrongful deaths of his wife and son. In an out-of-court settlement, the government agreed to 3.1 million dollars but admitted no wrongdoing.[52]

For the extreme right wing, the Weaver standoff was not merely an issue of one man avoiding a trial date and paying a horrific price. Rather, it symbolized just how far the American government would go to impose its tyranny on its citizens. And the man who jumped at this opportunity to organize a better resistance network among Patriot groups lived two states south, just outside Fort Collins, Colorado.[53]

Within days of Weaver's surrender, Pastor Pete Peters, an Identity minister in the small town of LaPorte, mailed personal letters to a broad spectrum of conservative (extreme and not) writers, leaders, and ministers. Peters invited these leaders to Estes Park, Colorado (a resort town approximately fifty miles northwest of Boulder) for a conference that would discuss and confront what he perceived as the injustice and tyranny exhibited in the deaths of Vicki and Sammy Weaver. Peters even went so far as to invite United States Attorney General William Barr to attend and explain the government's actions at Ruby Ridge. Barr declined the invitation, but 160 white Christian men from 30 states said they would attend the conference scheduled 2 months after the Ruby Ridge standoff and, indeed, some 150 did. Among those in attendance was ex-Klan leader and Aryan Nations "ambassador" Louis Beam.[54]

Some researchers have claimed this 1992 meeting as the "birthplace" of the modern militia movement. Others have refined their thinking about the importance of the meeting. More likely, it was touted as the birthplace in the wake of media attention. Mark Pitcavage, an expert on the American militia movement, does not see this gathering as the beginning of the militia movement because hardly any of the early militia leaders showed up, though John Trochmann, leader of MOM, was present.[55] Indeed, to suggest that this meeting created the modern militia movement may be overstating the case; groups in Idaho were already organizing in response to Ruby Ridge, and Bo Gritz had already begun to promote his special operations training (dubbed SPIKE for "Specially Prepared Individuals for Key Events").[56]

Rightists of all stripes getting together to discuss and demonize the government is nothing new. What was different about the Estes Park conference is that members of groups and individuals with differing views that normally would not have anything to do with each other were suddenly in the same room expressing similar views. Neo-Nazis, Identity adherents, antiabortion activists, Klan members, and even Larry Pratt of Gun Owners of America came together and attempted to devise a battle plan for future conflicts with the government.[57]

A "Special Report" emerged from the conference; it reprinted the entire text of Louis Beam's "Leaderless Resistance." Beam advocated legal, aboveground groups with underground smaller units that could engage in illegal activities that, in turn, could not be traced back to the parent organization. All units would operate independently and would never report to a central headquarters or single leader. Beam referred to these units as "phantom cells," and his essay became a blueprint of sorts not only for militias, but also for other antigovernment and white supremacist groups that wished to carry on an underground war with minimal repercussions to their members.[58] By 1994, Beam's principles for white supremacist response to Ruby Ridge had become the model structure for many American militia groups.

The October 1992 conference both revitalized the type of paramilitary organization the right had spawned in the 1980s, like The Order, and used the groups in attendance to promote "Leaderless Resistance." Peters' meeting laid much of the groundwork for the formation of modern militias by providing an organizational structure and solidifying connections between longtime white supremacists and Identity followers and others, such as Gun Owners of America. It was not until the following year that a large-scale, decentralized movement would appear. It did so in response to specific events.[59]

Compound Fractures

Waco hunkers on the rolling, humid plains of central Texas. Home of Baylor University and a large population of devout Baptists, Waco also provided a home to a group of cultists who took up residence in a compound just north of the small city. Dubbed Mount Carmel by its residents, members of the Branch Davidian Church (a separatist Adventist sect) stockpiled weaponry and foodstuffs and waited for the coming apocalypse.

Not newcomers, Branch Davidians had been in Texas since 1935 and had preached doom and gloom since the group's inception. Founder Victor Houteff prophesied a new era would begin on 22 April 1959, and 900 followers came to Texas to wait for the end. When the world continued, most of the 900 eventually left, but the Branch Davidian Church continued to prepare for the end.[60]

In 1981, a shy young man with a stutter came to Texas and joined the group. By 1990, Vernon Howell had transformed himself into a charismatic leader. He changed his name to David Koresh and continued the church's policy of millennium preparation. The self-proclaimed leader of the church believed he was an "anointed" messenger from God, chosen and inspired to reveal to his followers and to the world the meaning of Revelation and of 2,500 years of Jewish and Christian apocalyptic prophecy. Koresh also believed that it was his job to interpret the seven seals of Revelation to reveal the time and manner in which the end of the world would occur.[61] For Koresh and the other Branch Davidians, the beginning of the end occurred on 28 February 1993.

On that Sunday, ATF and FBI agents converged on Mount Carmel and attempted to serve Koresh with a warrant for the illegal purchase and possession of firearms, explosives, and other weaponry. The Ruby Ridge standoff had made law enforcement officials leery of separatists, and when word got out that the Branch Davidians were stockpiling heavy weaponry it added fuel to the fire. The confrontation turned violent, and four ATF agents and perhaps as many as six Davidians died in an exchange of gunfire. Four other Davidians, including Koresh, were wounded.[62] As a result of this wild-west-style shootout, both sides dug in and for the next month and a half were locked in a standoff.

As the story circulated through the American media, Patriots and burgeoning militia groups used the tragic events in Waco as proof that the federal government was seeking to prevent Americans from owning guns and that it sought to imprison those same Americans in the name of a Jewish-controlled New World Order. The Branch Davidians, though not part of the racist right, nevertheless became a symbol for the Patriot movement and its members' claims that the federal government was out of control and on its way to tyranny.[63]

The ATF and FBI had known for at least a year about Koresh's activities and the impressive arsenal he and his followers had been amassing. Even when Koresh found out about the impending warrant and raid, he refused to surrender. After all, in his eyes, federal agents were serving as tools of Satan as they sought to disrupt the Davidians' existence at Mount Carmel. The actions of the federal government only solidified Koresh's belief that the end of the world was fast approaching. The ATF soon learned that Koresh knew about the scheduled raid; nevertheless, they went ahead with it.[64]

For the next fifty-one days, tensions mounted as the ATF and FBI attempted to talk Koresh out of the compound. The FBI Hostage Rescue Team (HRT) that had seen action at Ruby Ridge was called in, and its members tried to end the standoff peacefully, especially in the wake of the fiasco in Idaho. Twenty-one children and two older women eventually left the compound; a few others trickled out as March turned to April. Life inside had become increasingly difficult; federal agents had cut the electricity and, in an attempt to drive Davidians out, had set up speakers to blast all manner of music and sounds at the compound.[65]

It was the HRT that lost patience first. With the approval of Attorney General Janet Reno, the team decided to force Koresh into surrendering. Its members would, they decided, converge on Mount Carmel in armored vehicles and use

Fire engulfs the Branch Davidian compound near Waco, Texas, on 19 April 1993. Over eighty members of the group, including leader David Koresh, died as federal agents tried to drive them out of the compound. Four ATF agents had died in a shootout at the site a few weeks earlier. Copyright © Associated Press.

tear gas to force the Davidians out. On 19 April 1993, the attack commenced. Davidians inside the compound refused to surrender and instead fired on the HRT. In response, the HRT broke through a wall of the compound with one of their tanks and fired its tear gas canisters. Flames broke out in the compound and, fueled by strong spring winds, an inferno quickly consumed the building, killing all but nine of the Davidians inside. The dead included twenty-two children under the age of fifteen.[66]

Debate continues to this day about how the flames started (and how many Davidians died); Patriots maintain that the HRT deliberately fired into the building to start a fire. The official government position is that the Davidians started the flames and point to recordings from listening devices planted in the compound that seem to support this theory. Regarding children in the compound, several families did reside in Mount Carmel and, according to government investigations, these children were subjected to child abuse and possibly molestation by Koresh. However, depending on which reporter or federal mouthpiece you ask, the evidence for and against child abuse takes on a "he-said/she-said" character.[67]

The horrible and tragic occurrence outside Waco galvanized right-wing groups around the country. Like Ruby Ridge, it was proof positive that the federal government was out of control. Moreover, the raid received criticism from more moderate circles about the way in which it was handled. After all, over eighty people were dead, some of whom were children. What kind of government advocated violent raids on its own citizens? More so than Ruby Ridge, the raid at Mount Carmel seemed to exemplify the actions of a government gone mad, of an FBI and ATF out of control and waging war on Americans. And perhaps because Koresh's group did not have a white supremacist reputation, they painted a more benign picture in the media than white separatist Randy Weaver, who was known to have attended Aryan World Congresses at the Aryan Nations Compound.

After Mount Carmel had burned to the ground and the remains of the Davidians were recovered, questions about the government's strategy in dealing with Koresh began to circulate through the American media. Koresh had learned of the impending attack that April morning. The ATF discovered that Koresh knew about the attack, but the assembled agents went ahead with it. Critics of the strategy wanted to know why such a large force was used, especially since so many children were housed in the compound. Koresh was known to leave Mount Carmel on occasion, even after run-ins with local law enforcement. The FBI and ATF had been investigating the Davidians for more than a year before the standoff. Why had he not been arrested or served with the warrant when he was on one of his trips into Waco? Koresh had cooperated with federal officials earlier; he had volunteered documents that pertained to the purchase of his weapons and had invited agents into the compound. Why, then, was this confrontation necessary? And why did it have to end in such a manner?[68]

Nine Davidians survived the fire. Five of them, in addition to six other cult members, stood trial on a variety of charges that included murder, conspiracy, and weapons violations. Three were acquitted, five received forty years in prison, and the remaining Davidians received lesser sentences, ranging from three to twenty years. In the aftermath of the botched siege, it soon became apparent to members of the media and the American public alike that problems had plagued the operation from the beginning. FBI negotiators continually clashed with FBI tacticians; negotiators wanted to use diplomacy but tacticians chose psychological warfare. A preassault evaluation of Koresh warned that, as a messianic figure, he was likely to end the siege by fulfilling his apocalyptic visions. FBI leaders ignored the review.[69]

Several months after the siege ended, ATF Director Stephen Higgins was forced into early retirement after it was discovered that top officials lied to the public about the initial February raid. Although Koresh knew about it and ATF personnel were aware that he knew, ATF officials claimed in press releases that

Koresh was unaware that he was to be served with a warrant. Five other ATF supervisors were fired for their roles in the initial raid (two were later reinstated), and FBI Director Louis Freeh claimed that the procedures and structures that the FBI relied on at Mount Carmel were "inadequate."[70]

Waco, more than Ruby Ridge, struck a chord among Patriot and militia groups because even the mainstream American media was questioning government procedures during the standoff. During the latter days of the siege and in the days after the government bulldozed the charred compound, various Davidian sympathizers (rarely numbering more than twenty at a time) held vigils and protests at the site. Many were members of racist Patriot and militia groups, who had come to see the fulfillment of their own prophecies about the American government.[71]

Among those protestors was a young Gulf War veteran originally from New York state who was already steeped in far-right paranoia and antigovernment sentiment. Timothy McVeigh left the Mount Carmel protest before the final ATF attack; he heard about it while visiting the Decker, Michigan, farm of James Nichols, another antigovernment sympathizer and brother of Terry Nichols. It affected McVeigh deeply. He, Waco, and Oklahoma City would forever be linked two years later by the vagaries of a calendar date imbued with horrible symbolism. Not only did the Branch Davidian siege galvanize the formation of numerous Patriot and militia groups in this country, it also fueled the intense racist and antigovernment paranoia and fascination with violence that McVeigh harbored.[72]

Two years to the day after Mount Carmel burned, McVeigh parked his rented Ryder truck in front of the Alfred P. Murrah Federal Building in Oklahoma City. The two-ton fertilizer and ammonium nitrate bomb hidden in the back of the vehicle exploded shortly after 9:00 A.M., its force shearing off the front of the eight-story structure, killing 168 men, women, and children. Somehow, in the twisted and dark labyrinth of his thinking, McVeigh took revenge on the federal government for its actions at Waco.[73]

In the bombing's horrific aftermath, many Patriot groups laid blame on the federal government, even going so far as to suggest that the government itself blew up the building in order to blame militias and Patriot groups, especially after the bad publicity the ATF and FBI generated at Ruby Ridge and Waco.[74] Some militias and Patriot groups did distance themselves from the violent rhetoric of the Patriot movement after Oklahoma City, but the growth of the movement did not stop, even after the intense scrutiny all facets of the right faced following Oklahoma City.

Two months after the bombing, the Militia Task Force, a research group that is part of the Southern Poverty Law Center, had identified 224 militias and support groups in 39 states. A year later, 809 groups had been identified. In 1997, according to the Task Force's statistics, 858 known groups were active. Patriot activity—including militias, tax protesters, common-law courts, and sovereign citizen groups—also increased in all fifty states, with the heaviest concentrations in the Midwest, Southwest, and along the Pacific coast.[75]

The Oklahoma City bombing, along with Waco and Ruby Ridge, created a perception among Patriot groups that the federal government was at war with its own citizens. Because of the extreme paranoia and conspiracy-driven belief system of many Patriot groups, Oklahoma City has become a "government set-up" to sway public opinion against militias and against "true Americans"—all part of the Jewish world plan to fool white Americans into complacency until the imminent takeover of this country and, ultimately, the world.[76]

These three events fueled the growth of the Patriot movement during the early and mid-1990s. But they also taught law enforcement officials a thing or two about disgruntled Americans and the paranoia that seems rooted in the very soil beneath our feet. Consequently, when the next rightist standoffs occurred, the results were very different.

Turning Points: The Freemen and the Republic of Texas

According to year 2000 census data, Jordan, Montana, is home to 364 people, roughly 99 percent of whom are white. The town sits at the intersection of State Highway 200 and Route 59 in Garfield County, a flat, wind-burnished ranching region of the state. According to Ken Toole, director of the Montana Human Rights Network based in Helena, his state seems to have become a haven for people wanting to hide from something.[77]

In the 1990s, it did seem that way. The Militia of Montana, the Unabomber, and then the Freemen took turns in the media, lending some credence to the notion that the state was a good place to "get lost." It is, after all, the third most sparsely populated state in the nation. Fewer than half a dozen people per spare mile inhabit Montana, and there is no daytime speed limit.[78] These vast, relatively unpopulated areas of the Rocky Mountain West became a refuge of sorts for a variety of right-wing extremists looking to not only avoid detection, but also spark a revolution.[79]

In an April 1996 New York Times article, Richard E. Nicholls links the extremist activity in Montana to the complex history and stereotypes of the American

West: the homesteader, the vigilante, and the outlaw. These figures, Nicholls suggests, "embody the principles of the West": self-reliance, avoidance of the perceived toxic effects of a meddling government, and the joys inherent in living close to the land. In 1990s Montana, it seemed the "outlaw" myth was finding expression through a group called the Freemen.[80]

On 25 March 1996, LeRoy Schweitzer, who was fifty-six, and Daniel E. Petersen, Jr., then fifty-three, along with Lavon Hansen, were arrested just off a ranch some thirty miles from Jordan. They were indicted in schemes that involved fraudulent checks and money orders. Schweitzer and Petersen also faced charges of felony criminal syndicalism—the advocacy of violence for political goals.[81]

The three men were members of a Patriot group known as the Freemen. The day after the arrest (Schweitzer was one of the leaders), several other members refused to vacate the ranch house and instead barricaded themselves within and vowed not to be taken alive. ATF, FBI, and local law enforcement officials set up a perimeter and began negotiations. Thus began an eighty-one-day standoff on the lonely plains of eastern Montana. This time, however, no one died and the Freemen standoff at their so-called Justus Township ended without major incident.

When the standoff first began, "Justus" was misinterpreted by the media and others to be a misspelling of "justice." In fact, the term is biblical, found in Colossians 4:11. Justus was an obscure follower of Christ. He took the name Justus because his original name was Jesus as well. In Hebrew, Justus means "righteous." According to Dale and Connie Jakes, the Montana Freemen misinterpreted the verse. They seemed to think that Justus actually *was* the Christ when in fact he seems to have been a converted Jew. Ironically, the anti-Semitic Freemen named their compound after him. The Jakes also say the Freemen liked the play on words Justus offered: "Just us."[82]

Like the Posse, the Freemen bombarded their neighbors and government and local officials with liens and various court documents. Members also rejected anything having to do with government control: taxes, drivers' licenses, car insurance, Social Security numbers, building inspections, even ZIP codes.[83] The Montana Freemen subscribed to Christian Identity, though their interpretation differed in some ways from those of other white supremacist groups. A twenty-page treatise filed with local courts by Freemen leader Rodney Skurdal suggests one of the major differences. Not only did God grant land to His people, but Skurdal takes the interpretation a bit further and suggests that God also granted ownership and control over that land to the exclusion of others. Freemen thus believe that they are the "chosen people"—"true" descendants of Anglo-Saxons—and that land is a sacred

Justus Township, the headquarters of the Montana Freemen, 30 miles outside Jordan.
This image was taken 29 March 1996. Authorities believed that the Freemen may have
constructed bunkers in the forested area in the background. Copyright © Associated
Press.

trust from God. Therefore, the government has no right to dictate land ownership
or levy property taxes. Their theology also incorporates an apocalyptic vision of a
final showdown between forces of good and evil, which sets the stage for confrontation between government forces (evil) and Freemen (good).[84]

On closer examination, the ideology is a mixture of a variety of rightist rhetoric and white supremacist beliefs. Most agree on these points: white Christian
males have special "Freeman" citizenship status while nonwhite men, non-
Christians, and women are second-class or worse. The government has no right
to tax or prosecute Freemen, and U.S. currency has no intrinsic value, so the
Freemen are under no obligation to repay loans. The federal government, according to Freemen beliefs, is controlled by Zionists and is therefore illegitimate.
The only legitimate authority is the common-law court.[85]

The Montana Freemen operated under the auspices of Schweitzer, a former
crop duster and tax delinquent; Rodney Skurdal, an ex-Marine from Wyoming;
and brothers Ralph and Emmett Clark. Skurdal had moved to Montana sometime after 1988 and bought a small ranch near the town of Roundup, perhaps
fifty miles southeast of Jordan. He was already steeped in Posse rhetoric and
promptly refused to pay any taxes of any kind. The IRS tried to confiscate his
property in 1993, but, because of Skurdal's antigovernment activities and growing belligerence, local authorities were loath to try to take it by force. The farm
was "auctioned" twice, but no one offered to buy it. Skurdal had filed cases in
which he outlined some sort of grievance against local and federal governments
in all fifty-six counties of Montana, garnering a reputation as a troublemaker
with possibly violent intentions. Through his activities, Skurdal met Schweitzer

and Petersen. Late in 1994, the two men had moved into Skurdal's farm, where they continued their paper harassment.[86]

Meanwhile, outside Jordan, Ralph and Emmett Clark had fared badly in the 1980s farm crisis. In 1981, they stopped making payments on their farm loans. By 1995, the two owed nearly two million dollars. Throughout the 1980s and 1990s, the Clark brothers turned more and more to rightist rhetoric as answers to their farm woes. Through their own journeys into antigovernment ideology, the Clark brothers, along with Ralph's son Edwin and nephew Richard, came into contact with Schweitzer.[87]

About the time the IRS tried to repossess Skurdal's property, a bank foreclosed on Ralph Clark's 960-acre wheat farm, located some thirty miles outside Jordan. In response to the foreclosure, the Clarks set up a common-law court in January 1994. Three dozen Freemen, including Skurdal and Petersen, along with sympathizers like the Militia of Montana's founder John Trochmann, took over the Garfield County Courthouse, where they held a meeting in which they created their own county government. The Freemen then began issuing million-dollar bounties for the arrests of the county sheriff, attorney, and judge.[88]

After the courthouse incident, the Freemen escalated their threats of violence against all local government officials and continued bombarding courts with liens and various complaints, an effective ploy to keep county officials and neighbors constantly scrambling to undo the damage. Phony liens have proven remarkably effective in the Patriot movement as a way to clog up court systems, as well as a technique to defraud the government and various banks of money. If a lien is filed against various property owners or a government official, for example, banks can transfer money against these assets until they are proven false. Consequently, the Freemen created fake checks and money orders they would write against a lien they had filed. With the funds they accrued this way they would purchase equipment to further their activities, pay off debts, or buy whatever they felt they needed, including guns, computers, and even an airplane. When the dust settled on the standoff, the Freemen had managed to collect 1.8 million dollars by defrauding banks, credit card companies, and mail order houses.[89]

The Freemen would use bad checks for anything and everything. Townspeople in Jordan and Roundup began demanding cash only from Freemen and their family members in the months before the showdown because it was the only way they could ensure compensation for goods and services. By Tuesday, 26 March, the U.S. Attorney's office in Los Angeles estimated that the federal government had received thirty million dollars' worth of bad checks from various Freemen groups and people who had taken their seminars (for which the Freemen charged).[90]

By March 1996, Jordan and Roundup locals were fed up with Freemen. For months, they had filed complaints with state and federal authorities to do something about the group, whose members were constantly threatening people with whom they disagreed. They had been passing bad checks, creating backlogs in local courts, and filing bogus liens on unsuspecting neighbors. About the time Schweitzer, Petersen, and Hansen were arrested, locals had already implemented plans to get together a group of as many able-bodied citizens as they could and force the Freemen to leave the Clark ranch.[91] When the three men were finally arrested on the twenty-sixth and twenty-one other Freemen (including five women and three girls) barricaded themselves inside the ranch, it was the culmination of several years of conflict between locals and the extremist group. But, because of Ruby Ridge and Waco, authorities were reluctant to move too quickly against the Freemen and possibly trigger another tragedy. Consequently, though local residents were glad that something was finally being done about the Freemen, many felt that most of the problems could have been avoided had law enforcement authorities acted earlier.

As it was, nearly three months passed before the Freemen surrendered. The government employed new tactics a year in the making that included assigning various agents, behavioral specialists, and negotiators to Jordan. They wore civilian clothing and maintained a perimeter a good distance from the ranch and ensured that media could not approach. They kept phone lines open with the Freemen and did not engage in displays of force.[92] On 11 April, two Freemen surrendered without incident. Two weeks later, Bo Gritz, Randy Weaver, and Jack McLamb arrived in Jordan, offering their services as negotiators. At first rebuffed, Gritz eventually was granted access to the compound, but he gave up in frustration in early May.[93]

On 1 June, the FBI brought in armored vehicles and a helicopter to Justus Township, as they considered a plan to occupy part of the property. Two days later, Bureau agents cut the power to the ranch and announced plans to scramble radio and television signals. The Freemen had rejected all overtures, instead patrolling their compound with their weapons in plain sight. On the twelfth, sixteen-year-old Ashley Taylor left the compound and surrendered. She was the daughter of Dana Dudley, a Patriot holed up at the ranch who was wanted for check fraud schemes in Colorado. Also that day, in an unprecedented move, the FBI allowed Edwin Clark to leave the compound. They flew him to Billings to confer with Schweitzer. Clark was accompanied by members of the CAUSE

Randy Weaver (center) with other Freemen sympathizers at an April 1996 town meeting in Brussett, Montana, during the standoff. Bo Gritz is standing to Weaver's right holding a baseball cap. Gritz and Weaver went to the site of the standoff to see if they could help negotiate with the Freemen and bring about a peaceful resolution. Authorities politely declined Weaver's offer, but Gritz was given a chance to talk with Freemen leaders, which did not resolve the situation. Gritz and Weaver are long-time associates; Gritz went to Weaver's standoff at the latter's request and attempted to negotiate terms between Weaver and federal authorities. Copyright © Associated Press.

Foundation, a North Carolina group active in pursuing litigation against the federal government on behalf of Waco survivors. Clark was brought back that day and released to the compound. The next day, the Freemen surrendered.[94]

Peace, however, was a long time coming. Although the kinder, gentler tactics law enforcement authorities employed did ensure that no one died or sustained injury, the length of the standoff wore heavily on locals' nerves. Many residents of Jordan, though glad that the Freemen were derailed, felt that the process had taken much too long. The Freemen, after all, weren't a bunch of outsiders who had suddenly descended on the area (though a few were). They were life-long residents of the community, and most everyone in Jordan had a friend or relative barricaded in the compound. Their antigovernment activities had created deep rifts between themselves and townspeople. Splits occurred among locals as well—those who felt sympathetic toward the Freemen and those who did not. Most, however, felt that the group's members were "freeloaders" insofar as they had not paid taxes and had tried to bilk the community with fake checks and false liens.[95]

Ultimately, the standoff in Montana left wounds in its wake. But it also made apparent that not all members of the Patriot movement are fringe dwellers. They are often disaffected members of communities with ties to their neighbors and families. Caught up in forces they feel they cannot control, they turn their frustrations to something tangible, however misguided, and focus on the government as enemy. Those who end up in the Patriot movement, whether in Posse chapters, militias, or Freemen groups, do have a point about continued economic deterioration in parts of this country and about the systematic expansion of the state's repressive apparatus, as exemplified by previous standoffs with groups and individuals since the early 1980s. During the past twenty years, there has been a decline in real wages for millions of Americans and the farm belt has been particularly hard hit through globalization and domestic and foreign policy.[96]

The northern plains have been particularly hard-hit as more people move away seeking a livelihood other than agriculture. This in itself is nothing new; the Plains areas have always been economically strapped and people have spent more time going than coming since the nineteenth century.[97] But the realities of twentieth- and twenty-first-century economics are indicative of real political and economic inequalities central to U.S. policy. As Chip Berlet and Matthew Lyons note, antielitism, properly directed, would be a healthy response to these global shifts. Unfortunately, the Patriot movement diverts attention from real systems of power and instead scapegoats and reduces complex reasons for social and economic conditions to simple conspiracies.[98]

The myths ingrained in the expanses of the American West create a conundrum for right-wing groups. Members cling to an ideology that is born of myth, not reality, and when faced with situations that do not jibe with the myths of frontier and nostalgia, many find solace instead in conspiracies that threaten to tear them from their communities and roots. The Freemen standoff marked a turning point in not only how the government deals with rightist groups, but also how rural communities perceive a Patriot response to real issues. The Freemen garnered little support from fellow rightists when it became apparent that law enforcement authorities were just going to wait them out. There was no ammunition for rightist revolution in the standoff, and the actions and attitudes of the Freemen themselves served to turn public opinion against them.[99]

A view west down Texas Highway 166 as it wends its way to the entrance of the Davis Mountains Resort road, where the Republic of Texas' headquarters was located. The group engaged in a standoff with law enforcement officers on 1 May 1997. Copyright © Associated Press.

A year later, another standoff in response to a community's efforts to oust a rightist group did result in tragedy, but by that time, many rightists themselves had little sympathy for the barricaded group.

"A Whole Other Country"

Fort Davis, Texas, is about 175 miles west of El Paso. State Highways 117 and 18 intersect at the town, which is the seat of Jeff Davis County. Fort Davis was established as a military camp in 1854; by the early twentieth century, it had become a popular destination for wealthy Gulf Coast families enjoying the mild climate in the Davis Mountains.[100] As of 2000, 1,050 people lived in Fort Davis, about half of the county's population. Of that count, roughly half are white and half identify as Hispanic, though a few people do not identify as either.[101]

Texas, like Montana, has lots of wide open spaces and places to get lost. That may have been what Richard McLaren ultimately was trying to do when he moved to west Texas from Wilmington, Ohio, in the late 1970s. He graduated from high school in 1972 and apparently attended some college but seemed not to find it to his liking. After seeing an article in *Texas Highways* magazine about the spectacular scenery in the western parts of the state, he decided to move to the Fort Davis region. McLaren admitted a fascination with Texas since writing a third-grade book report on the Alamo. Upon arrival, he worked a variety of odd jobs and then landed employment at an organic winery at Davis Mountains Resort. Eventually, he came to own the operation.[102]

At some point during the years he resided in Fort Davis, McLaren became a daily presence at the county courthouse, where he filed lawsuits, affidavits, and contestations of land surveys and deeds of trust against his neighbors. For roughly fourteen years, McLaren used these common-law tactics to tie up court systems and attempt to wrest land from his neighbors without resorting to buying it. Consequently, McLaren's reputation among Fort Davis locals was not conducive to so-called western hospitality.[103] Those folks who opted to fight his court filings ended up spending thousands of dollars in legal fees to prove him wrong. McLaren, however, generally ignored judgments against him.

Paralleling the actions of the Montana Freemen and other common-law Patriots, McLaren and his colleagues peppered Texas with bogus liens. On 13 December 1995, McLaren founded the Republic of Texas at a meeting in San Antonio, stating that Texas is, in fact, a sovereign nation and was never legally annexed by the United States in 1845.[104] Consequently, the federal government had no jurisdiction over the Republic's residents. In August of the following year, after McLaren served a stint in jail for refusing to cease and desist filing bogus liens, the group sent a letter to the United Nations notifying it of the official flag and military insignia of their "sovereign country."[105] Members were already convening common-law courts and filing hundreds of liens against government officials and private citizens,[106] including then-Governor George W. Bush, other state officials, and even Pope John Paul II.[107]

Unlike other Patriot groups, and indicative of the variety of approaches that the Patriot movement employs, the Republic of Texas under McLaren did not feature racism or anti-Semitism as a plank in its platform, though it did advocate independence from America and revolutionary, perhaps violent, means to achieve it. Consequently, I place McLaren under the "extreme" label because of his stockpiling of weaponry and the fact that he and his followers took hostages.

Stephen Atkins points out that the original intent of the Republic's movement was to restructure state government. McLaren wanted a common-law government, providing citizens few laws to worry about. Without laws, attorneys and politicians would be obsolete. Drivers' licenses would not be required, and there would be no speed limits on Texas highways. All financial transactions would be based on gold and silver and homeowner and farm debt would be wiped out. All taxes except import and export would be abolished, all schools would be local, and state universities would be privatized. McLaren also wanted a state militia to provide a military force, loosely based on the Swiss canon model.[108]

McLaren declared himself the leader of the Republic of Texas and took up residence in an abandoned volunteer firefighter building he dubbed "The Embassy" off a dirt road in the Davis Mountains. Members of the group began creating their own checks, passing at least three million dollars' worth throughout Texas. McLaren continued to ignore cease and desist orders while his neighbors chafed at his continued lien-filing and property boundary disputes. Like the residents of Jordan, Fort Davis locals tried to get law enforcement authorities to do something about the Republic of Texas and McLaren. Many had been subjected to the erstwhile leader's legalese and a few had spent thousands of dollars to disprove the claims. The hostility Fort Davis had for McLaren could itself have been dangerous; locals were outraged that McLaren had been allowed to create so much trouble for so long.[109]

Finally, in April 1997, the situation came to a head. Two Republic of Texas members were arrested for their common-law activities and fraud. In retaliation, members from "The Embassy" invaded the nearby home of Joe and Margaret Ann Rowe, firing gunshots and taking them hostage. Joe Rowe was the head of a property owners' association who was vocal in his opposition to the Republic's actions. He had himself been involved in legal battles for years with McLaren. In the incident, Rowe was hit by flying glass and one of the Republic's members struck him with the butt of a rifle, breaking his arm. The two were taken by force to "The Embassy," where McLaren prepared for a siege.[110]

Declaring that the Republic was at war with the United Nations and all foreign entities, including the American federal government, McLaren demanded the release of the two Republic members who had been detained earlier that day. Furthermore, Governor Bush and other state leaders were to agree to a referendum on independence for the state's eighteen million residents. The vote would allow people to decide whether they wanted to belong to the United States or be a sovereign republic. With increasing bravado, McLaren also stated that paramilitary groups across the nation were en route to Texas to defend him and that plans were underway to take Texas state officials hostage, though authorities claimed there was no evidence of the latter claim.[111]

Tensions increased as surrounding residents were evacuated and law enforcement officials moved in. The following day, McLaren freed the Rowes in exchange for the release of one of the Republic's members from jail. Robert Sheidt had to be

Richard McLaren, self-styled leader of the Republic of Texas, walking outside his
home, which he designated the "Embassy of the Republic of Texas, Office of Foreign
Affairs." McLaren considered himself an ambassador of sorts with duties similar to
the secretary of state on the federal level. This photo was taken 6 March 1997.
Copyright © Associated Press.

convinced to do the swap, because he apparently had come to realize the serious-
ness of the situation. Five days later, he would surrender, claiming that he had to
get out; he couldn't take it anymore.[112]

By 29 April, eighty residents from the surrounding area had been evacuated
and other locals were demanding immediate action. Thirteen adults were holed
up at McLaren's "Embassy." If granted diplomatic immunity, McLaren stated,
they would surrender.[113] However, McLaren abruptly broke off negotiations the
next day. Eighty miles away in Pecos, seven men were arrested with weapons, including explosive devices. They were apparently on their way to Fort Davis to help
the Republic of Texas. This development proved worrisome to law enforcement
officials. Two days later, they would tighten the perimeter around the Republic's headquarters, which included a ramshackle trailer (in which McLaren and
supporters were barricaded) and a run-down outbuilding, sparking a frantic

"Mayday!" call from McLaren on his shortwave radio, pleading for intervention from "any nation."[114]

The day after McLaren's radio entreaty, on 3 May, he and three Republic of Texas members walked out of the trailer in which they had been holed up and surrendered. Two others—Mike Matson and Richard Keyes—fled into the surrounding woods. McLaren's wife Evelyn (the two had been married in a Republic-sanctioned ceremony the preceding December) had surrendered a few hours earlier; her grown daughters convinced her to do so.[115] Matson was killed in a mountain gun battle with law enforcement the next day. Keyes remained a fugitive until September, when he was finally captured.[116]

Rightist outrage at Matson's death failed to materialize as it had after Ruby Ridge and Waco. As in the Montana standoff, many rightists around the country felt that McLaren and his vision of the Republic of Texas were not helping the Patriot cause. The Republic split three ways in the months prior to the crisis in the Davis Mountains. When McLaren's group took hostages, one competing faction posted a statement on its website that McLaren and those acting with him "have gone completely off the deep end."[117]

The notoriety following the McLaren standoff damaged the Republic of Texas movement as a whole and may have led other Patriots to distance themselves from the incident and the group. Some extreme rightists saw McLaren's and the Freemen's wars against their neighbors as one of the reasons their movements failed. Some extreme rightists have begun to feel that, to create a revolution, building bridges within the communities of residence is a more effective way to garner support for their other right-wing ideas.[118] Members of the two other factions were indicted for fraud and served some jail time. The Texas legislature also passed an emergency law making it a criminal offense to file fraudulent liens, simulate the legal process, or impersonate public officials. This law has made it much easier to arrest and prosecute Republic members, which has derailed the group's efforts to subvert legal and political processes in the state.[119]

Nevertheless, the wounds remain in this small Texas community. Some residents lost thousands of dollars in legal battles with McLaren, and others lost land because they couldn't afford the legal battles to prove his contestations were false. Many Fort Davis residents were angry that law enforcement had not acted sooner to deal with the situation. After his surrender, more than a few of his neighbors expressed disappointment that McLaren hadn't been killed.[120] Although the self-styled leader of the Republic is serving a ninety-nine year sentence (with an additional twenty-two years tacked on in 1998 for federal firearms violations and fraud), the damage he inflicted on Fort Davis hasn't been forgotten.[121]

McLaren had gone west looking for a new beginning. Most of his Fort Davis contingent were themselves not Texas natives.[122] Feeling disaffected, they bought into McLaren's promises and conspiracy theories and hitched a ride on his rhetoric, looking for answers to larger political and economic questions. Instead of finding solutions, their actions further alienated them from their immediate community as well as potential sympathizers. The Montana Freemen and McLaren's Republic of Texas were modern Western outlaws, attempting to enact their own visions of how things should be, based on misconceptions of how things were and where they are headed. Some of the Freemen had been battling shifting economic situations for years; they came to their conclusions through their actual experiences with financial hardships and perceived government meddling in agricultural affairs. McLaren tapped into disaffection to boost his own stature.

Regardless of whether the Patriot movement harbors truly aggrieved Americans with genuinely legitimate complaints or self-styled wannabe leaders taking advantage of others' issues, the results are the same. Local communities can and do suffer when people use extreme right ideology and conspiracy as solutions to problems.

CHAPTER 6

Conclusion: From Sheets to Shirts

New Frontiers for Right-Wing Extremism

Michael Kimmel stated in 2004 that "[t]he white supremacist movement is animated by and populated by downwardly mobile lower-middle-class men (and their female counterparts)." He continued, "[M]en . . . grew up believing that this was 'their' country and that all they had to do was to follow the same rules their fathers and grandfathers did and they too could reap the rewards of their entitlement." As Kimmel stated, many followed those rules, but the rewards seemed to go to others—nonwhites and immigrants.[1]

A global economy created its own problems: banks foreclosed on farms, and corporations began moving their factories overseas to save money and avoid American taxes. The sons and grandsons of the men who were reasonably successful "playing by the rules" discovered that the rules no longer granted them the same entitlements they saw their ancestors reaping. Kimmel noticed "three entangled streams" that have come together in the white supremacist movement: "racial entitlement, class-based rage, and the shame of emasculation."[2]

There is no doubt that when outside political and economic forces coalesce to create anxieties and stresses in local communities, some people will seek answers in extremist movements. However, I do not agree with Kimmel that the movement is populated by downwardly mobile lower-middle-class men. Certainly, men who fit this profile are involved in white supremacist groups or have white supremacist beliefs, but the evolution of the movement in the late-twentieth and early twenty-first century tells a slightly different story. Indeed, even the 1920s Klan demonstrated its propensity for attracting educated, middle-class professionals to its ranks. To suggest, therefore, that white supremacists can be typecast is misleading.

Kathleen Blee's work with the extremist right demonstrates that there is no set profile—at least not for women who are involved with white supremacist groups or beliefs—for participants. Many are from middle-class or upwardly mobile households that cut across rightist and leftist political leanings.[3] In 2002, Carol Swain revealed a new development (during the mid- and late 1990s) in the white supremacist movement: the growth of so-called white nationalism, which uses rhetoric far more palatable to a mainstream audience and proclaims that its supporters "don't hate" anyone who isn't white; they merely "love" the white race and wish to "celebrate its history."[4]

Swain noted that white nationalists tend to "reject the kind of violence and intimidation once advocated by the older racist right." They instead seek to expand their influence through argument and rational discourse aimed at an audience of white Americans who "have become embittered or aggrieved over what they perceive to be a host of racial double standards in the areas of affirmative action and crime reporting" and in large-scale immigration from third-world countries. White nationalists aggressively seek and desire a more mainstream audience, and to meet those goals, they are developing new tactics.[5] Think here of the image that David Duke presents: clean-cut, polite, educated, articulate.

During the course of her research and interviews, Swain discovered that white nationalist leaders do tend to be educated, articulate, and personable, which serves to make their arguments more persuasive than earlier extreme right groups.[6] White nationalists use the rhetoric of national self-determination and national self-assertion to protect what they believe is their "God-given natural right to their distinct cultural, political, and genetic identity as white Europeans."[7] The movement includes a slick publication called *American Renaissance,* published since 1991. Many of the articles *AR* posts on its website deal with domestic and foreign affairs, presented in a benign format that resembles standard news magazines like *Time.*[8]

Converts to white nationalism extend into academia. They include Professors Michael Levin (philosophy, City University of New York Graduate Center and City College), J. Philippe Rushton (psychology, University of Western Ontario), and Glayde Whitney (deceased 2002; behavioral genetics, Florida State University). Hart has called for the geographical partitioning of the United States for various racial groups (providing a homeland for whites), and Levin has written that African Americans have such difficulties today establishing stable families, succeeding in school, and controlling violence because of their "differential genetic endowment." To Levin, evolution produced a racial hierarchy in terms of abstract reasoning ability and the ability to control emotions, delay gratification, and plan for the future. Of course, whites are at the top of the hierarchy. Rushton has attempted to discredit the theory that biological race has no validity, and Whitney wrote an introduction to David Duke's autobiography and worked to further his theories about racial differentiation and the genetic propensities of certain races.[9]

Couching views in a "scientific" format with the backing of an academic title or institution can do wonders for furthering one's views, particularly among college students. So can a professional-looking website. White nationalists such as Don Black, who launched the first white nationalist website, Stormfront, in 1995, make a very clear distinction between white supremacists and white nationalists. In an interview with Swain, Black stated that all he and others who share his beliefs are demanding is the preservation of the kind of white America that many great statesmen of the past envisioned. Black referred to the Founders as men who believed that blacks and whites simply could not live together and argued that, in fact, some of the Founders attempted to send blacks back to Africa through the American Colonization Society.[10]

My purposes here are not to argue semantics or contexts about what the Founders did or did not intend with regard to African Americans and whites. The primary and secondary literature on the subject is massive and a reader can access it at his or her leisure. What is important with regard to Black's statements is how white nationalists use the past to buttress their views, creating a new package for an increasingly separatist message. Stormfront's Black advocates white separatism and a white homeland somewhere in the country and mentioned the Pacific Northwest in his interview with Swain and Nieli.[11]

None of this is to suggest that white *supremacists* have faded away. Far from it. The movement is evolving, like social and political movements do, and white nationalism is but a new facet of a larger supremacist context. We can vilify extreme rightists as "haters" and "loonies" until we run out of breath. To do so, however, serves only to dismiss the thousands of people in this country who either are directly involved in groups or sympathize with some of or all of the goals and messages. Individuals are maddeningly multifaceted and have many reasons for what they do.

Certainly, the movement has attracted a few men who clearly would have benefited from psychological intervention: Benjamin Smith went on a shooting spree in Chicago and Bloomington, Indiana, on the Fourth of July weekend in 1999, killing two in addition to himself; Buford Furrow walked into a Jewish daycare center in Los Angeles on 10 August 1999 and opened fire. No one died at the daycare center, but Furrow did shoot and kill a Filipino American mail carrier later that day.[12] Smith had fallen under the sway of the World Church of the Creator, a white supremacist group led by Matthew Hale formerly based in Illinois, while Furrow had ties to Aryan Nations.[13]

Eric Rudolph, the rather infamous survivalist steeped in Christian Identity who disappeared into the North Carolina wilderness for five years, carried out a string of bombings in the southeastern United States. He pleaded guilty (and will serve two life sentences) to the 1996 Olympic park bombing in Atlanta that killed one woman and injured a hundred; he also pleaded guilty to the 1997 bombings of an Atlanta abortion clinic and a gay bar and the 1998 bombing of a

Birmingham abortion clinic that killed an off-duty police officer and maimed a nurse.[14]

Rudolph had been steeped in antigovernment and racially charged rhetoric since childhood; his mother was also a Christian Identity follower. In 1981, following the death of her husband (Rudolph's father), she moved the family to a largely rural isolated area of western North Carolina with a history of antigovernment sentiment since bootlegging days. Rudolph's mother networked with other extreme right leaders and movement members and home-schooled her son, thus solidifying his views by an early age.[15]

In spite of these "loose cannons," most white supremacists and white nationalists are not people who will "go off" at any minute. Invariably, their rhetoric can cause those who are unstable to carry out violence—after all, if someone hears "evil Jews" or "abortion is murder" enough and is already unstable, he (or she) could construe such statements to mean that it is thus acceptable and in fact justifiable to use violence against those the extreme right targets.

It is also important to remember, as Chip Berlet has stated, right-wing groups, whether extremist or not, do not *cause* prejudice in the United States. They exploit it.[16] As I write this, on 15 July 2005, members of the National Vanguard (formerly part of the white supremacist National Alliance) submitted papers to the Secretary of State of Nevada documenting the formation of the so-called White People's Party (WPP). The party needs 7,914 signatures by August 2006 to qualify for ballot access.

Chaired by Michael O'Sullivan, a forty-one-year-old Las Vegas real estate broker, the WPP promises to "build real political clout for whites" and help work for the goal of a "whites-only living space"[17] in the country. O'Sullivan claims that "many minorities agree" with the WPP; he states that minorities "don't want their race mixed with ours."[18] The director of the Nevada chapter of the Anti-Defamation League of B'nai B'rith, Cynthia Luria, stated that the party's ranks are growing "amid a resurgence of racism in the Southwest" fueled by anxieties over immigration from Mexico and other Latin American countries.[19]

Luria fears that issues that are important to more mainstream Americans, who perhaps have legitimate concerns about economic downturn and increased illegal immigration in the Southwest, will support the WPP, though they may not be aware of the rest of the party's platform, which states that "all policies and decisions to be made shall be governed and decided by whether it is good for our people, non-Jewish people of wholly European descent."[20]

White nationalists, thus, are better than older white supremacist groups at taking current political and social issues of the day, spinning an exclusionist message, and making their views more palatable to mainstream Americans. Illegal immigration is an issue of which most mainstream Americans are aware and about which many are concerned.

The horrific events of 9/11 have also provided white supremacist and nationalist groups anti-Semitic fodder. Most support the idea that 9/11 occurred because of American support of Israel and that somehow, Jews are behind the catastrophe to force the United States to intervene in the Middle East and bring about Israeli (Jewish) dominance in the region. A few, like the National Alliance, have their own "yellow-ribbon" campaign in which they call for "bringing our troops home and putting them on the Mexican border."

This is not to suggest that all mainstream white Americans are going to buy into the views. However, because some do and because the movement is garnering media attention (the Nevada WPP received a mention in *Newsweek*), others who might share more extreme views become aware of groups such as the WPP and begin supporting them, passing the message along. Word of mouth can be an effective tool in spreading extreme rightist views.

Another factor in the evolution of the movement is the Internet. Interested parties can find out about local chapters, communicate with like-minded individuals all over the world, download membership applications, e-mail leaders, shop for white supremacist tee shirts and books online, get tips about how to disseminate information and leaflets, and avoid police detection or, if confronted by police, provide suggestions about what to say and do.[21] Many, like Aryan Nations and the National Vanguard, have readily downloadable anti-Semitic and racist leaflets that can be easily printed out. Other leaflets might extol the virtues of white women and call for white men to protect them so they may continue to propagate the race. Still others have a more modern, updated look that often includes such symbols as the American flag.

In other words, one no longer has to attend formal meetings to be involved with an extreme right-wing organization. One can check e-mail, go to chat rooms, and hold online discussions with like-minded others. The movement, thus, has become more widespread and flexible than in the past, as people in one part of the country (or world) can link up with others in another and spread news about events, racist music shows and CDs, where to purchase items, and who in the area might be sympathetic to exclusionist views. The web, unfortunately, doesn't offer checks and balances or research the validity of information, nor does it train people on how to vet material or question sources.

Consequently, someone who is anxious about rising gas prices, the war on terror, or a stagnant economy might take some comfort in easy, "either/or"

White nationalists developed their own yellow ribbon magnet. The yellow ribbon magnet was very popular following the U.S. invasion of Iraq in March 2002. Most say "support our troops," while others say "bring our troops home." The National Alliance
wanted to bring them home and put them on the Mexican border to stop illegal immigration. From the National Alliance online store, located at www.natvanbooks.com. The
National Alliance sells books and paraphernalia through its publishing arm, National
Vanguard Books (not to be confused with the National Vanguard group that split
from the Alliance).

answers. The extreme right has always provided clear targets based on a dualis-
tic view of the world ("evil" versus "good") for feelings like this, and, as Abby
Ferber stated in 2004, "[i]n this world of complex information overload, con-
flicting opinion, and feelings of threat, it can be a comfort to simply cut through,
or avoid, complexities, and rest on what feel like truths."[22]

This is how the extreme right spreads its message. It focuses on specific issues
that have resonance among more mainstream Americans and offers "a solution"

Aryan Nations, like many white supremacists and nationalists in the wake of 9/11, were certain that Jews (specifically Israel) were responsible for the attacks on the World Trade Center in New York City. This image exemplifies that belief. A white hand pulls a curtain back to reveal a plane flying into a tall building. Hovering above the cityscape is a stereotypical image of a Jewish man with a hooked nose. From August Kreis' Aryan Nations website, located at www.aryan-nations.org. This is a downloadable flyer.

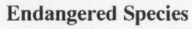

Earth's Most Beautiful
Endangered Species

The life of a race is in the wombs of its women.
The White race faces extinction now!
Only 2% of the earth's population
is young White female.

Look long and hard, White man.
Images like hers may soon cease to exist forever.

Judeo-Christianity & Judeo-controled world governments
perpetuate genocide through doctrines of Universalism.
No race can survive without nations of its own. America denies
us White nations, White schools, White neighborhoods, White
organizations and everything necessary for racial survival,
then promotes inter-racial mating.

The highest law of nature is the preservation of one's own kind.
There is no time remaining for White men to indulge in reality
denial or cowardice. If our women are not worth fighting for,
then I ask you, "What Is?"

Live The 14 Words

*"We must secure the existance of our people
and a future for White children"*

ARYAN NATIONS

http://aryan-nations.org

Here is why:
*"because the beauty of the White Aryan
woman must not perish from the earth*

"Earth's Most Beautiful Endangered Species" is, according to white supremacists and nationalists, white women. This flyer, available for download and dissemination at www.aryan-nations.org, exhorts white men to oppose the international Jewish conspiracy and fight for a white nation and, more important, white women. The term "14 words" is in reference to what has become a rallying cry for some white supremacist groups. The phrase was coined by David Lane, an imprisoned member of The Order.

in the form of a white homeland or "white rights." White Americans who perhaps are frustrated by larger domestic and foreign economic and social currents might buy into the message and begin spending more and more time absorbing nothing but extremist views, conspiracies, and websites. A steady diet of that can eventually lead one into deeper involvement, which invariably means spreading the message among friends or family members who might be receptive to the "solutions" extreme rightists offer for real-world problems.

The Order's Robert Mathews' White American Bastion has yet to come to fruition, though weblogs exist that promulgate the idea.[23] Some extreme rightist groups continue to push for a white homeland, which is nothing more than segregation reinvented. They are not as specific as Aryan Nations' Richard Butler and The Order's Bob Mathews were with regard to geographical location, though there seems to be a tacit understanding that the Midwest or the West would be good places for this homeland, since the eastern seaboard seems heavily populated and largely occupied and doesn't seem to offer much for an Aryan infrastructure.[24]

The West still offers wide open spaces, great swaths of forested mountains, and land into which dreams are sown. But the myths that have surrounded the West as created and disseminated through white, Protestant, and masculine filters have been co-opted to further extremist agendas. The dangers of rightist rhetoric are that it taps into extant grievances and longstanding anger and offers no solutions beyond violence. What's more, when groups like the Freemen and

An image available for screensaver use or dissemination at the National Vanguard website. It attempts to appeal to patriotic Americans by including the image of the flag in the background along with the figure of what appears to be a hiker. The Vanguard split from the National Alliance in 2005 in the wake of infighting in the Alliance. As of August 2005, the Vanguard was working to put the so-called White People's Party on the ballot in Nevada. Image available at www.nationalvanguard.org.

the Republic of Texas isolate themselves from their communities within the rubric of their own beliefs, they can lose all perspective on the truth.

The extremist right has come to recognize that wide open spaces and a place of one's own could be good things for one's well-being. However, it is possible to take rugged individualism to an extreme even too far outside the bounds of white supremacist beliefs. They have moved beyond the rugged individualist model for their white state and begun instead tapping into the homesteading and community-building model as a way to serve a more palatable form of racism to the rest of America.

What I hope to have conveyed here is that the extreme right in this country is an organic, home-grown movement. Groups and individuals that espouse white supremacist rhetoric and call for a "racial homeland" are not anomalies on the American landscape or in American history. This country was founded on exclusionist principles and national myths surrounding the Protestant mission into the wilderness. The fabled "city on a hill" and impulses that became national policy like Manifest Destiny can be used to justify rightist sentiments and actions.

The underlying causes of extreme rightist activity can be either real or perceived. What many Americans who are not sympathetic to the right tend to do, however, is dismiss it as a lunatic fringe when, in reality, less extreme rightists and even some conservatives and libertarians share some of their viewpoints in areas such as immigration, affirmative action, welfare, and religion.

Extreme rightists are our fellow Americans. The views they hold are a deep part of American history, though they have tapped the darker side of our cherished national myths. Their views are not part of some lunatic fringe, and the overwhelming majority of people who subscribe to extreme rightist ideology live and work in our communities. Most want pretty much what we all want: food, shelter, a good job, a secure future for themselves and their children, a comfortable retirement. When something threatens these desires, people's responses depend on a variety of circumstances. Extremist rhetoric has always been a part of American history, part of who we all are as Americans. Some people have found short-term solutions to long-term problems in the right. We owe it to ourselves and to the greater vision of this country, thus, to open more dialogues between each other, and genuinely address underlying problems in our communities. Extremism thrives on unspoken fears and sensationalism. The sooner we can air the former and defuse the latter, the better our chances for really derailing the white supremacist movement and, one hopes, for coming together as Americans to solve the problems of a new century.

Notes

Preface

1. The text of Amendment 2 reads: "Neither the State of Colorado, through any of its branches or departments, nor any of its agencies, political subdivisions, municipalities or school districts, shall enact, adopt, or enforce any statute, regulation, ordinance, or policy whereby homosexual, lesbian, or bisexual orientation, conduct, practices or relationships shall constitute or otherwise be the basis of or entitle any person or class of persons to have or claim minority status, quota preferences, protected status or claim of discrimination." This copy of the text comes from Judge Jeffrey Bayless, "Findings of Fact, Conclusions of Law and Judgment," *Evans v. Romer* (1992), case number 93SA17, folder 6, City and County Building, Denver, Colorado.

2. I presented the paper, titled "Lifestyles of the Rich and Shameless ... Not E/specially Queer: Colorado for Family Values, Amendment 2, and the Ku Klux Klan" at the "InQueery, InTheory, InDeed" Conference, 17–20 November in Iowa City, Iowa. I later retitled the piece "From Bibles to Buggery: The Historical Continuity of Right-Wing Ideology."

3. Sociologist Jessie Daniels points out—and correctly, I think—that what white supremacists conjure up in their publications shares the white supremacist discourse produced by elected officials, mainstream political debate, popular culture, and academic intellectuals (p. 2), *White Lies: Race, Class, Gender, and Sexuality in White Supremacist Discourse* (New York: Routledge, 1997).

4. I am indebted to Jessie Daniels for pointing this out in her *White Lies*. See especially Chap. 6.

Chapter 1

1. Kathleen M. Blee, *Inside Organized Racism: Women in the Hate Movement* (Berkeley: University of California Press, 2002), 112–113.

2. Jane Tompkins, *West of Everything: The Inner Life of Westerns* (New York: Oxford University Press, 1992), 5.

3. Ibid., 17 and Chap. 2, "Women and the Language of Men." Regarding historiography on the "frontier" as a man's world, sources are plentiful. Beginning with Frederick Jackson Turner's 1893 "The Significance of the Frontier in American History," in *The Frontier in American History,* ed. Martin Ridge (Tucson: University of Arizona Press, 1986), the role of men in the West has overshadowed that of women. See also Ray Allen Billington, *America's Frontier Heritage* (Albuquerque: University of New Mexico Press, 1966), and Walter Prescott Webb, *The Great Frontier* (Boston: Houghton and Mifflin, 1952). For ways in which western history intertwines with myth and romance, see Henry Nash Smith, *Virgin Land: The*

American West as Symbol and Myth (Cambridge, Mass.: Harvard University Press, 1950); and Robert Athearn, *The Mythic West in Twentieth-Century America* (Lawrence: University Press of Kansas, 1986). This androcentric model of western history came under critique with the rise of western women's history. See, for example, Julie Roy Jeffrey, *Frontier Women: The Trans-Mississippi West 1840–1880* (New York: Hill and Wang, 1979); Joan M. Jensen and Darlis A. Miller, "The Gentle Tamers Revisited: New Approaches to the History of Women in the American West," *Pacific Historical Review* 49 (May 1980), 173–213; Susan Armitage and Elizabeth Jameson, eds., *The Women's West* (Norman: University of Oklahoma Press, 1987), and Elizabeth Jameson and Susan Armitage, *Writing the Range: Race, Class, and Culture in the Women's West* (Norman: University of Oklahoma Press, 1997). Both are collections of essays that analyze popular perceptions of western women. See also Lillian Schlissel, *Women's Diaries of the Westward Journey* (1982; New York: Schocken Books, 1992); Lillian Schlissel, Vicki L. Ruiz, and Janice Monk, eds., *Western Women: Their Land, Their Lives* (Albuquerque: University of New Mexico Press, 1988).

4. Gene Autry, "The Cowboy Code." I found it on the web at http://courses .cs.vt.edu/~cs3604/lib/WorldCodes/ Cowboy.Code.html. This version was taken from Delta Airways *Sky* magazine, August 1998. The Code, a short, itemized list, is copyrighted by the Gene Autry Survivors' Trust, 1994.

5. The most recent example of this is a conversation I had via "snail mail" with Richard Scutari, imprisoned for his role in the murder of Jewish talk-show host Alan Berg in Denver (1984). Mr. Scutari explained to me that he has no "ill will" against people who aren't white. He just thinks nonwhites and whites should not mix. Notwithstanding the fact that he joined a group that actively created a list of people who should die for their actions against the "white race." Richard Scutari, personal correspondence with author, 15 October 2003. Mr. Scutari is serving his sentence at the maximum security facility in Florence, Colorado.

6. Abby L. Ferber, "Introduction," in *Home-Grown Hate: Gender and Organized Racism,* ed. Abby L. Ferber (New York: Routledge, 2004), 12.

7. Kathleen M. Blee, *Inside Organized Racism: Women in the Hate Movement* (Berkeley: University of California Press, 2002), 27–28.

8. Ibid., 49–50.

9. Abby L. Ferber, *White Man Falling: Race, Gender, and White Supremacy* (New York: Rowman and Littlefield, 1998).

10. Kathleen M. Blee, *Women of the Klan: Racism and Gender in the 1920s* (Berkeley: University of California Press, 1991), 1.

11. Ibid., 48–49.

12. James Coates, *Armed and Dangerous: The Rise of the Survivalist Right* (New York: Hill and Wang, 1987); and James W. Gibson, *Warrior Dreams: Violence and Manhood in Post-Vietnam America* (New York: Hill and Wang, 1994), 212–230.

13. For Aryan Nations, see James Ridgeway, *Blood in the Face: The Ku Klux Klan, Aryan Nations, Nazi Skinheads, and the Rise of a New White Culture* (1990; New York: Thunder's Mouth Press, 1995), Chap. 3, 350–352, and James Coates, *Armed and Dangerous,* Chap. 5.

14. One of the best overviews of British-Israelism and its subsequent mutation into Christian Identity among American

white supremacist groups is Michael Bar-kun, *Religion and the Racist Right: The Origins of the Christian Identity Movement* (Chapel Hill: University of North Carolina Press, 1994). For the information here, see 3–5, 17–24, 199–201.

15. See especially Michael Barkun, *Religion and the Racist Right* and James Aho, *The Politics of Righteousness: Idaho Christian Patriotism* (Seattle: University of Washington Press, 1990), Chap. 4.

16. Anti-Defamation League of B'nai B'rith (hereafter ADL), *Extremism on the Right: A Handbook* (New York: Anti-Defamation League of B'nai B'rith, 1988), 58.

17. Ridgeway, *Blood in the Face,* Chap. 4; David H. Bennett, *The Party of Fear: The American Far Right from Nativism to the Militia Movement* (1988; New York: Vintage Books, 1995), 352–355. See also Kenneth S. Stern, *A Force upon the Plain: The American Militia Movement and the Politics of Hate* (New York: Simon & Schuster, 1996), 50–53, and Morris Dees, with Jim Corcoran, *Gathering Storm: America's Militia Threat* (New York: HarperCollins, 1996), 3.

18. Ridgeway, *Blood in the Face,* 138–142 and James Corcoran, *Bitter Harvest: Gordon Kahl and the Posse Comitatus: Murder in the Heartland* (New York: Viking Penguin, 1990).

19. Stern, *A Force upon the Plain,* Chap. 4, Dees, *Gathering Storm,* Chap. 5; Neil A. Hamilton, *Militias in America: A Reference Handbook* (Santa Barbara, Calif.: ABC-Clio, 1996), 30–31.

20. Stephen E. Atkins, *Encyclopedia of Modern American Extremists and Extremist Groups* (Westport, Conn.: Greenwood Press, 2002), 71–72.

21. Stern, *A Force upon the Plain,* 54–56; Ridgeway, *Blood in the Face,* 110–111.

22. John George and Laird Wilcox. *Nazis, Communists, Klansmen, and Others on the Fringe: Political Extremism in America* (Buffalo: Prometheus Books, 1992), 23.

23. Seymour Lipset and Earl Raab, *The Politics of Unreason: Right-Wing Extremism in America, 1790–1970* (New York: Harper & Row, 1970), 3.

24. Sara Diamond, *Roads to Dominion: Right-Wing Movements and Political Power in the United States* (New York: Guilford Press, 1995), 6–7.

25. Lisa McGirr, *Suburban Warriors: The Origins of the New American Right* (Princeton, N.J.: Princeton University Press, 2001), 9–11. See also Chip Berlet's discussion with regard to terminology and not painting all conservatives with an extremist brush in "Mapping the Political Right: Gender and Race Oppression in Right-Wing Movements," in *Home-Grown Hate: Gender and Organized Racism,* ed. Abby L. Ferber (New York: Routledge, 2004), 19–21.

26. Ibid., 10.

27. A classic analysis of paranoia and American politics is Richard Hofstadter, *The Paranoid Style in American Politics and Other Essays* (New York: Knopf, 1965).

28. Bennett, *The Party of Fear,* 17. See also John Tracy Ellis, *Catholics in Colonial America* (Baltimore: Helicon Press, 1965); H. R. Trevor-Roper, *Catholics, Anglicans, and Puritans: Seventeenth Century Essays* (Chicago: University of Chicago Press, 1988); John Higham, *Strangers in the Land: Patterns of American Nativism, 1860–1925* (1955; New York: Atheneum, 1975), 6–7.

29. James Hennessey, *American Catholicism: A History of the Roman Catholic*

Community in the United States (New York: Oxford University Press, 1981), 36–37; Thomas More Brown, "The Image of the Beast: Anti-Papal Rhetoric in Colonial America," in Richard O. Curry and Thomas M. Brown, eds., *Conspiracy: Fear of Subversion in American History* (New York: Holt, Rinehart, and Winston, 1972), 7–8.

30. John Ellis, *Perspectives in American Catholicism* (Baltimore: Helicon Press, 1963), 43; Alan Heimart and Perry Miller, eds., *The Great Awakening: Documents Illustrating the Crisis and Its Consequences* (Indianapolis: Bobbs-Merrill, 1967), 323–325; Bennett, *Party of Fear,* 20.

31. Thomas McAvoy, *The Formation of the American Catholic Minority, 1820–1860* (1948; Philadelphia: Fortress Press, 1967), 41; Hennessey, *American Catholics,* 59–60, 63, 68; Bennett, *Party of Fear,* 21.

32. Bennett, *Party of Fear,* 21; see also Bernard Bailyn, ed., *Pamphlets of the American Revolution.* Vol. 1: 1775–1776 (Cambridge, Mass.: Harvard University Press, 1965), 204–210, 213, 239–245.

33. Higham, *Strangers in the Land,* 9.

34. See, for example, Richard White, *"It's Your Misfortune and None of My Own": A New History of the American West* (Norman: University of Oklahoma Press, 1991), Chap. 4, which deals with the federal government and Indian policy. Other works that deal with this topic include Francis Paul Prucha, *The Great Father: The United States Government and the American Indians* (Lincoln: University of Nebraska Press, 1984); and Robert Utley, *The Indian Frontier of the American West* (Albuquerque: University of New Mexico Press, 1984).

35. Bennett, *The Party of Fear,* 48–49; Lipset and Raab, *The Politics of Unreason,* 38–41.

36. Lipset and Raab, *The Politics of Unreason,* 53–54, 59, 60.

37. Bennett, *Party of Fear,* 111–112, 114–115, 131–133.

38. Blee, *Women in the Klan.* Blee notes that when the Klan began to charter its new women's organizations, it emphasized that the role of women was as a helpmate to Klansmen. The KKK press referred to the women's Klan often as its "auxiliary" and billed it as an appropriate means of participating in the Klan's political agenda without sacrificing "womanly dignity" (p. 31). For a more recent discussion of a woman's activity in the Klan and a skinhead group, see Andrea Barnett, "The Girl Next Door Could Be the Next Leader of the Colorado KKK," in *Westword* (Denver, Colorado), 16–24 March 1994 edition, 24–30. The woman in question, Brooke Wolff, did not join because of a boyfriend or husband, but she did have a male skinhead friend who encouraged her to join the movement during her freshman year at a Denver high school.

39. David M. Chalmers, *Hooded Americanism: The First Century of the Ku Klux Klan, 1865–1965* (Garden City, New York: Doubleday & Company, 1965), 9; William Pierce Randel, *The Ku Klux Klan: A Century of Infamy* (Philadelphia: Chilton Books, 1965), 6. Other scholars of the Reconstruction-era Klan include Allen W. Trelease, *White Terror: The Ku Klux Klan Conspiracy and Southern Reconstruction* (Westport, Conn.: Greenwood Press, 1971), and Stanley F. Horn, *Invisible Empire: The Story of the Ku Klux Klan* (New York: W. W. Norton, 1981).

40. Blee, *Women in the Klan,* 12–13; Chalmers, *Hooded Americanism,* 17–19; Wyn Craig Wade, *The Fiery Cross: The Ku Klux Klan in America* (New York: Simon and Schuster, 1987), 57–79.

41. Blee, *Women of the Klan,* 11.

42. Ibid.

43. Ibid., 13–14.

44. Ibid., 14–16.

45. Ibid., 16.

46. Nancy MacLean, *Behind the Mask of Chivalry: The Making of the Second Ku Klux Klan* (New York: Oxford University Press, 1994), 114.

47. Ibid., 117.

48. Catherine McNicol Stock, *Rural Radicals: Righteous Rage in the American Grain* (Ithaca, N.Y.: Cornell University Press, 1996), 91.

49. For example, strikes in Cripple Creek (1894 and 1904) and Ludlow (1913), both in Colorado, illustrate violence against miners attempting to unionize. In both cases, miners faced mine owners and their allies and the confrontations resulted in casualties on both sides. Ludlow was particularly notorious because two women and eleven children (associated with the miners) were killed in the strike. Regarding Cripple Creek, see Elizabeth Jameson, *All That Glitters: Class, Conflict, and Community in Cripple Creek* (Urbana: University of Illinois Press, 1998). See also White, *"It's Your Misfortune,"* 339–347, and Richard E. Lingenfelter, *The Hardrock Miners: A History of the Mining Labor Movement in the American West, 1863–1893* (Berkeley: University of California Press, 1974). On anti-Chinese violence, see Alexander Saxton, *Indispensable Enemy: Labor and the Anti-Chinese Movement in California* (Berkeley: University of California Press, 1971), and Liping Zhu, *A Chinaman's Chance: The Chinese on the Rocky Mountain Mining Frontier* (Niwot: University of Colorado Press, 1997).

50. See Billington, *America's Frontier Heritage,* 147. He states that "vigilantes sometimes degenerated into lynching mobs that took the life of many an innocent man."

51. Stock, *Rural Radicals,* 93–94; George and Wilcox, *Nazis, Communists, Klansmen, and Others on the Fringe,* 16; Richard Maxwell Brown, *The South Carolina Regulators* (Cambridge, Mass.: Belknap Press of Harvard University Press, 1963), 40–52.

52. Stock, *Rural Radicals,* 97. See also Brown, *South Carolina Regulators,* 83–95.

53. Richard Maxwell Brown, *Strain of Violence: Historical Studies of American Violence and Vigilantism* (New York: Oxford University Press, 1975), 96. Also cited in Stock, 97. See also Richard Maxwell Brown, "Western Violence: Structure, Values, Myth," *Western Historical Quarterly* 24:1 (February 1993), 5–20.

54. White, *"It's Your Misfortune,"* 332.

55. Ibid., 333. See also Roger D. McGrath, *Gunfighters, Highwaymen, and Vigilantes: Violence on the Frontier* (Berkeley: University of California Press, 1984), and Brown, *Strain of Violence.*

56. An instance in which vigilantes restored law and order had to do with the Plummer gang in Montana, which robbed and murdered with impunity. The leader of this gang, Henry Plummer, happened to be the sheriff of Bannock. The vigilante movement that sprang up to confront the problem dispatched the gang and then disbanded. See White, *"It's Your Misfortune,"* 333; Duane A. Smith, *Rocky Mountain West: Colorado, Wyoming, and Montana, 1859–1915* (Albuquerque: University of New Mexico Press, 1992), 30–31; and Thomas Dimsdale, *The Vigilantes of Montana* (1866; Norman: University of Oklahoma Press, 1953).

57. White, *"It's Your Misfortune,"* 333.

58. W. S. Harwood, "Secret Societies in America," *North American Review* 164 (May 1897), 620–623. Cited also in Mark C. Carnes, *Secret Ritual and Manhood in Victorian America* (New Haven, Conn.: Yale University Press, 1989), 1. See also Mary Ann Clawson, *Constructing Brotherhood: Class, Gender, and Fraternalism* (Princeton, N.J.: Princeton University Press, 1989).

59. Carnes, *Secret Ritual and Manhood*, 2.

60. Clawson, *Constructing Brotherhood*, 13.

61. Ibid., 15.

62. For Clawson's findings, see *Constructing Brotherhood*, 96–98.

63. Carnes, *Secret Ritual and Manhood*, 2.

64. Clawson, *Constructing Brotherhood*, 109.

65. Clawson draws the same conclusion: "In class terms, American fraternal orders seem to have been quite representative of the population they took for their own: white men of British and Northern European descent. Theirs was an egalitarianism made possible by the exclusion of women, blacks, and ethnic minorities from the relevant social universe, a universe whose boundaries fraternal institutions helped to demarcate and guard." *Constructing Brotherhood*, 110.

66. Michael Kimmel, *Manhood in America: A Cultural History* (New York: Free Press, 1996), 172–173.

67. Carnes, *Secret Ritual and Manhood*, 79. See also Dorothy Ann Lipset, *Freemasonry in Federalist Connecticut* (Princeton, N.J.: Princeton University Press, 1977), 329–338, for an analysis of women's role in crippling Freemasonry in the 1820s and 1830s.

68. Carnes, *Secret Ritual and Manhood*, 79. In *Constructing Brotherhood*, Clawson notes that temperance campaigns of the 1820s, 1830s, and 1840s exerted an enormous effect on American culture. Drinking lost respectability and declined; most affected were men. After the Civil War, white Protestant men in particular sought companionship within fraternal lodges and male rituals rather than at taverns (161–162). See also W. J. Rorabaugh, *The Alcoholic Republic: An American Tradition* (New York: Oxford University Press, 1979).

69. Margaret Lamberts Bendroth, *Fundamentalism and Gender, 1875 to the Present* (New Haven, Conn.: Yale University Press, 1993), 16–17. See also Nancy Cott, *The Bonds of Womanhood: "Women's Sphere" in New England, 1780–1835* (New Haven, Conn.: Yale University Press, 1977).

70. Peter Filene, *Him/Her/Self: Sex Roles in Modern America* (Baltimore: Johns Hopkins University Press, 1986), 69–70; Bendroth, *Fundamentalism and Gender*, 17; and Clyde Griffen, "Reconstructing Masculinity from the Evangelical Revival to the Waning of Progressivism: A Speculative Synthesis," in *Meanings for Manhood: Constructions of Masculinity in Victorian America*, ed. Mark C. Carnes and Clyde Griffen (Chicago: University of Chicago Press, 1990), 183–204. Griffen notes that by the 1850s, young men and boys "had reason to be troubled by the now-sharp contrast between gender spheres and the dominance of the gentle virtues within the home" and the proportion of males aged fifteen through nineteen who remained at home increased dramatically. Consequently, a delay in young men's careers

and marriage resulted concurrently with a loss of excitement within Evangelical Protestantism. A more anxious focus on future career and survival in an increasingly unpredictable economic focus replaced evangelicalism's emphasis on missions of reform. In a world where fathers spent longer days away from home, younger men still at home journeyed to manhood amid uncertainty (p. 190). See also Anthony Rotundo, "Body and Soul: Changing Ideals of American Middle-Class Manhood, 1770–1920," *Journal of Social History* 16 (1983), 23–35.

71. Carnes, *Secret Ritual and Manhood,* 81.

72. Ibid., 86. Carnes cites Paschal Donaldson, *The Odd-fellows' Pocket Textbook,* revised ed. (Philadelphia: Moss and Co., 1867). See also Clawson, *Constructing Brotherhood,* Chap. 6.

73. Carnes, *Secret Ritual and Manhood,* 85.

74. Ibid., 86.

75. Ibid. Carnes notes that Sarah J. Fairman was Grand Matron of the Order of the Eastern Star in Vermont. She reported that, when she searched for an explanation of the decree, she could find no answer. See also Clawson, *Constructing Brotherhood,* 193–199.

76. Ibid., 83.

77. Ibid., 86.

78. Ibid. Clawson proposes that the women's auxiliaries provided another networking sphere for women beyond church and home.

79. Blee, *Women of the Klan,* 13.

80. Ibid., 13–14. See also Chalmers, *Hooded Americanism,* 21.

81. Ibid.; Chalmers, *Hooded Americanism,* 21.

82. Blee, *Women of the Klan,* 127–128.

83. Lipset and Raab note that extremism arises from some kind of discontent: "The nature of anxiety, as it touches on the development of political movements in this country, has typically been related to a sense of power and status deprivation." People who participate in right-wing movements or who believe in rightist ideology feel "deprived" in the sense that their once-secure position of power — social, economic, political — is somehow threatened by changes in any of those three categories (*The Politics of Unreason,* 23).

84. For a brief historiographical analysis, see Robert Goldberg's preface in *Hooded Empire: The Ku Klux Klan in Colorado* (Urbana: University of Illinois Press, 1981), vii–xv. John Mecklin, one of the earliest documenters of the 1920s Klan, acknowledges that the Klan was not confined merely to the South, but that it was primarily a small-town or rural movement, the values of which were transported to urban areas by recent migrants. *The Ku Klux Klan: A Study of the American Mind* (New York: Harcourt, Brace and Company, 1924), 104–109. See also Chalmers, *Hooded Americanism,* 114; Richard Hofstadter, *The Age of Reform: From Bryan to F.D.R* (New York, 1955), 294; Lipset and Raab, *The Politics of Unreason.*

Charles Alexander, in keeping with the Klan as a small-town phenomenon, discovered that the organization's growth in Texas, Oklahoma, Louisiana, and Arkansas was in response to violations of the law and moral codes. *The Ku Klux Klan in the Southwest* (Lexington: University of Kentucky Press 1966). Kenneth T. Jackson, on the other hand, researched the Klan in cities and argued that the group was extremely successful in urban recruiting and also in influencing state and national policymaking. The crux of his argument is that the Klan grew in cities because of the clash between diverse groups of racial, ethnic, and religious peoples congregating in urban areas. The Klan was a white Protestant reaction— primarily among those who lived in the areas between urban ghettos and affluent white neighborhoods—to nonwhites and non-Protestants residing in the area. *The Ku Klux Klan in the City, 1915–1930* (New York: Knopf, 1967), 245.

85. See Alexander, *The Ku Klux Klan in the Southwest*, 18–19, and Goldberg, *Hooded Empire*. Goldberg's study offers an opportunity to examine the membership of the Klan across rural and urban areas of Colorado; he discovered that membership varied across class lines according to local issues in the communities he studied. See also MacLean, *Behind the Mask of Chivalry*, Chap. 3.

86. Chalmers, *Hooded Americanism*, 110–111; MacLean, *Behind the Mask of Chivalry*, 29–35; Higham, *Strangers in the Land*, Chap. 9.

87. See David Kennedy, *Over Here: The First World War and American Society* (New York: Oxford University Press, 1980); William Leuchtenburg, *The Perils of Prosperity, 1914–32* (Chicago: University of Chicago Press, 1958); John Braeman, Robert H. Bermner, and David Brody, eds., *Change and Continuity in Twentieth-Century America: The 1920s* (Columbus: Ohio State University Press, 1968); and Ellis W. Hawley, *The Great War and the Search for a Modern Order: A History of the American People and Their Institutions, 1917–1933* (New York: St. Martin's Press, 1979).

88. Arnold Rice, *The Ku Klux Klan in American Politics* (Washington, D.C.: Public Affairs Press, 1962), 15–16.

89. Leonard J. Moore, "Historical Interpretations of the 1920s Klan: The Traditional View and Recent Revisions," in *The Invisible Empire in the West: Toward a New Historical Appraisal of the Ku Klux Klan of the 1920s*, ed. Shawn Lay (Urbana: University of Illinois Press, 1992), 22. For urban Klan activities, see Jackson, *The Ku Klux Klan in the City*.

90. Jackson, *The Ku Klux Klan in the City*, 24–25.

91. Rice, *The Ku Klux Klan in American Politics*, 2. Rice uses Simmons' testimony during Congressional hearings that took place in 1921 in his attempt to reconstruct his past.

92. Rory McVeigh, "Structural Incentives for Conservative Mobilization: Power Devaluation and the Rise of the Ku Klux Klan 1915–1925," *Social Forces*, vol. 77 (1999), 1463–1464.

93. Rice, *The Ku Klux Klan in American Politics*, 3–5. See also Bennett, *The Party of Fear*, 208–209. Bennett states that the Stone Mountain meeting took place in October but Arnold S. Rice claims that it occurred in November, on Thanksgiving eve. I am more inclined to lean toward Rice's date, as it is cited in Congressional hearings regarding the Klan's activities. See *The Ku Klux Klan*, 67th Congress, 1st Session (Washington, D.C.: Government Printing Office, 1921). The hearings were held before the House Committee on Rules, 11–17 October, 1921. See also Rice, *The Ku Klux Klan in American Politics*, 1.

94. McVeigh, "Structural Incentives for Conservative Mobilization," 1465.

95. Bennett, *The Party of Fear*, 208–209.

96. Ibid., 209.

97. Ibid., 210.

98. Ibid., 211.

99. Ibid., 1466–1467, 1473.

100. Dr. H. W. [Hiram Wesley] Evans, "Where Do We Go From Here," in *Papers Read at the Meeting of Grand Dragons: Knights of the Ku Klux Klan At their First Annual Meeting held at Asheville, North Carolina, July 1923,* 17. On file at the Denver Public Library, Western History Archives (hereafter DPL).

101. Excerpt from "A Klansman's Obligation as Patriot to His God, His Country, His Home, and His Fellowmen," in *Papers Read at the Meeting of Grand Dragons,* Asheville, North Carolina, July 1923. On file at DPL. This particular paper was attributed to "the Grand Dragon, Realm of Colorado," probably John Galen Locke.

102. Goldberg, *Hooded Empire,* 7.

103. Ibid., 7–8.

104. I found a concise biography of Stephenson online at Wikipedia at http://en.wikipedia.org/wiki/ D._C._Stephenson; accessed June 2005.

105. http://en.wikipedia.org/ wiki/ D._C._Stephenson; accessed June 2005.

106. Ridgeway, *Blood in the Face,* 62; Lipset and Raab, *The Politics of Unreason,* 162–164; Leo P. Ribuffo, *The Old Christian Right: The Protestant Far Right from the Great Depression to the Cold War* (Philadelphia: Temple University Press, 1983), 25–29, 32–34. Ribuffo's second chapter is devoted solely to William Dudley Pelley.

107. Ridgeway, *Blood in the Face,* 62. For a description of Pelley's revelation, see Ribuffo, *The Old Christian Right,* 48–49.

108. For Pelley's organizational attempts and his anti-Semitism and racism, see Ribuffo, *The Old Christian Right,* 52–70. For a description of the Silver Legion uniforms and the hierarchy, see 63–64.

109. Ridgeway, *Blood in the Face,* 63–64; Ribuffo, *The Old Christian Right,* 76–78. Pelley's claims about his membership were probably inflated. His claims have yet to be verified.

110. Ridgeway, *Blood in the Face,* 64; Ribuffo, *The Old Christian Right,* 80–81; 86–87. Ribuffo's Chap. 3 is a short biography of Winrod's life. Regarding Winrod and the *Protocols of the Learned Elders of Zion,* see Ribuffo, *The Old Christian Right,* 109–116. See also Lipset and Raab, *The Politics of Unreason,* 160–162.

111. Ridgeway, *Blood in the Face,* 64–65; Ribuffo, *The Old Christian Right,* 126–127.

112. Ridgeway, *Blood in the Face,* 65–66; Ribuffo, *The Old Christian Right,* 128–129, 135–139. Ribuffo's Chap. 4 deals exclusively with Smith. See also Isabel B. Price, "Gerald L. K. Smith and Anti-Semitism" (M.A. thesis, University of New Mexico, 1965), 3–4, 9. See also "Gerald Lyman Kenneth Smith," *Current Biography* (New York: H. W. Wilson Co., 1944) and "Huey Long's Nation-Wide Share Our Wealth Organization," *Literary Digest* 119:12 (16 March 1935), 12–13. The latter discusses Smith's work with Long and his work on the Share Our Wealth program.

113. Ridgeway, *Blood in the Face,* 67; Ribuffo, *The Old Christian Right,* 140–148; Price, "Gerald L. K. Smith and Anti-Semitism," 42–43, 52–55, 57–60. See also William Bradford Huie, "Gerald Smith's Bid for Power," *American Mercury* 55 (August 1942), 147–157.

114. Ridgeway, *Blood in the Face,* 68; Ribuffo, *The Old Christian Right,*

148–157; Price, "Gerald L. K. Smith and Anti-Semitism," 82–89, 91.

115. Ridgeway, *Blood in the Face*, 69–70; Ribuffo, *The Old Christian Right*, 161–66; Price, "Gerald L. K. Smith and Anti-Semitism," 91, 98–108. Smith actually petitioned against World War II. Regarding this petition, see *Congressional Record*, vol. 86, pt. 10, 76th Congress, 3rd Session, 19 August 1940 (Washington, D.C.: Government Printing Office, 1941). Regarding Smith's descent into virulent anti-Semitism after World War II, see Price, Chap. 4. During these years, Smith formed the "America First Party" and advocated Christian Identity. By 1953, Smith was advocating the abolition of the United Nations, an ideological stance that remains a major ideological plank in the American extremist right now. See Price, 129–140.

116. James W. Gibson, "Is the Apocalypse Coming? Paramilitary Culture after the Cold War," in Charles B. Strozier and Michael Flynn, *The Year 2000: Essays on the End* (New York: New York University Press, 1997), 180–81; Gibson, *Warrior Dreams*.

Chapter 2

1. Richard White, "The Current Weirdness in the West," *Western Historical Quarterly*, 28:1 (spring 1997), 5.

2. Richard White, *"It's Your Misfortune and None of My Own": A History of the American West* (Norman: University of Oklahoma Press, 1991), 61–85, 137–155, 395–430; Patricia Nelson Limerick, *The Legacy of Conquest: The Unbroken Past of the American West* (New York: W. W. Norton, 1987), 78–97, 293–320; see also Gerald Nash, *The American West in the Twentieth Century: A Short History of an*

Urban Oasis (Englewood Cliffs, N.J.: Prentice-Hall, 1973).

3. Richard White, "The Current Weirdness in the West," 8, 9.

4. Jeffrey Roche, "Cowboy Conservatives," in *The Conservative Sixties*, ed. Jeffrey Roche and David Farber (New York: Peter Lang Publishing, 2003), 79. For a more detailed analysis of the rise of conservative political culture in the American West, see Roche's *Cowboy Conservatism: The Emergence of Western Political Culture, 1933–1984* (New York: Peter Lang Publishing, forthcoming).

5. Patricia Nelson Limerick, "Believing in the American West," in *Something in the Soil: Legacies and Reckonings in the New West* (New York: W. W. Norton, 2000), 314.

6. Ibid.

7. Ibid., 314–315.

8. Miriam Horn, "How the West was Really Won," *U.S. News and World Report* 108:20 (21 May 1990), 56.

9. See Patricia Nelson Limerick, "The Adventures of the Frontier in the Twentieth Century," in *Something in the Soil*, 74–92.

10. David M. Wrobel, *The End of American Exceptionalism: Frontier Anxiety from the Old West to the New Deal* (Lawrence: University Press of Kansas, 1993), 145.

11. Richard G. Butler, ed., "The Sword on the Land," *Calling Our Nation*, no. 26 (1981), 1; Roy N. Eddy, "Evacuation Part I," *Calling Our Nation*, no. 26 (1981), n.p. Both located in folder 1, Wilcox Collection, Spencer Research Library, University of Kansas (hereafter Wilcox Collection), stamped 1981 by the collections manager.

12. "George Lincoln Rockwell: A Candid Conversation with the Fanatical Führer of the American Nazi Party," *Play-*

boy (n.d.), 80. This article is on file in the Keith Stimely Collection, box 30, folder 4, Knight Library, University of Oregon, Eugene, Oregon (hereafter KS). Rockwell was assassinated in 1968, and the American Nazi Party folded after Rockwell's death. See also Frederick J. Simonelli, *American Fuehrer: George Lincoln Rockwell and the American Nazi Party* (Urbana: University of Illinois Press, 1999). Anonymous, *The Talon* 3:26 (December 1978), 3–4, KS, box 35, no. 2. The Euro-American Alliance was still in existence in 1992; *Arizona Republic,* "Secret War: 'Patriots' Have Loose Ties to Rightists Nationwide," 21 December 1986.

13. John C. Calhoun, "What It Means to be a Klansman," in *Inter-Klan Newsletter and Survival Alert* (hereafter *IKNSA*), ca. 1983, 2. Aryan Nations, Folder 1, Wilcox Collection. Although this newsletter bills itself as "Klan" (Inter-Klan), it was ostensibly billed as a newsletter for white men who were concerned with the future of the white race: "It is the policy of this publication to carry the news and views of all the Klans. We are not concerned in the least with the particular name or affiliation of an individual group" (Editor, *INKSA,* no. 4, March 1984). I suspect that it appears in the Aryan Nations collection because, during the mid-1980s, Louis R. Beam, leader of the Texas Knights of the Ku Klux Klan, had become deeply involved at the Hayden Lake, Idaho, compound as an organizer and computer networker. I do not believe that the Calhoun who authored this piece is related to the secessionist South Carolinian Calhoun of the nineteenth century, but I suspect that the modern Calhoun knew of him.

14. *INKSA* states, "Despair not, true Patriot!… WE shall prevail. We have the promise of a just God that THEIR system shall not hold sway over this earth. Period," (1984), 4, Aryan Nations, folder 2, Wilcox Collection. Louis Beam and John C. Calhoun claim that "the eternal war, which can most properly be called a Conflict of the Ages, has taken a final turn. The age-long conflict approaches the last battle—Ragnarok, Armageddon—is about to be fought, and there will be only one survivor of this struggle," *INKSA,* no. 5 (1984), Aryan Nations, p. 3, folder 2, Wilcox Collection.

15. The original meaning of "millennium" refers to the passage in the Book of Revelation (20:4–6) that envisions a thousand years of peace after the upheaval of Christ's Second Coming. After this thousand-year reign, all earthly existence is to give way before the Last Judgment. See Michael Barkun, *Disaster and the Millennium* (New Haven, Conn.: Yale University Press, 1974), 26–27.

16. For a description of how the idea of the year 2000 played out in America, See Charles B. Strozier, "Introduction," in *The Year 2000: Essays on the End,* ed. Charles B. Strozier and Michael Flynn (New York: New York University Press, 1997), 1.

17. See, for example, Bryan R. Wilson, *Magic and the Millennium: A Sociological Study of Religious Movements of Protest among Tribal and Third-World Peoples* (London: Heineman Educational, 1973). For a discussion about more recent millenarian movements, see Eric J. Hobsbawm's classic *Primitive Rebels: Studies in Archaic Forms of Social Movement in the 19th and 20th Centuries* (Manchester: University of Manchester Press, 1959). See also Norman Cohn, "How Time Acquired a Consummation," in *Apocalypse Theory and the Ends of the World,* ed. Malcolm Bull (Cambridge, Mass.: Blackwell, 1995),

21; and Mark Fenster, *Conspiracy Theories: Secrecy and Power in American Culture* (Minneapolis: University of Minnesota Press, 1999), Chap. 6.

18. Cohn has perhaps written the definitive work on European millenarianism during the Middle Ages. See *The Pursuit of the Millennium: Revolutionary Millenarians and Mystical Anarchists of the Middle Ages* (1957; New York: Oxford University Press, 1970).

19. Barkun, *Disaster and the Millennium*, 27–28. For Barkun's discussion about France, see 28–30. See also Ernest Lee Tuveson, *Redeemer Nation: The Idea of America's Millennial Role* (Chicago: University of Chicago Press, 1968).

20. Paul Boyer, *When Time Shall Be No More: Prophecy Belief in Modern American Culture* (Cambridge, Mass.: Belknap Press of Harvard University Press, 1992), 68.

21. Ruth H. Bloch, *Visionary Republic: Millennial Themes in American Thought, 1756–1800* (Cambridge: Cambridge University Press, 1985), 11.

22. Ibid., 69.

23. Bloch, *Visionary Republic*, 69.

24. Boyer, *When Time Shall Be No More*, 70–71. See also Alan Heimert, *Religion and the American Mind from the Great Awakening to the Revolution* (Cambridge, Mass.: Harvard University Press, 1966).

25. Boyer, *When Time Shall Be No More*, 72.

26. Bloch, *Visionary Republic*, 47.

27. Ibid., 54, 82.

28. Jeffrey Kaplan, *Radical Religion in America: Millenarian Movements from the Far Right to the Children of Noah* (Syracuse, N.Y.: Syracuse University Press, 1997), xiv–xv. For a discussion of nineteenth- and early twentieth-century premillennialism, see Timothy P. Weber, *Living in the Shadow of the Second Coming: American Premillennialism, 1875–1925* (Oxford: Oxford University Press, 1979). See also Richard T. Hughes, *Myths America Lives By* (Urbana: University of Illinois Press, 2003), Chap. 4.

29. "Aryan Nationalist Army Code of Conduct," *Aryan Nations Newsletter*, no. 18 (1980), Aryan Nations, p. 6, folder 1, Wilcox Collection.

30. Reginald Horsman, *Race and Manifest Destiny: The Origins of American Racial Anglo-Saxonism* (Cambridge, Mass.: Harvard University Press, 1981), 189.

31. Gary Grestle, "Liberty, Coercion, and the Making of Americans," *Journal of American History* 84:2 (September 1997), 536–559.

32. White, *"It's Your Misfortune and None of My Own"*, 73, 74.

33. John O'Sullivan, "The Great Nation of Futurity," *United States Democratic Review* 6:23 (November 1839), 426–430. The pages on which these quotations can be found are, respectively, 426, 427, and 430. O'Sullivan coined the phrase in 1845 in an article called "Annexation," which appeared in *United States Magazine and Democratic Review*, vol. 17 (July 1845), 5–10.

34. Frederick Merk, *Manifest Destiny and Mission in American History* (1963; Cambridge, Mass.: Harvard University Press, 1995), 33.

35. Ibid., 74.

36. James Baldwin, "On Being 'White' ... and Other Lies," in *Black on White: Black Writers on What It Means to Be White*, ed. David R. Roediger (New York: Schocken Books, 1998), 177–180.

37. Horsman, *Race and Manifest Destiny*, 9.

38. Ibid.

39. Ibid., 9–10.

40. Ibid., 10–15. See also Richard T. Vann, "The Free Anglo-Saxons: A Historical Myth," *Journal of the History of Ideas,* 19 (April 1958), 265–266.

41. Horsman, *Race and Manifest Destiny,* 14.

42. Ibid., 15.

43. Ibid. Regarding the impact of Whig views of Anglo-Saxons on eighteenth-century Americans, see H. Trevor Colbourn, *The Lamp of Experience: Whig History and the Intellectual Origins of the American Revolution* (Chapel Hill: University of North Carolina Press, 1965); Gordon S. Wood, *The Creation of the American Republic, 1776–1787* (Chapel Hill, University of North Carolina Press, 1969). See also Bernard Bailyn, *The Ideological Origins of the American Revolution* (Cambridge, Mass.: Belknap Press of Harvard University Press, 1967).

44. Horsman, *Race and Manifest Destiny,* 24. See also T. H. Breen, "Ideology and Nationalism on the Eve of the American Revolution: Revisions *Once More* in Need of Revising," *Journal of American History* 84:1 (June 1997), 13–39; William P. Hoar, "Manifest Destiny: Many 19th-Century Americans Believed Their Young Nation Was Destined to Extend the Benefits of Freedom and Opportunity across the Continent—From Sea to Shining Sea," *New American,* vol. 19 (28 July 2003; originally in *American Opinion,* June 1981), 33+.

45. Horseman, *Race and Manifest Destiny,* 24.

46. Edward N. Saveth, ed., *Understanding the American Past: American History and Its Interpretations* (New York: Little, Brown, 1958), 12–13. For a more detailed explanation of the Teutonic Hypothesis,

see Edward N. Saveth, *American Historians and European Immigrants, 1875–1925* (New York: Columbia University Press, 1948), Chap. 1.

47. Saveth, *Understanding the American Past,* 12. Herbert Baxter Adams' writings include "The Germanic Origin of New England Towns," a paper presented before the Harvard Historical Society on May 9, 1881; "Saxon Tithing Men of America," also presented at the American Antiquarian Society on 21 October, 1881. Adams' seminars at Johns Hopkins University trained many of the next generation of American historians, including Frederick Jackson Turner.

48. Saveth, ed., *Understanding the American Past,* 14.

49. Saveth, *American Historians and European Immigrants,* 90.

50. Ibid., 92.

51. Ibid., 97.

52. For a superb analysis of these discussions about Manifest Destiny among American politicians, policymakers, and the media, see Merk, *Manifest Destiny and Mission in American History.* See also Elliott West, "Reconstructing Race," *Western Historical Quarterly* 34:1 (spring 2003), 9.

53. Kaplan, *Radical Religion in America,* 3.

54. See Gerald L. K. Smith, *Besieged Patriot,* ed. Elma M. Smith and Charles F. Robinson (Eureka Springs, Ark.: Elma M. Smith Foundation, 1978), 238–239.

55. Kaplan, *Radical Religion in America,* 4.

56. Ibid.

57. Emerson Hough, *The Passing of the Frontier: A Chronicle of the Old West* (New Haven, Conn.: Yale University Press, 1918), 1.

58. Frederick Jackson Turner, "The Significance of the Frontier in American History," in *History, Frontier, and Section,* ed. and with introduction by Martin Ridge (Albuquerque: University of New Mexico Press, 1993), 59–92.

59. Hough, *The Passing of the Frontier,* 1.

60. Horsman, *Race and Manifest Destiny,* 99–100. Merk also examines the influence of the rhetoric and ideology of Manifest Destiny in the popular and political press. He finds that it was prevalent after 1844. See Merk, *Manifest Destiny and Mission in American History,* 41–60.

61. Horsman, *Race and Manifest Destiny,* 100. Richard Drinnon, in *Facing West: The Metaphysics of Indian-Hating and Empire Building* (1980; Norman: University of Oklahoma Press, 1997), charts the westward impetus of white American expansion since the Puritan settlements and its repercussions in American institutions.

62. Horsman, *Race and Manifest Destiny,* 100–101.

63. Horsman addresses the issue of opposition to Manifest Destiny. See *Race and Manifest Destiny,* 255–60.

64. Richard Slotkin, *Gunfighter Nation: The Myth of the Frontier in Twentieth-Century America* (New York: Atheneum Books, 1992), 10.

65. Ibid. See also Limerick, *Legacy of Conquest,* Chaps. 1, 8, and 9; and Jay Gitlin, "On the Boundaries of Empire: Connecting the West to Its Imperial Past," in *Under an Open Sky: Rethinking America's Western Past,* ed. William Cronon, George Miles, and Jay Gitlin (New York: W. W. Norton & Company, 1992), 71–89.

66. Slotkin, *Gunfighter Nation,* 10.

67. Ibid., 16–17. Slotkin traces the evolution of the frontier myth since the

arrival of Anglo settlers in New England. See his *Regeneration through Violence: The Mythology of the American Frontier, 1600–1860* (1973; New York: Harper Perennial, 1996) and *Fatal Environment: The Myth of the Frontier in the Age of Industrialization 1800–1890* (1985; New York: HarperPerennial, 1994). For his discussion of the rapid social, cultural, and economic changes that occurred between 1815 and 1870, see especially Chaps. 6 and 7.

68. Slotkin, *Fatal Environment,* 140.

69. Ibid., 139.

70. Henry Nash Smith, *Virgin Land: The American West as Symbol and Myth* (Cambridge, Mass.: Harvard University Press), 100–105.

71. Ibid., 187.

72. Gail Bederman, *Manliness and Civilization: A Cultural History of Gender and Race in the United States, 1880–1917* (Chicago: University of Chicago Press, 1995), 171.

73. Ibid., 178. See also Theodore Roosevelt, *The Winning of the West,* 4 vols. (New York: G. P. Putnam's Sons, 1889–1896), 1:114–115; and Slotkin, *Gunfighter Nation,* 42–51.

74. Bederman, *Manliness and Civilization,* 187–188.

75. Ibid., 191.

76. Michael Kimmel, *Manhood in America: A Cultural History* (New York: Free Press, 1996), 89–91.

77. Frederick Jackson Turner, "The Significance of the Frontier in American History," in *The American Frontier: Opposing Viewpoints,* ed. Mary Ellen Jones, American History Series (San Diego: Greenhaven Press, 1984), 25.

78. See, for example, Smith, *Virgin Land;* William W. Savage, Jr., *The Cowboy Hero: His Image in American History and Culture* (Norman: University of

Oklahoma Press, 1979); Slotkin's trilogy, *Regeneration through Violence, The Fatal Environment*, and *Gunfighter Nation*; William H. Goetzmann and William N. Goetzmann, *The West of the Imagination* (New York: W. W. Norton, 1986); Robert Athearn, *The Mythic West in Twentieth-Century America* (Lawrence: University Press of Kansas, 1986); Gerald D. Nash, *Creating the West: Historical Interpretations, 1890–1990* (Albuquerque: University of New Mexico Press, 1991), Chap. 5; White, *"It's Your Misfortune and None of My Own,"* Chap. 21; Donald Worster, "Beyond the Agrarian Myth," in *Trails: Toward a New Western History*, ed. Patricia Nelson Limerick, Clyde Milner II, and Charles E. Rankin (Lawrence: University Press of Kansas, 1991), 3–26; Ann Fabian, "History for the Masses: Commercializing the Western Past," in *Under an Open Sky*, ed. Cronon, Miles, and Gitlin, 223–238; Jane Tompkins, *West of Everything: The Inner Life of Westerns* (Oxford: Oxford University Press, 1992); William W. Savage, Jr., *Cowboy Life: Reconstructing an American Myth* (1975; Niwot: University Press of Colorado, 1993); Michael L. Johnson, *New Westers: The West in Contemporary American Culture* (Lawrence: University Press of Kansas, 1996); and Richard Aquila, ed., *Wanted Dead or Alive: The American West in Popular Culture* (Urbana: University of Illinois Press, 1996).

Chapter 3

1. Butler quoted in Kim Murphy, "Last Stand of an Aging Aryan," *Los Angeles Times*, 10 January 1999, A1.

2. Tom Engelhardt, *The End of Victory Culture: Cold War America and the Disillusioning of a Generation* (New York: Basic Books, 1995), 254. Numerous sources about the effects of the Vietnam War on American culture and politics exist. See, for example, David Farber, *The End of Great Dreams: America in the 1960s* (New York: Hill and Wang, 1994); Andrew J. Rotter, ed., *Light at the End of the Tunnel: A Vietnam War Anthology* (New York: St. Martin's Press, 1991); William H. Chafe, *The Unfinished Journey: America since World War II* (New York: Oxford University Press, 1986); Marilyn Young, *The Vietnam Wars, 1945–1990* (New York: HarperCollins 1991); John Hellman, *American Myth and the Legacy of Vietnam* (New York: Columbia University Press, 1986); and John Carlos Rowe and Rick Berg, eds., *The Vietnam War and American Culture* (New York: Columbia University Press, 1991).

3. James William Gibson, *Warrior Dreams: Violence and Manhood in Post-Vietnam America* (New York: Hill and Wang, 1994), 1. Gibson states elsewhere that "defeat also created a cultural crisis, in that much of American national identity, and masculine identity in particular, had been shaped by the country's long history of victory in warfare. Men's identity was further challenged by the feminist movement, which grew phenomenally in the 1970s and 1980s." See also Gibson, "Is the Apocalypse Coming? Paramilitary Culture after the Cold War," in *The Year 2000: Essays on the End*, ed. Charles B. Strozier and Michael Flynn (New York: New York University Press, 1997), 180.

4. Arnold R. Isaacs, *Vietnam Shadows: the War, Its Ghosts, and Its Legacy* (Baltimore: Johns Hopkins University Press, 1997), 3.

5. Ibid., 6.

6. Ibid., 9–11; Charles Neu, "The Vietnam War and the Transformation

of America," in *After Vietnam: Legacies of a Lost War,* ed. Charles Neu (Baltimore: Johns Hopkins University Press, 2000), 3.

7. Isaacs, *Vietnam Shadows,* 14, 28.

8. Ibid., 23–24.

9. Ibid., 39.

10. Loren Baritz, "Military Mismanagement," in *Light at the End of the Tunnel: A Vietnam War Anthology,* ed. Andrew J. Rotter (New York: St. Martin's Press, 1991), 330–332, 336–337.

11. Isaacs, *Vietnam Shadows,* 42, 56.

12. Ibid., 48; Brian Balogh, "From Metaphor to Quagmire: The Domestic Legacy of the Vietnam War," in *After Vietnam,* ed. Neu, 34.

13. Balogh, "From Metaphor to Quagmire," 47–48.

14. Gibson, "Is the Apocalypse Coming?" 180.

15. Ibid.

16. Randy Shilts, *Conduct Unbecoming: Lesbians and Gays in the U.S. Military, Vietnam to the Persian Gulf* (New York: St. Martin's Press, 1993), 33, 74–75, 417.

17. Gibson, "Is the Apocalypse Coming?" 181.

18. Ibid.

19. Philip Lamy, *Millennium Rage: Survivalists, White Supremacists, and the Doomsday Prophecy* (New York: Plenum Press, 1996), 70.

20. Ibid., 71–72, 82.

21. "Ear to the Ground," *Outside* (August 1997), 28.

22. From "Idaho Facts: Information and Statistics about Idaho's People and Economy" website at http://imnh.isu.edu/digitalatlas/geog/demogrphc/idfacts.pdf (accessed 26 June 2005).

23. This information is available

through the Idaho State government website at http://gov.idaho.gov/fyi/kidbook/Demographics.pdf (accessed 27 June 2005).

24. See the U.S. Census, available at http://factfinder/census.gov (accessed 27 June 2005). See also http://www.northwest-national.com/mt.htm, a real estate site that provides some accurate numbers for population in the state (accessed 27 June 2005).

25. See http://nris.state.mt.us, one of the state's official websites. The maps, available as jpg and pdf formats, provide the topographic break-down of the state (accessed 28 June 2005).

26. See census data at http://quickfacts.census.gov/qfd/states/53000.html (accessed 26 June 2005).

27. For information on topography, see the U.S. Forest Service website at http://www.fsfed.us/pnw/fia/maps/pages/BaileysEcoRegionBoundariesWashington.shtml (accessed 26 June 2005).

28. In 1983, the compound included Butler's house, a school for the education of children, and a print shop. "Unknown Subjects; Members of Aryan Nation [*sic*], Coeur d'Alene, Idaho," report filed 20 October 1983, field office file no. BT 177A-21, U.S. Department of Justice, Federal Bureau of Investigation, Freedom of Information-Privacy Acts (hereafter FOIPA) no. 435860/190–hg-1258584.

29. See the Northwest Area Foundation's Indicator website. For Idaho's population in 1970, the link is http://www.indicators.nwaf.org/ShowOneRegion.asp?IndicatorID=1&FIPS=16000 (accessed 26 June 2005).

30. Anti-Defamation League of B'nai B'rith (hereafter ADL), biography of Richard Butler. Available on the ADL website at

http://www.adl.org/learn/Ext_US/butler
.asp?xpicked=2&item=2, hereafter ADL
Richard Butler web biography (accessed
5 December 2003).

31. "Racists Seek to Form White Home-
land in Northwest," *Albany Democrat-
Herald* (Oregon), 12 June 1986, 8; "Aryans
Plan NW Homeland," *Albany Democrat-
Herald*, 14 July 1986, 10.

32. See the Network's website at http://
nnlm.gov/pnr/characteristics/index.html
(accessed 27 June 2005).

33. Richard Butler quoted in *The
Oregonian*'s Sunday magazine, *Northwest
Magazine* (hereafter *Northwest Maga-
zine*), 18 November 1984, 8.

34. James Aho, *The Politics of Righteousness: Idaho Christian Patriotism* (Seattle:
University of Washington Press, 1990),
56–57.

35. Aho, *Politics of Righteousness*, 57.
The name of the church, "Church of Jesus
Christ, Christian," comes from Butler's
pointed attempt to disavow any connection Christ has with Judaism. See the Portland *Oregonian*, "Meeting Draws Leaders
of Neo-Nazi Groups," 12 July 1986, B7.

36. Richard Mauer, "Aryan Nations,"
Idaho Statesman, 14–17 September 1980;
"The New Nazis: Rifles, Religion, and
Racism," *Spokesman-Review*, 14 April
1985, A1, A10, and 21 April 1985, A1, A8,
A14; Joshua Hammer, "Trouble," *People*,
29 August 1983, 44–48; Elly Everitt, "A
Light for the White Race," *Twin Falls
News-Times*, 3 January 1983, A9–A10;
John Harris, "Hitler's Legacy," *Seattle
Post-Intelligencer*, 5 January 1985, F1, F5.

37. Aho, *Politics of Righteousness*, 56–57.

38. Butler, "The Aryan Warrior,"
http://www.twelvearyannations.com/
aryanwarrior.html.

39. Henry Nash Smith, *Virgin Land:

The American West as Symbol and Myth
(Cambridge, Mass.: Harvard University
Press, 1950), 123.

40. Ibid.

41. ADL, Richard Butler web biography.

42. Ibid.

43. ADL, *Extremism on the Right: A
Handbook*, Anti-Defamation League
of B'nai B'rith (New York: ADL, 1988),
70–71.

44. Ibid., 17.

45. "Racists Seek to Form White Homeland," *Albany Democrat-Herald*. They
plan to do so by "outbreeding" their
foes.

46. Fafnir, "The Birth of a Nation,"
Inter-Klan Newsletter and Survival Alert,
p. 12, n.d., Keith Stimely Collection, box
31, folder 6, Knight Library, University
of Oregon, Eugene, Oregon (hereafter
KS). I put the date of this particular
issue as sometime around 1980 because
of Fafnir's writings in other issues about
this time. The ADL notes that Fafnir is
an alias for Robert E. Miles, who was a
longtime advocate of Christian Identity.
He started his racist career in the Ku Klux
Klan during the 1950s. He founded a
church ("Mountain Church") in Cohoc-
tah, Michigan, where he served as its
pastor. Miles advocated a variation of
Identity that claimed that God's elder son
was Satan, who rebelled against the father
and subsequently has been fighting Jesus
since the dawn of time. See ADL, *Extremism on the Right*, 130–132. Miles died in
the early 1990s.

47. Mike Sager, "A Journey to the Heart
of Whiteness," *Gentleman's Quarterly*,
66:3 (March 1996), 249. I find it intrigu-
ing that this article appeared in a men's
magazine that caters mostly to fashion
and lifestyle concerns.

48. Ibid.

49. Ibid., 280.

50. "The Aryan Warriors [*sic*] Stand," in "Calling Our Nation" insert, no. 10, 1979, Aryan Nations, folder 1, Wilcox Collection.

51. Ibid.

52. Ibid.

53. Ibid.

54. Ibid.

55. Ibid.

56. John C. Calhoun, "What It Means To Be A Klansman," *Inter-Klan Newsletter and Survival Alert*, 1983, Aryan Nations, folder 1, Wilcox Collection. Some of the newsletters did not include issue numbers.

57. Cindy Cutler [resident of the Aryan Nations compound], "News Media Interview," reprinted in "Calling Our Nation" no. 27, ca. 1980, Aryan Nations, folder 1, Wilcox Collection.

58. Pastor R. G. Butler, reporter interview, 1980, in "Calling Our Nation," no. 27, Aryan Nations, folder 1, Wilcox Collection.

59. Bryan Denson, *The Oregonian* (Portland), 27 January 1999; for another report about the suit, see Kevin Peraino, "Aryan Nations in the Dock," *Newsweek* 136:10 (4 September 2000), 26.

60. Ibid. The case number is CV-99–441, filed in the District Court of the First Judicial District, Idaho, in Kootenai County. The Acrobat files can be found at the Southern Poverty Law Center at http://www.splcenter.org/legal/docket/files.jsp?cdrID=30&sortID=0 (accessed 5 December 2003).

61. ADL, "Bertollini and Story: 11th Hour Remnant Messenger," *Extremism in America*. Available for viewing at http://www.adl.org/learn/Ext_US/

bertollini.asp?xpicked=2&item=1. For more information on the business dealings and background of Bertollini and Story, see Kim Murphy, "Hate's Affluent New Godfathers," *Los Angeles Times*, 10 January 1999, A14.

62. Nicholas K. Geranios, "Richard Butler Said to Have Left the Property He Lost in Lawsuit," *Seattle Post-Intelligencer*, 24 October 2000; "Aryan Nations Leader Moves," *Albuquerque Journal*, 24 October 2000.

63. *Seattle Times*, accessed online at http://seattletimes.nwsource.com/html/localnews/2002030871_butlerobito9m.html (accessed 28 June 2005).

64. David Foster, "Group Dismantling Aryan Nations Site," *Albuquerque Journal*, 24 May 2001.

65. "Ex-Neo-Nazi Complex May Burn," *Albuquerque Journal*, 17 May 2001.

66. Geranios, "Richard Butler Said to Have Left." I contacted Pastor Butler several times via e-mail in July and August, 2003. I finally did receive a response from him, but he did not answer any of my questions about the compound or its history. Instead, he provided two short paragraphs that mentioned Aryan Nations philosophy and the continuing race war. Personal correspondence, 8 August 2003. He did not respond to my follow-up e-mail in which I thanked him and asked for elaboration about the history of the compound.

67. The twelve Aryan nations are the United States, Great Britain, Holland, Iceland, Sweden, Denmark, Finland, Norway, Germany, France, Italy, and Spain. These nations are considered "white." Sager, "Journey to the Heart of Whiteness," 251.

68. For Kreis' plans, see Dan Lewerenza,

"Aryan Nations looking to move to Pennsylvania," Education and Vigilance Network, http://www.evnetwork.net/fallkreis.html (accessed August 2003).

69. The Southern Poverty Law Center website posted this update at http://www.splcenter.org/intel/intelreport/article.jsp?aid=37, headlined "Squabbling Aryans Hail the New Dawn" (accessed 5 December 2003). I tried to contact Charles Juba via the Internet in May and June of 2003 but never received a response.

70. See Mary Ann Clawson, *Constructing Brotherhood: Class, Gender, and Fraternalism* (Princeton, N.J.: Princeton University Press, 1989).

71. Howard L. Bushart, John R. Craig, and Myra Barnes, *Soldiers of God: White Supremacists and Their Holy War for America* (New York: Kensington Books, 1998), 209.

72. Robert Jay Mathews, from his last letter as reprinted in James Ridgeway, *Blood in the Face: The Ku Klux Klan, Aryan Nations, Nazi Skinheads, and the Rise of a New White Culture* (1990; New York: Thunder's Mouth Press, 1995), 114–115; ADL, *Extremism on the Right*, 51–52.

73. Kevin Flynn and Gary Gerhardt, *The Silent Brotherhood: The Chilling Inside Story of America's Violent Anti-Government Militia Movement* (1989; New York: Signet Books, 1995), Chaps. 4–5. This is probably the best-known and most comprehensive account of Mathews and The Order. See also Thomas Martinez (he pronounced it Mar-tin-EZ, so as to disassociate himself from his father's Mexican surname during Thomas' involvement with the racist right) and John Guinther, *Brotherhood of Murder: How One Man's Journey through*

Fear Brought The Order—The Most Dangerous Racist Gang in America—to Justice (New York: McGraw-Hill, 1988), Chaps. 10–12; Jeffrey Kaplan, *Radical Religion in America: Millenarian Movements from the Far Right to the Children of Noah* (Syracuse, N.Y.: Syracuse University Press, 1997), 61–67; Ridgeway, *Blood in the Face*, 107–118; James Coates, *Armed and Dangerous: The Rise of the Survivalist Right* (1987; New York: Hill and Wang, 1995), Chap. 2; David H. Bennett, *The Party of Fear: The American Far Right from Nativism to the Militia Movement* (1988; New York: Vintage Books, 1995), 348–349, 351–353, 441–442.

74. Evelyn A. Schlatter, "'Extremism in the Defense of Liberty': The Minutemen and the Radical Right," in *The Conservative Sixties*, ed. David Farber and Jeffrey Roche (New York: Peter Lang Publishing, 2003), 37–50.

75. Kaplan, *Radical Religion in America*, 61.

76. Flynn and Gerhardt, *The Silent Brotherhood*, 35–42.

77. Ibid., 43–44.

78. Ibid., 44–46.

79. Coates, *Armed and Dangerous*, 47.

80. Flynn and Gerhardt, *The Silent Brotherhood*, 56–57.

81. This is the story that Richard Kemp, a former member of The Order, told me about how Mathews ended up in Washington state. Kemp is currently serving time in an Oregon prison for his activities with the group in the early 1980s. Personal correspondence, 6 August 2003.

82. Flynn and Gerhardt, *The Silent Brotherhood*, 58–60.

83. I have been unable to find that advertisement.

84. Ibid., 96–104.

85. Ibid., 47–48, 105–107. For a brief background on William Pierce and the National Alliance and a description of *The Turner Diaries*, see the ADL, *Extremism on the Right*, 39–40.

The Turner Diaries is now available in large bookstores, reprinted by a libertarian publisher, but its first (1978) and second editions (through the sixth printing) were published through the National Alliance's publishing house, National Vanguard Books. My copy is one of those published by National Vanguard Books, and I acquired it in 1996 at a gun show in Albuquerque, New Mexico.

86. The Anti-Defamation League of B'nai B'rith provides a biography on their website: http://www.adl.org/ Learn/ Ext_US/pierce.asp (accessed August 2005).

87. Richard Scutari, Order member, claimed that the media's attention on The Order's use of *The Turner Diaries* is unfounded. He claims that, though members thought it was a great read, it was a novel and not a blueprint for Order activities. He states that Simpson's work was Mathews' bible and that the battle plans came from *The Road Back*. He was interviewed by letter on overthrow.com, 13 September 2003. http:// www.overthrow.com/lsn/news.asp? articleID=5971 (accessed 11 December 2003). According to overthrow.com, the story originated in the *Libertarian Socialist News*. William Gayley Simpson, *Which Way Western Man* (Cooperstown, N.Y.: Yeoman Press, 1978). I have been unable to locate a copy of *The Road Back*.

88. Andrew MacDonald [William Pierce], *The Turner Diaries* (1978; Hillsboro, W.V.: Vanguard Books, 1995). Turner's bombing of the FBI national headquarters allegedly served as the inspiration for Timothy McVeigh's 1995 bombing of the Alfred P. Murrah Federal Building in Oklahoma City.

89. Flynn and Gerhardt, *The Silent Brotherhood*, 109–110.

90. Ibid. I have been unable to find out who that couple was.

91. Mathews, in a speech delivered at the National Alliance summer convention in 1983. The speech is available through the National Alliance or at http:// www.vanguardnewsnetwork.com/ timeline/RobertMathews_call_to _arms.ra (accessed April 2003). From my research, it doesn't appear that any members of The Order were actually farmers.

92. Flynn and Gerhardt, *The Silent Brotherhood*, 119–122.

93. Personal correspondence with Kemp, 6 August 2003, and with Scutari, 15 October 2003.

94. Flynn and Gerhard, *The Silent Brotherhood*, 125–126; it is also reprinted in Ridgeway, *Blood in the Face*, 107, as the Aryan Nations Oath of Allegiance. I believe it is the oath used at Aryan Nations and that Mathews adopted it for The Order. The eight other men in that meeting included Richard (Richie) Kemp, William (Bill) Soderquist, Ken Loff, and David Lane. Those from Aryan Nations included Dan Bauer, Denver Parmenter, Randy Duey, and Bruce Pierce. I have been able to correspond with Kemp and Lane. The others either never responded or politely declined. The child was Ken Loff's six-week-old daughter, Jamie Anne.

95. See Flynn and Gerhardt, *The Silent Brotherhood*, 205–208. Richard Kemp has never mentioned this incident in his correspondence with me.

96. The ADL has a biography of Richard

Scutari posted online at their website, adl.org. Scutari was indicted for Berg's murder but never convicted. Instead, he is serving a sixty-year sentence for racketeering and criminal conspiracy.

97. Flynn and Gerhardt, *The Silent Brotherhood*, 310–313. The man who had purchased the gun was Andrew Barnhill.

98. Ibid., 440–442.

99. Ibid., 446. The ADL reports that the fire started as a result of the "ammunition with which he barricaded himself." See ADL, *Danger: Extremism—The Major Vehicles and Voices on America's Far-Right Fringe* (New York: ADL, 1996), 271. My research indicates that Flynn and Gerhardt's account is actually correct.

100. Ridgeway, *Blood in the Face*, 115–117; Martinez and Guinther, *Brotherhood of Murder*. Martinez was the informant. See also "U.S. Alleges Overthrow Plot … White Supremacists Linked to Scheme to Take Over Government," *Washington Post*, 12 December 1984, A3. Courtesy of the United States Department of Justice, Federal Bureau of Investigation, Washington, D.C., Office of Public and Congressional Affairs, FOIPA, no. 435860/ 190–hg-1258584.

101. See, for example, www.freetheorder .com and www.pyramidprophecy.net. A search in any search engine on The Order will yield more hits.

102. Martinez and Guinther, *Brotherhood of Murder*, 55–56. Martinez claims, "Racists, I've found, are great fans of Eastwood's vengeful cop stories" (p. 55). James Gibson cites Martinez's statements in his discussion of Mathews and he links Mathews' apparent fascination with movies like this to the New War that burgeoned in survivalist culture after the Vietnam War. See Gibson, *Warrior Dreams*, 228. Mathews, though aware of

Christian Identity, followed Odinism, derived from Norse mythology. He also chose tenets from other faiths and grafted them onto Odinism. See Flynn and Gerhardt, *The Silent Brotherhood*, 109, 123. For information about Odinism, see Kaplan, *Radical Religion in America*, 69–72; Betty A. Dobratz and Stephanie L. Shanks-Meile, *"White Power, White Pride!" The White Separatist Movement in the United States* (1997; Baltimore: Johns Hopkins University Press, 2000), 140–143; and Mattias Gardell, *Gods of the Blood: The Pagan Revival and White Separatism* (Durham, N.C.: Duke University Press, 2003).

103. "Links of Anti-Semitic Band Provoke 6-State Parley," *New York Times*, 12 December 1984, B7. See also Gibson, *Warrior Dreams*, 224–230.

104. Kemp, one of the members of The Order who is in prison, actually cited Gibson's work as indicative of how he, Kemp, was feeling in the 1980s: displaced, undervalued, and worried about the state of the nation. Personal correspondence, 12 July 2003.

105. Flynn and Gerhardt, *The Silent Brotherhood*, 79, 80.

106. Ibid.

107. Ibid., 81–82.

108. "Violence on the Right: A Handful of New Extremists Disturbs the Peace," *Newsweek*, 4 March 1985, 23.

Chapter 4

1. North Dakota Governor George A. Sinner, 9 February 1987, *Examination of Problems Affecting the Farm Community*, Hearings before the Committee on Agriculture, Nutrition, and Forestry, United States Senate, One Hundredth Congress, 1st Session (Washington, D.C.: Government Printing Office, 1988), 47.

2. Catherine McNicol Stock, *Rural Radicals: Righteous Rage in the American Grain* (Ithaca, N.Y.: Cornell University Press, 1997).

3. Lawrence Goodwyn, *The Populist Moment: A Short History of the Agrarian Revolt in America* (New York: Oxford University Press, 1978), 55. Goodwyn traces the ideological roots of the Populist Party from the 1892 Omaha Platform back to 1886, when a new culture of a people's politics materialized in Texas. See also Peter H. Argersinger, *The Limits of Agrarian Radicalism: Western Populism and American Politics* (Lawrence: University Press of Kansas, 1995), 2–10; John D. Hicks, *The Populist Revolt: A History of the Farmers' Alliance and the People's Party* (1931; Lincoln: University of Nebraska Press, 1961), Chaps. 2–3; George McKenna, ed., *American Populism* (New York: G. P. Putnam's Sons, 1974); David B. Griffiths, *Populism in the Western United States, 1890–1900*, 2 vols. (Lampeter, Dyfed, Wales: Edwin Mellen Press, 1992); Jeffrey Ostler, *Prairie Populism: The Fate of Agrarian Radicalism in Kansas, Nebraska, and Iowa, 1880–1892* (Lawrence: University Press of Kansas, 1993); Robert W. Larson, *Populism in the Mountain West* (Albuquerque: University of New Mexico Press, 1986).

4. Elizabeth Sanders, *Roots of Reform: Farmers, Workers, and the American State, 1877–1917* (Chicago: University of Chicago Press, 1999), 1.

5. See Goodwyn, *The Populist Moment*, Chap. 2; and Hicks, *The Populist Revolt*, 21, 23–25, 60–61, 67, 74.

6. Larson, *Populism in the Mountain West*, Chaps. 1, 5, 6; and James Edward Wright, *The Politics of Populism: Dissent in Colorado* (New Haven, Conn.: Yale University Press, 1974).

7. Larson, *Populism in the Mountain West*, 26, 43, 44, 47, 60, 90–92, 139.

8. Argersinger, *The Limits of Agrarian Radicalism*, 2.

9. Ibid., 4.

10. Richard White, *"It's Your Misfortune and None of My Own": A New History of the American West* (Norman: University of Oklahoma Press, 1991), 373; see also Wright, *The Politics of Populism*.

11. White, *"It's Your Misfortune and None of My Own"*, 373; Larson, *Populism in the Mountain West*.

12. Sanders, *Roots of Reform*, 131.

13. Ibid. See also Richard Hofstadter, *The Age of Reform: From Bryan to F.D.R.* (New York: Vintage Books, 1960), 94.

14. Elizabeth Jameson, *All That Glitters: Class, Conflict, and Community in Cripple Creek* (Urbana: University of Illinois Press, 1998), 172–175.

15. White, *"It's Your Misfortune and None of My Own"*, 375.

16. See Robert C. McMath, Jr., *American Populism: A Social History, 1877–1898* (New York: Hill and Wang, 1993), and Sanders, *Roots of Reform*, 138–147.

17. C. Vann Woodward, *Tom Watson: Agrarian Rebel* (New York: MacMillan, 1938).

18. Ibid. See also Argersinger, *The Limits of Agrarian Radicalism*, 10; and McMath, *American Populism*.

19. Larson, *Populism in the Mountain West*, Chap. 10; Argersinger, *The Limits of Agrarian Radicalism*, Chaps. 1–3; Goodwyn, *The Populist Moment*, Chaps. 2–3.

20. Hofstadter, *The Age of Reform*, 61.

21. Sara Diamond, *Roads to Dominion: Right-Wing Movements and Political Power in the United States* (New York: Guilford Press, 1995), 262–265.

22. Hofstadter, *The Age of Reform*, 70, 77–78.

23. Ibid., 80.

24. Ibid., 82–92.

25. Walter T. K. Nugent, *The Tolerant Populists: Kansas Populism and Nativism* (Chicago: University of Chicago Press, 1963), 3–15.

26. See Larson's discussion with regard to Montana and anti-Chinese sentiment in *Populism in the Mountain West*, 91–93, and Goodwyn, *The Populist Moment.*

27. See, for example, Griffiths, *Populism in the Western United States;* Bernadette Brexel, *The Populist Party: A Voice for the Farmers in Industrialized Society* (New York: Rosen Publishing, 2003); and O. Gene Clanton, *A Common Humanity: Kansas Populism and the Battle for Justice and Equality, 1854–1903* (Lawrence, Kansas: Sunflower University Press, 2004).

28. Hofstadter, *The Age of Reform,* 74.

29. Michael Kazin, *The Populist Persuasion: An American History* (New York: Basic Books, 1995), 10, 12. See also Argersinger, *The Limits of Agrarian Radicalism,* 2; Allen D. Hertzke, *Echoes of Discontent: Jesse Jackson, Pat Robertson, and the Resurgence of Populism* (Washington, D.C.: Congressional Quarterly Press, 1993), 40.

30. Kazin, *The Populist Persuasion,* 36–37.

31. Stock, *Rural Radicals,* 20.

32. Stock, *Rural Radicals,* 22, 23–24. See also Gordon S. Wood, *The Radicalism of the American Revolution* (New York: Knopf, 1992).

33. Stock, *Rural Radicals,* 15.

34. Ibid., 15–16. See also White, *"It's Your Misfortune and None of My Own",* 370; Hertzke, *Echoes of Discontent,* 241; Argersinger, *The Limits of Agrarian Radicalism,* 102; Margaret Canovan, *Populism* (New York: Harcourt, Brace, Jovanovich, 1981), 232–233, 284–285; Goodwyn, *The Populist Moment,* xxi; Hicks, *The Populist Revolt,* Chap. 3; McKenna, *American Populism,* xviii; Norman Pollack, *The Populist Response to Industrial America* (New York: W. W. Norton, 1966), 11–12.

35. Kazin, *The Populist Persuasion,* 104, 260–272. Regarding rightist populist sentiment, see Harry C. Boyte, Heather Booth, and Steve Max, eds., *Citizen Action and the New American Populism* (Philadelphia: Temple University Press, 1986); Hertzke, *Echoes of Discontent;* and Diamond, *Roads to Dominion,* 262–265.

36. Kazin, *The Populist Persuasion,* 14.

37. Ibid., 15.

38. Jameson, *All That Glitters,* 140–141.

39. Ibid., 143.

40. Ibid., 160. See also Chaps. 7–8.

41. Chip Berlet and Matthew N. Lyons, *Right-Wing Populism in America: Too Close for Comfort* (New York: Guilford Press, 2000), 214.

42. Jean Hardisty, "The Resurgent Right: Why Now?" *Public Eye* (fall–winter 1995), 1–13.

43. Berlet and Lyons, *Right-Wing Populism in America,* 219–220.

44. Ibid., 220; see also Diamond, *Roads to Dominion,* Chap. 4.

45. Berlet and Lyons, *Right-Wing Populism in America,* 220.

46. Ibid., 220–221.

47. There is some discrepancy with regard to the founding date. The Anti-Defamation League of B'nai B'rith has 1984 as the date in question while Stephen E. Atkins, author of the *Encyclopedia of Modern American Extremists and Extremist Groups* (Westport, Conn.: Greenwood Press, 2002), 247, lists the date as 1982. I am inclined to use the 1982 date.

48. Anti-Defamation League of B'nai B'rith (ADL), "The Populist Party," from the web biography of Willis Carto, available on their website at www.adl.org (accessed 16 August 2005).

49. Atkins, *Encyclopedia*, 247.

50. Ibid., 248, 87–88. For more on Duke, see Douglas D. Rose, ed., *The Emergence of David Duke and the Politics of Race* (Chapel Hill: University of North Carolina Press, 1992), and Tyler Bridges, *The Rise of David Duke* (Jackson: University Press of Mississippi, 1994).

51. Atkins, *Encyclopedia*, 248.

52. Henry Nash Smith, *Virgin Land: The American West as Symbol and Myth* (1950; Cambridge, Mass.: Harvard University Press, 1970), 123.

53. Smith, *Virgin Land,* 124.

54. Matt Koehl, in his twelve-point program of the NSWPP, *White Power* 95 (n.d., but probably September 1980), 7, folder 2, box 50, Keith Stimely Collection, Knight Library, University of Oregon, Eugene, Oregon (hereafter Stimely Collection).

55. Koehl, "America Needs Small Farmers," *White Power* 40 (June 1973), 5, box 49, folder 17, Stimely Collection. Koehl had been a member of George Lincoln Rockwell's American Nazi Party and was a protegé of Rockwell. He founded the NSWPP after Rockwell's 1967 assassination. *White Power* was the NSWPP's publication.

56. Roderick Nash, *Wilderness and the American Mind* (1967; New Haven, Conn.: Yale University Press, 1982), 67.

57. Brian Dippie, "The Winning of the West Reconsidered," *Wilson Quarterly* 14:3 (summer 1990), 74.

58. Annette Kolodny, *The Land before Her: Fantasy and Experience of the Ameri-*can Frontiers, *1630–1860* (Chapel Hill: University of North Carolina Press, 1984), 54.

59. Reginald Dyck, "Frontier Violence in the Garden of America," in Eric Heyne, ed., *Desert, Garden, Margin, Range: Literature on the American Frontier* (New York: Twayne Publishers, 1992), 56.

60. Anne F. Hyde, "Cultural Filters: The Significance of Perception in the History of the American West," *Western Historical Quarterly* 24:3 (August 1993), 353.

61. Ibid., 358–359.

62. Hyde, "Cultural Filters," 361, 362–364.

63. Robert G. Athearn, *The Mythic West in Twentieth-Century America* (Lawrence: University Press of Kansas, 1986), 29. See also Richard Slotkin, *Gunfighter Nation: The Myth of the Frontier in Twentieth-Century America* (New York: Atheneum Books, 1992), 17. For specific discussions of the growth of farming in specific western regions, see Gilbert C. Fite, *The Farmers' Frontier: 1865–1900* (1966; Albuquerque: University of New Mexico Press, 1974).

64. Thomas Jefferson, *Writings,* ed. Merrill D. Peterson (New York: Literary Classics of the United States, 1984), 818 (letter to John Jay).

65. William P. Browne, Jerry R. Skees, Louis E. Swanson, Paul B. Thompson, and Laurian J. Unnevehr, *Sacred Cows and Hot Potatoes: Agrarian Myths in Agricultural Policy* (Boulder, Colo.: Westview Press, 1992), 9. See also Wendell Barry, *The Unsettling of America: Culture and Agriculture* (1977; San Francisco: Sierra Club Books, 1986), 143. "In the mind of Thomas Jefferson, farming, education, and democratic liberty were indissolubly linked."

66. Browne et al., *Sacred Cows and Hot Potatoes*, 9.

67. Leo Marx, *The Machine in the Garden: Technology and the Pastoral Ideal in America* (New York: Oxford University Press, 1967), 3. Marx's Chapter 3 traces the pastoral/agrarian myth from the eighteenth century and Chapter 4 discusses the rise of industrial America and the tensions between pastoral myth and urbanizing reality.

68. James R. Shortridge, *The Middle West: Its Meaning in American Culture* (Lawrence: University Press of Kansas, 1989), 27–28.

69. See Athearn, *The Mythic West*, 33–39.

70. Athearn, *The Mythic West*, 53–54. Emerson Hough, indicative of many of these periodicals, loudly lamented the "passing of the frontier" during the early years of the twentieth century and he also wrote on the alleged "dilution" of the American bloodstream. See his *Passing of the Frontier: A Chronicle of the Old West.* Vol. 26: Chronicles of America Series (New Haven, Conn.: Yale University Press, 1926).

71. Slotkin states that, "as the political struggles of the twentieth century intensified, the genres of mass culture became crucial as a common site in which Americans could imagine (or observe others imagining) the basis for a new (or renewed) cultural consensus on the meaning and direction of American society," *Gunfighter Nation*, 24. It was no accident that dime Westerns, detective and science fiction stories, serial novels published in magazines, and later genre movies emphasized white heroes (active) and heroines (passive). For more on Anglo-Saxon presence in popular culture, see Slotkin, *Gunfighter Nation*; Athearn, *The Mythic West*, Chap. 8; Ralph Brauer and Donna Brauer, *The Horse, the Gun and the Piece of Property: Changing Images of the TV Western* (Bowling Green, Ohio: Bowling Green University Press, 1975); Les Adams and Buck Rainey, *Shoot-'em-Ups: The Complete Reference Guide to Westerns of the Sound Era* (Metuchen, N.J.: Scarecrow Press, 1985); Barbara Howard Meldrum, ed., *Under the Sun: Myth and Realism in Western Popular Classics* (Troy, N.Y.: Whitston, 1985); Lee Clark Mitchell, "'When you call me that …': Tall Talk and Male Hegemony in *The Virginian,*" *PMLA* 102:1 (1987), 66–77; Christine Bold, *Selling the Wild West: Popular Western Fiction, 1860–1960* (Bloomington: Indiana University Press, 1991); Jane Tompkins, *West of Everything: The Inner Life of Westerns* (New York: Oxford University Press, 1992); and Richard W. Etulain, *Re-Imagining the American West: A Century of Fiction, History, and Art* (Tucson: University of Arizona Press, 1996).

72. Bronwen J. Cohen, "Nativism and Western Myth: The Influence of Nativist Ideas on the American Self-Image," *Journal of American Studies* 8:1 (1974), 23–24, 25, 26–27.

73. Cohen, "Nativism and the Western Myth," 28–29. The historiography of the debate over whether the West is a place or a process is extensive. I will summarize here. The debate stems from later interpretations of Frederick Jackson Turner's essay "The Significance of the Frontier in American History," in which he states, "Up to our own day American history has been in a large degree the history of the colonization of the Great West. The existence of an area of free land, its con-

tinuous recession, and the advance of
American settlement westward, explain
American development." In Martin
Ridge, ed., *History, Frontier, and Section:
Three Essays by Frederick Jackson Turner*
(Albuquerque: University of New Mexico
Press, 1993), 59. Since Turner's 1893 essay,
scholarly debate and interpretations about
what or why the West is the way it is and
why it plays the role it does (if it does) in
American history has tangled modern
twentieth-century historiography. See, for
example, Ray Allen Billington, *The West-
ward Movement in the United States* (New
York: D. Van Nostrand, 1959) and *Amer-
ica's Frontier Heritage* (1963; Albuquerque:
University of New Mexico Press, 1974); C.
Merton Babcock, *The American Frontier:
A Social and Literary Record* (New York:
Holt, Rinehart, and Winston, 1965). More
recent interpretations include Patricia
Nelson Limerick, *The Legacy of Conquest:
The Unbroken Past of the American West*
(New York: W. W. Norton, 1987); William
Cronon, "Revisiting the Vanishing Fron-
tier: The Legacy of Frederick Jackson
Turner," *Western Historical Quarterly* 18:2
(April 1987), 157–176; Michael P. Malone,
"Beyond the Last Frontier: Toward a New
Approach to New Western History,"
Western Historical Quarterly 20:4
(November 1989), 409–427; Patricia
Nelson Limerick, Clyde A. Milner II, and
Charles E. Rankin, eds., *Trails: Toward
a New Western History* (Lawrence: Uni-
versity Press of Kansas, 1991); Donald
Worster, *Under Western Skies: Nature and
History in the American West* (New York:
Oxford University Press, 1992); William
Cronon, George Miles, and Jay Gitlin,
eds., *Under an Open Sky: Rethinking
America's Western Past* (New York: W. W.
Norton, 1992); Allan G. Bogue, "The
Significance of the History of the Ameri-

can West: Postscripts and Prospects,"
Western Historical Quarterly 24:1 (February 1993), 45–68; Clyde A. Milner II, *A
New Significance: Re-envisioning the History of the American West* (New York:
Oxford University Press, 1996); and
Valerie J. Matsumoto and Blake Allmendinger, eds., *Over the Edge: Remapping the American West* (Berkeley: University of California Press, 1999).

74. See Earl Pomeroy, "Computers in
the Desert: Transforming the Simple
Life," *Western Historical Quarterly* 25:1
(spring 1994), 7. See also Limerick, *The
Legacy of Conquest.*

75. Pomeroy, "Computers in the
Desert," 7.

76. R. Douglas Hurt, *Problems of Plenty:
The American Farmer in the Twentieth
Century* (Chicago: Ivan R. Dee, 2002),
ix, xi.

77. Stuart W. Shulman, "The Origin of
the Federal Farm Loan Act: Issue Emergence and Agenda-Setting in the Progressive Era Print Press," in *Fighting for the
Farm: Rural American Transformed,* ed.
Jane Adams (Philadelphia: University of
Pennsylvania Press, 2003), 113.

78. Hurt, *Problems of Plenty,* 41–42.

79. Hofstadter, *The Age of Reform,* 119;
see also John D. Black, *Parity, Parity, Parity* (Cambridge, Mass.: Harvard University Press, 1942), Chap. 5.

80. Bruce L. Gardner, *American Agri-
culture in the Twentieth Century: How It
Flourished and What It Cost* (Cambridge,
Mass.: Harvard University Press, 2002), 50.

81. David E. Hamilton, *From New Day
to New Deal: American Farm Policy from
Hoover to Roosevelt, 1928–1933* (Chapel
Hill: University of North Carolina
Press, 1991), 10.

82. Ibid.

83. Ibid., 11.

84. Ibid., 12.

85. Wessels Living History Farm website, located at http://www .livinghistoryfarm.org/farmingin the30s/ money_10.html (accessed 19 July 2005). The site details the first penny auction, held in 1931 in Madison County, Nebraska. See also T. H. Watkins, *The Great Depression: America in the 1930s* (Boston: Back Bay Books, 1995).

86. Wessels Living History Farm website.

87. Hurt, *Problems of Plenty*, 58, 93.

88. Gardner, *American Agriculture in the Twentieth Century*, 94–95.

89. Ibid., 51.

90. Hurt, *Problems of Plenty*, 110, 122, 130, 135.

91. For an intimate and in-depth portrait of the effects of the 1980s crisis on a Midwestern farming community, see Kathryn Marie Dudley, *Debt and Dispossession: Farm Loss in America's Heartland* (Chicago: University of Chicago Press, 2000). For a discussion of the mechanics of the 1980s crisis, see Barry J. Barnett, "The U.S. Farm Financial Crisis of the 1980s," in *Fighting for the Farm*, 160–171.

92. Cornelia Butler Flora, "Presidential Address: Rural Peoples in a Global Economy," *Rural Sociology* 55:2 (summer 1990), 161–162. See also F. Larry Leistritz and Steve H. Murdock, "Financial Characteristics of Farms and of Farm Financial Markets and Policies in the United States," in *The Farm Financial Crisis: Socioeconomic Dimensions and Implications for Producers and Rural Areas*, ed. Steve H. Murdock and F. Larry Leistritz (Boulder, Colo.: Westview Press, 1988), 14–27; and United States Department of Agriculture (hereafter USDA), Economic Research Service, "The Current Financial Condition of Farmers and Farm Lend-

ers," *Agriculture Information Bulletin*, no. 490 (March 1985), vi.

93. Neil E. Harl, *The Farm Debt Crisis of the 1980s* (Ames: Iowa State University Press, 1990), 7, 15.

94. Flora, "Presidential Address," 163–165. See also J. B. Penn, "The Structure of Agriculture," and E. M. Babb, "Some Causes of Structural Change in U.S. Agriculture," both in USDA, Economics, Statistics, and Cooperative Service, *Structure Issues of American Agriculture: Setting, Farm Production, Public Policies, Marketing, Rural America, The Experience of Others* (Agricultural Economic Report 438, 1979); USDA, Economic Research Service, "The Current Financial Condition of Farmers and Farm Lenders," vi–vii.

95. USDA, "The Current Financial Condition of Farmers and Farm Lenders," vi.

96. Ibid., viii.

97. Harl, *The Farm Crisis of the 1980s*, 13–15.

98. Limerick, *The Legacy of Conquest*, 29. See also Anne Hyde, "Cultural Filters," *Western American Quarterly* 24:3 (August 1993), 467–469, and Albert L. Hurtado, "The Proffered Paradigm: Finding the West in Time and Space," *Western Historical Quarterly* 25:4 (Winter 1994), 467. Hurtado notes that "the West—even western culture—was a product of, or a reaction to, industrial and corporate America: it was not created by a frontier process or a result of environmental influences. Even the central myth of the West as land of new beginnings was a construction that confirmed the power of the eastern elites who controlled the industrial economy." William Deverell also discusses the high expectations and the reality of western settlement. See

"Fighting Words: The Significance of the American West in the History of the American West," *Western Historical Quarterly* 25:2 (summer 1994), 200. "Studies departing from the old scripts of western history tell us about these difficulties, these failures. They call into question the narrow tale of western history that promises reward and independence for the patriotic hardy."

99. ADL, *Extremism on the Right: A Handbook* (New York: ADL, 1988), 106–107. See also Ridgeway, *Blood in the Face*, 141–142; James Corcoran, *Bitter Harvest: Gordon Kahl and the Posse Comitatus: Murder in the Heartland* (New York: Viking Books, 1990).

100. ADL, *Extremism on the Right*, 58–59, 96–97.

101. Daniel Levitas, *The Terrorist Next Door: The Militia Movement and the Radical Right* (New York: Thomas Dunne Books, 2002), 2–3.

102. Ibid., 3.

103. Ibid., 8.

104. Ibid., 8. See James Coates, *Armed and Dangerous: The Rise of the Survivalist Right* (1987; New York: Hill and Wang, 1995), 104–105. I spoke with Chip Berlet on 10 March 1999 via telephone about Gale's work with Beach's original organization. Berlet informed me that all the Posse members with whom he has spoken about Gale and Beach indicate that Beach was the workhorse of the group. Berlet is the senior research analyst at Political Research Associates, a Somerville, Massachusetts–based watchdog group that monitors the right.

105. Coates, *Armed and Dangerous*, 104–105.

106. Levitas, *The Terrorist Next Door*, 9.

107. Posse Comitatus information pamphlet, n.d., p. 16., Wilcox Collection, Kenneth Spencer Research Library, University of Kansas, Lawrence, Kansas (hereafter Wilcox Collection). I assume the author is Beach, since the address that is listed on the pamphlet is in Portland and the organization listed is C.L.E.R.C., Beach's acronym for the Posse.

108. Loren J. B. Nedley, "Public Notice: The Time Has Come," leaflet signed and dated 24 April 1974 by Captain Nedley, who is calling for more Posse members. The leaflet is reprinted in Ridgeway, *Blood in the Face*, 134. See also Jim Scott, "The Vigilantes are Back!" *Argosy* 281:2 (February 1975), 30–32. Scott deliberately invokes the nineteenth-century image of vigilante mobs hanging alleged lawbreakers in his discussion of the Posse. This particular article is on file in the Wilcox Collection.

109. Posse information sheet, on file in the Wilcox Collection.

110. Information packet, Posse Comitatus (Sheriff's Posse Comitatus), n.d., Wilcox Collection. Given that the address listed to write for more information is Portland, Oregon, and the acronym used is C.L.E.R.C, I believe this particular handbook was originally published soon after Beach began propagandizing the group, perhaps 1970. The date the archivist stamped on the front page is smudged and illegible.

111. Quoted in Coates, *Armed and Dangerous*, 105.

112. Ibid.

113. Ibid., 106. See also ADL, *Extremism on the Right*, 58; ADL, *Special Report: Paranoia as Patriotism: Far-Right Influences on the Militia Movement* (New York: ADL, 1995), 29–30; ADL, *Hate Groups in America: A Record of Bigotry and Violence* (New York: ADL, n.d.), 44–45; *Kansas City Star*, "Posses Take On

Government," 5 September 1976; *Seattle Post-Intelligencer,* "Are they the Good Guys or the Bad Guys?" 4 March 1981.

114. Elaine Markoutsas, "Wisconsin Posse Digs in for the 'Bloodbath' to Come," *Chicago Tribune,* 20 August 1980, 3.

115. See ADL, *The Freemen Network: An Assault on the Rule of Law* (New York: ADL, 1996), 1, 11. For a succinct explanation and analysis of the common-law movement, see Mark Pitcavage, "Common Law and Uncommon Courts: An Overview of the Common Law Court Movement," the Militia Watchdog website: http://www.militia-watchdog.org/common.htm, 1–22, July 1997.

116. Pseudonym.

117. Colorado State Case No. 98-D-1196: *John Doe, De Jure Plaintiff, vs. O. Edward Schlatter, John and Jane Does, One through unlimited. De Facto Defendants;* Objection to order dismissing complaint and request to correct order, and issue judgment, 22 June 1998, author's private files.

118. Susan Hansen, "A Rule of Their Own," *American Lawyer* 18 : 4 (May 1996), 54; *Wasau Herald,* 20 February 1980. On file in the Wilcox Collection.

119. Hansen, "A Rule of Their Own," 54.

120. Corcoran, *Bitter Harvest,* 29.

121. Markoutsas, "Wisconsin Posse Digs in for the 'Bloodbath' to Come," 2.

122. Ibid.

123. Pamphlet, n.d., p. 1. On file in the Wilcox Collection. The date of this publication is probably the early 1970s, since the address listed is C.L.E.R.C. in Portland. Though the inference here is that women can join—"citizens," "volunteers"—the stipulation is that only men between eighteen and forty-five can be a part of the Sheriff's posse (i.e., the Posse Comitatus).

124. Wickstrom has joined the information age with a vengeance. For his recent views (many of which have not changed at all in terms of his Identity background), interested parties can check his website located at http://www.jameswickstrom.com. His posse-comitatus.org has been subsumed under the website http://www.aryan-nations.org.

125. Markoutsas, "Wisconsin Posse Digs in for the 'Bloodbath' to Come," 2.

126. Reverend Tom Mason, Pastor, First United Methodist Church, Claxton, Georgia, 9 February 1987, *Examination of Problems Affecting the Farm Community,* Hearings before the Committee on Agriculture, Nutrition, and Forestry, United States Senate, 100th Cong., 1st Sess. (Washington, D.C.: Government Printing Office, 1988), 196, 197.

127. Joel Dyer has provided one of the more poignant recent accounts of the effects of the Farm Crisis. See *Harvest of Rage: Why Oklahoma City Is Only the Beginning* (Boulder, Colo.: Westview Press, 1997), 20–26.

128. Maureen Wade, Jay, Oklahoma. Letter reprinted in Dyer, *Harvest of Rage,* 21–22.

129. Speaker #2 at a town meeting on rural stress, Tonkawa, Oklahoma, 1991. Reprinted in Dyer, *Harvest of Rage,* 22–23.

130. Berry addresses the connections in *The Unsettling of America.* See especially 29–30.

131. Abby L. Ferber and Michael Kimmel, "'White Men Are This Nation': Right-Wing Militias and the Restoration of Rural American Masculinity," in *Home-Grown Hate: Gender and Organized Racism,* ed. Abby L. Ferber (New York: Routledge, 2004), 145–146.

132. Smith, *Virgin Land,* 190–193.

133. Browne et al., *Sacred Cows and Hot Potatoes,* 13–15.

134. Dyer, *Harvest of Rage,* 27–36; Mark Lee, "Study Shows Suicide High Among Farmers," *Tulsa World,* 12 September 1989, C1; Mark Lee, "High Suicide Rate Linked to Farm Financial Stress," *Tulsa World,* 16 September 1989, A1; Charlene Finck, "The 80s Are Over But … Farmers are Still Killing Themselves," *Farm Journal,* 114:12 (October 1990), 36–39; William Sinclair, "Grief Is Growing on Farmland," *Washington Post,* 24 May 1987, A3; Osha Gray Davidson, *Broken Heartland: The Rise of America's Rural Ghetto* (Iowa City: University of Iowa Press, 1996).

135. Dyer, *Harvest of Rage,* 15.

136. Flora, "Presidential Address," 166, 169; Dyer, *Harvest of Rage,* 13.

137. William R. Ritz, "Farmers to Protest Debt Sale, 300 Gather to Block Court-Ordered Auction of Farm," *Denver Post,* 4 January 1983, B5–B6; Ritz, "Farmers Jailed after Protest At Springfield, Deputies' Tear Gas Subdues Crowd at Auction of Land," *Denver Post,* 5 January 1983, A1, A14. The incident made other newspapers as well. See the *Chicago Tribune,* "200 Farmers Protesting Foreclosure in Springfield Colorado Dispersed by Tear Gas," 5 January 1983, A4; *Los Angeles Times,* "300 Farmers Protest Auction of Farm in Springfield," 5 January 1983, 16, 20; Tom Morganthau, Frank Maier, Marilyn Achiron, Jeff B. Copeland, "Again, the Fear of Foreclosure," *Newsweek,* 17 January 1983, 12–13.

138. William Ritz, "Bad Debts Followed Ag Activist, 11 Suits Filed in Last 14 Years," *Denver Post,* 6 January 1983, A1. The tractorcade that converged on Washington, D.C., ended in hearings before a Senate committee. See American Agriculture Movement, *Hearing before the Committee on Agriculture, Nutrition, and Forestry,* United States Senate, Congress, 1st Session, 9 February 1979 (Washington, D.C.: Government Printing Office, 1979); Terry Wooten, Wichita, Kansas *Eagle-Beacon,* "Economic Woes Lead Movement to Another Winter of Discontent," n.d., 8A. The date of this article, though it is absent on this clipping, is probably 11 January 1983. On page 8, Wooten states "Last Tuesday, in … Springfield … about 300 chanting farmers tried to shout down the auction.…"; William P. Browne and John Dinse, "The Emergence of the American Agricultural Movement, 1977–79," *Great Plains Quarterly* 5 (fall 1985), 221–236.

139. Morganthau et al., "Again, the Fear of Foreclosure," 13.

140. See Stock, *Rural Radicals,* 158–160.

141. *Denver Post,* "Split Rears in Farmer Movement," 11 January 1983, B1.

142. *Salina* (Kansas) *Journal,* clipping dated 2 February 1983 (headline missing); and *Salina Journal,* "Weskan Training School Taught 'Killer Team' Tactics?" 20 February 1983, 1, 3, and "Paramilitary Seminar Infiltrated in Kansas," 17 February 1983. All on file in the Wilcox Collection, Posse Comitatus files.

143. *Salina Journal,* 14 February 1983, clipping in Posse Comitatus files, Wilcox Collection.

144. Wichita *Eagle-Beacon,* "Economic Woes Lead Movement to Another Winter of Discontent," 11 February 1983, A8. His most recent denial is noted in Judy L. Thomas, "New Farm Parity Movement Quickly Encounters Criticisms," *Kansas City Star,* 24 March 1999, A9. Eugene Schroder and Micki Nellis, *Constitution: Fact or Fiction* (Cleburne, Tex.: Buffalo Creek Press, 1995).

145. "'Posse' Philosophy Raises Fears,"

Salina Journal, 20 February 1983, 00. Wallace County, in nearby western Kansas, harbored a known Posse branch. *Salina Journal,* "Colorado Farmer Sought On Explosives Charges," 18 February 1983. The Posse chapter in Kansas may have been part of the chapter operating in eastern Colorado or it may have been the same chapter; Springfield and Weskan sit fairly close on either side of the Colorado/ Kansas border. Lenny Zeskind, "The Far Right," *Shmate: A Journal of Progressive Jewish Thought,* No. 11–12 (summer 1985), 29.

146. Zeskind, "The Far Right," 29.

147. Coates, *Armed and Dangerous,* 120–122.

148. Kirk in a taped phone conversation with police during the 1984 standoff. Quoted in Ridgeway, *Blood in the Face,* 145–146.

149. Dyer, *Harvest of Rage,* 40–41, 44; Stock, *Rural Radicals,* 171–172; Coates, *Armed and Dangerous,* 121. See also Calvin Trillin, who wrote about Kirk in "I've Got Problems," *New Yorker,* 18 March 1985, 114.

150. Trillin, "I've Got Problems," 110–111.

151. Ibid., 112–114.

152. Ibid., 116.

153. Lynora Williams, executive director of the Center for Democratic Renewal, quoted in Corcoran, *Bitter Harvest,* 122. Williams supplied the warning after David Duke, former Imperial Wizard of the Ku Klux Klan, ran for the Louisiana state senate in 1989 and won. The prior year, Duke ran for president as a member of the Populist Party, a far-right manifestation of small "p" populism. Duke continued to run for various political offices throughout the 1990s; in 2001 he was arrested for mail and tax fraud and sentenced in March 2003 to fifteen

months in a federal prison. Upon his release, he will consider a run for Congress. See ADL at www.adl.org and "David Duke Considering a Run for Congress" at http://www.cnn .com/2004/ ALLPOLITICS/01/23/eleco4.h.duke.ap/ (accessed 10 July 2005).

154. See Corcoran, *Bitter Harvest,* 245–246; and Ridgeway, *Blood in the Face,* 142.

155. Corcoran, *Bitter Harvest,* Chap. 5.

156. Ibid., 173.

157. Ibid., 155–166. See also ADL, *Extremism on the Right.*

158. Levitas, *The Terrorist Next Door.* For Kahl, see especially pages 191–201. Corcoran, *Bitter Harvest,* 244–246. See also Steven P. Wagner, "Prof Says Theology Links Hate Groups." Available online at in-forum http://www.in-forum.com/ specials/gordonkahl/index.cfm?id+27460 (accessed 28 December 2005).

159. See Coates, *Armed and Dangerous,* 108.

160. "Ode to Gordon Kahl," by Louis R. Beam, Jr. Quoted in Ridgeway, *Blood in the Face,* 143. Louis Beam was a leader in a chapter of the Texas Ku Klux Klan. Sometime around 1982 he became affiliated with Aryan Nations in Idaho and worked as a paramilitary organizer for them. He was also their computer networker. He got Aryan Nations up and running on the Internet and then on the web. He has not been active with Aryan Nations since the early 1990s because he claims he has been suffering from the effects of Agent Orange, to which he was exposed during his military service in Vietnam.

161. Wallace Stegner, *The American West as Living Space* (Ann Arbor: University of Michigan Press, 1987), 69–70.

162. Stegner, *The American West as Living Space,* 68.

163. Donald Worster, "Freedom and Want: The Western Paradox," in his *Under Western Skies: Nature and History of the American West* (New York: Oxford University Press, 1992), 88–89.

164. Donald Worster, "Beyond the Agrarian Myth," in *Trails: Toward a New Western History*, ed. Patricia Nelson Limerick, Clyde A. Milner II, and Charles E. Rankin (Lawrence: University Press of Kansas, 1991), 19. See also Limerick, *The Legacy of Conquest*, 78–79.

165. Walter Prescott Webb, *The Great Frontier* (1952; Lincoln: University of Nebraska Press, 1986), 300–301.

166. Patricia Nelson Limerick, *The Legacy of Conquest: The Unbroken Past of the American West* (New York: W. W. Norton, 1987), 125–127.

Chapter 5

1. Thompson Smith, "The Patriot Movement: Refreshing the Tree of Liberty with Fertilizer Bombs and the Blood of Martyrs," *Valparaiso Law Review* (fall 1997), 3. See also *Webster's Dictionary*. I accessed the online version at http://www.m-w.com/cgi-bin/dictionary?book=Dictionary&va=vigilantism.

2. For information on the causes of the Revolutionary War, see, for example, Pauline Maier, *From Resistance to Revolution: Colonial Radicals and the Development of American Opposition to Britain, 1765–1776* (New York: Knopf, 1972); Alfred F. Young, ed., *The American Revolution: Explorations in the History of American Radicalism* (DeKalb: Northern Illinois University Press, 1976); Gary B. Nash, *The Urban Crucible: Social Change, Political Consciousness, and the Origins of the American Revolution* (Cambridge, Mass.: Harvard University Press, 1979); Gordon S. Wood, *The Radicalism of the*

American Revolution (New York: Knopf, 1992).

3. For a history of vigilante activity in America, see, for example, Richard Maxwell Brown's work in the subject: "Violence and Vigilantism in American History," in *American Law and the Constitutional Order: Historical Perspectives*, ed. Lawrence M. Friedman and Harry N. Schreiber (Cambridge, Mass.: Harvard University Press, 1988), 171–190; and *Strain of Violence: Historical Studies of American Violence and Vigilantism* (New York: Oxford University Press, 1975) and *The South Carolina Regulators* (Cambridge, Mass.: Belknap Press, 1963). See also Thomas P. Slaughter, *The Whiskey Rebellion: Frontier Epilogue to the American Revolution* (New York: Oxford University Press, 1986), and Catherine McNicol Stock, *Rural Radicals: Righteous Rage in the American Grain* (Ithaca, N.Y.: Cornell University Press, 1996).

4. Brown, "The History of Vigilantism in America," 94–95.

5. Lane Crothers, *Rage on the Right: The American Militia Movement from Ruby Ridge to Homeland Security* (New York: Rowman and Littlefield, 2003), Chaps. 2–3.

6. I will capitalize "Patriot" when I am referring to the rightist Patriot movement.

7. There are numerous sources on the Patriot movement and its origins. See, for example, Carolyn Gallaher, *On the Fault Line: Race, Class, and the American Patriot Movement* (New York: Rowman and Littlefield, 2003), Chap. 4; Crothers, *Rage on the Right*, Chaps. 2–3; Stephen E. Atkins, *Encyclopedia of Modern American Extremists and Extremist Groups* (Westport, Conn.: Greenwood Press, 2002), 239; and Wilson Huhn, "Political Alienation

in America and the Legal Premises of the Patriot Movement," *Gonzaga Law Review* 34 (1998–1999), 417–443.

8. James W. Gibson, *Warrior Dreams: Violence and Manhood in Post-Vietnam America* (New York: Hill and Wang, 1994), 196.

9. Ibid.

10. Susan Jeffords, *The Remasculinization of America: Gender and the Vietnam War* (Bloomington: Indiana University Press, 1989), 116. Tom Engelhardt also discusses the role of Vietnam in creating a sort of "victimhood" among Americans. See *The End of Victory Culture: Cold War America and the Disillusioning of a Generation* (New York: Basic Books, 1995), 274–278.

11. *Soldier of Fortune* became more discriminating with its ads following a 1988 lawsuit that charged the magazine with negligence. The magazine had run an ad in 1985 placed by John Wayne Heard, a self-proclaimed mercenary who was convicted of three contract murders. He had been hired by outside parties who saw his ad in *SOF*. The magazine was sued by a victim's relative for negligence and was fined ten million dollars. See Gibson, *Warrior Dreams*, 198–202.

12. Gibson, *Warrior Dreams*, 214.

13. *Newsletter* (n.d., but probably early 1980s), C-DPL files, Wilcox Collection. The C-PDL was associated with the Covenant, Sword, and Arm of the Lord (CSA) compound, located in Arkansas. It was active during the 1980s, but not as much so during the 1990s.

14. Daniel Junas, "The Rise of Citizen Militias: Angry White Guys with Guns," in *Eyes Right! Challenging the Right-Wing Backlash*, ed. Chip Berlet (Boston: South End Press, 1995), 228.

15. Atkins, *Encyclopedia of Modern American Extremists and Extremist Groups,* 239.

16. Richard Abanes, *American Militias: Rebellion, Racism, and Religion* (Downer's Grove, Ill.: InterVarsity Press, 1996), 69; David H. Bennett, *The Party of Fear: The American Far Right from Nativism to the Militia Movement* (1988; New York: Vintage Books, 1995), 443, 465; Neil A. Hamilton, *Militias in America: A Reference Handbook* (Santa Barbara, Calif.: ABC-Clio Books, 1996), 3–8; 61–62; Crothers, *Rage on the Right,* Chap. 2.

17. I would like to mention here that not all militias are racist. The 1st New Mexico Militia based in Hobbs (located in the southeastern corner of the state), for example, does not allow anyone into the group who members suspect is racist or who openly professes such views. As it currently stands, however, all members are white Protestant men whose average age is forty. Almost all have military backgrounds, and about half have served in Vietnam. The political philosophy of this organized militia leans more toward libertarianism—i.e., "keep the federal government out of people's private lives." The members are against gun control, and all are skilled with weaponry and conduct safety training courses for new members. The 1st New Mexico Militia justifies its existence through the New Mexico State Constitution, which states that the governor will have at his/her disposal a standing militia in cases of emergency. Personal communication with Colonel R. J. Wright, 1st New Mexico Militia, Hobbs, New Mexico, 12 January 1999.

18. Regarding white supremacist recruitment in modern law enforcement and the military, see Michael Novick, *White Lies, White Power: The Fight*

Against White Supremacy and Reactionary Violence (Monroe, Me.: Common Courage Press, 1995). See especially Chap. 4, "Blue by Day, White by Night: Organized White-Supremacist Groups in Law Enforcement Agencies and the Military," 59–91.

19. Free Militia, *Field Manual of the Free Militia* (Great Barrington, Mass.: Riverwalk Press, 1994). Skipp Porteus stated in his foreword that the militia movement is connected to Identity rightist groups and to the Radical Religious Right, which includes, for example, the Traditional Values Coalition (v). The Free Militia discussed biblical reasons for existence but did not bring up race, possibly so that it could appeal to a wider range of discontented Americans. See especially Section 1. Gail Stewart, *Militias* (San Diego: Lucent Books, 1998), states that, "although some militias do not make racist or terroristic statements publicly, their private agendas are becoming more and more extremist," 12. The Free Militia is based in Wisconsin. See also Abanes, *American Militias;* Morris Dees, with James Corcoran, *Gathering Storm: America's Militia Threat* (New York: HarperCollins, 1996); Hamilton, *Militias in America;* Crothers, *Rage on the Right.* Carolyn Gallaher supplies a detailed description of class, race, and the Patriot movement. See *On the Fault Line: Race, Class, and the American Patriot Movement* (New York: Rowman and Littlefield, 2003).

20. See James A. Aho, *The Politics of Righteousness: Idaho Christian Patriotism* (Seattle: University of Washington Press, 1990), 13–15.

21. Abanes, *American Militias,* 8–9. See also John K. Akins, "God, Guns, and Guts: Religion and Violence in Florida

Militias" (Ph.D. dissertation, University of Florida, 1998). Although Akins focused on Florida-based groups, the ideology and practices can be extrapolated to militias in other states.

22. Aho, *The Politics of Righteousness,* 13–15.

23. Ibid.; see also Chip Berlet and Matthew Lyons, "Militia Nation," *Progressive,* 59:6 (June 1995), 25; Jill Smolowe, "Enemies of the State," *Time,* 8 May 1995, 61; James Ridgeway and Leonard Zeskind, "Revolution U.S.A.: The Far Right Militias Prepare for Battle," *Village Voice,* 2 May 1995, 34–37.

24. David A. Neiwert, *In God's Country: The Patriot Movement and the Pacific Northwest* (Pullman: Washington State University Press, 1999), 4–5. See also Rebecca L. Frereichs, "Christian Patriots: A Comparative Historical Analysis" (M.A. thesis, University of New Mexico, Albuquerque, New Mexico, 1996), 32–39.

25. Scholarly and literary accounts and analyses of these myriad issues abound. For a few overviews, see Henry Nash Smith, *Virgin Land: The American West as Symbol and Myth* (Cambridge, Mass.: Harvard University Press, 1950); Roderick Nash, *Wilderness and the American Mind* (1967; New Haven, Conn.: Yale University Press, 1982), which deals with the ideological relationship Americans have had with the landscapes in which they settle—particularly those considered "Western"; Leo Marx, *The Machine in the Garden: Technology and the Pastoral Ideal in America* (New York: Oxford University Press, 1967); and Patricia Nelson Limerick, *The Legacy of Conquest: The Unbroken Past of the American West* (New York: W. W. Norton, 1987), especially Chap. 2, "Property Values"; Donald Worster, *Under Western Skies: Nature and History*

in the American West (New York: Oxford University Press, 1992), particularly Chaps. 3–7; see also Richard White, "It's Your Misfortune and None of My Own": A New History of the American West (Norman: University of Oklahoma Press, 1991), especially Chaps. 6 and 9. For a chilling description of military pollution in the West, see Mike Davis, "Dead West: Ecocide in Marlboro Country," in Over the Edge: Remapping the American West, ed. Valerie J. Matsumoto and Blake Allmendinger (Berkeley: University of California Press, 1999), 339–369.

26. White, "It's Your Misfortune and None of My Own", 567; Limerick, Legacy of Conquest, 46–47.

27. Michael P. Malone and Richard W. Etulain, The American West: A Twentieth-Century History (Lincoln: University of Nebraska Press, 1989), 286–287.

28. William Kevin Burke, "The Wise Use Movement: Right-Wing Anti-Environmentalism," in Eyes Right! Challenging the Right-Wing Backlash, ed. Chip Berlet (Boston: South End Press, 1995), 135.

29. Malone and Etulain, The American West, 136.

30. Ibid., 140.

31. Stewart, Militias, 59–61; Michael Novick, "Was Hitler an Ecologist?" in White Lies, White Power, 203–224.

32. Stewart, Militias, 59–61.

33. Aho, The Politics of Righteousness, 37–67.

34. Abanes, American Militias, 67–68. Adams and Madison quoted in Abanes.

35. Abanes, American Militias, 68.

36. Ibid., 68.

37. Wayne A. Ross, "Join a Militia—Break the Law?" Soldier of Fortune 20:4 (April 1995), 52–53. See also Mike Williams, "Citizen Militias: '... Necessary to the Security of a Free State ...'" Soldier of Fortune 20:4 (April 1995), 48–53, 81–82.

38. The Free Militia, Field Manual of the Free Militia, 84–95.

39. Jess Walter, Every Knee Shall Bow: The Truth and Tragedy of Ruby Ridge and the Randy Weaver Family (New York: ReganBooks, 1995), 1. I will refer to Randy and Vicki Weaver by their first names, to avoid confusion. Randy claims that there actually is no "Ruby" Ridge. Their house was on Caribou Ridge; "Ruby" was a name manufactured, he claims, by the press. Because that's how the location is known, however, I'll refer to it as Ruby Ridge. See Randy and Sara Weaver, The Federal Siege at Ruby Ridge: In Our Own Words (Marion, Mont.: Ruby Ridge, Inc., 1998), 18. Sara is Randy's eldest daughter.

40. Weaver claims that he was trained in Special Forces and earned a Green Beret. See Randy and Sara Weaver, The Federal Siege at Ruby Ridge, 13. In 1993, James L. Pate wrote in SOF that Weaver never passed the training for Special Forces; instead, he was a regular Army combat engineer assigned to a support role in a Special Forces unit and his basic duties included bridge building and other heavy construction work that involved some use of explosives. Pate states that Weaver became disillusioned with the military because he did not get posted to Vietnam. According to Pate, Weaver did not take any courses in demolitions. See James L. Pate, "Standoff in Idaho: The Randy Weaver Incident," Soldier of Fortune, 18:3 (March 1993), 63–65. Walter, Every Knee Shall Bow, 22–23. I was unable to track Weaver down to verify his biography. His last known addresses were in Montana and then Iowa.

41. Walter, Every Knee Shall Bow, 24–27. See also Kenneth Stern, A Force upon

the Plain: The American Militia Movement and the Politics of Hate (New York: Simon and Schuster, 1996), Chap. 1; Morris Dees with James Corcoran, *Gathering Storm: America's Militia Threat* (New York: HarperCollins, 1996), 10–12; Junas, "The Rise of Citizen Militias," 228–229; Stewart, *Militias,* 29–30.

42. Walter, *Every Knee Shall Bow,* 27–39. See also Dees and Corcoran, *Gathering Storm,* 10–12; Stern, *A Force upon the Plain,* Chap. 1; and Abanes, *American Militias,* Chap. 4.

43. Walter, *Every Knee Shall Bow,* 40–46.

44. Ibid., 48–49.

45. Anonymous writer, "Safety Valve," *Instauration* 7:6 (May 1982), 4, folders 1–3, box 38, Keith Stimely Collection, Knight Library, University of Oregon, Eugene, Oregon (hereafter Stimeley Collection). See also Aho, *The Politics of Righteousness,* 13–15.

46. Walter, *Every Knee Shall Bow,* 68–72.

47. Ibid., 99–100. See also Stern, *A Force upon the Plain,* 20–21.

48. Walter, *Every Knee Shall Bow,* 114–115.

49. Ibid., 165–170.

50. For a brief biography of Gritz and his work in the far right, see ADL, *Special Report: Paranoia as Patriotism: Far-Right Influences on the Militia Movement* (New York: ADL, 1995); Jim [James L.] Pate, "Bo Knows Politics: Klansmen, Christics, Clowns, and Gritz's Populist Party," *Soldier of Fortune* 17:9 (September 1992) 40–43, 74.

51. Walter, *Every Knee Shall Bow;* Stern, *A Force upon the Plain,* 33.

52. I base my description of the occurrences on Ruby Ridge as described in a variety of sources. See James L. Pate,

"Amateurs and Assassins II," *Soldier of Fortune* 21:1 (January 1996), 56–61 and 84–87; Tom Morganthau, "The Echoes of Ruby Ridge," *Newsweek,* 28 August 1995, 24–28; Kevin Keating, "Die-Hard Protesters Keep Roadblock Vigil," *Spokane Spokesman-Review,* 1 September 1992, A6; Kevin Keating and J. Todd Foster, "Rural Peace Shattered—and Some Blame Feds," *Spokane Spokesman-Review,* 22 August 1992, A1, A9; Kelly McBride, "Weaver Was Target of Arms Sting," *Spokane Spokesman-Review,* 26 August 1992, A4; Dee Norton, "Fugitive Guards Family, Beliefs Atop Sheer Cliff," *Seattle Times,* 24 August 1992, A1; Walter, *Every Knee Shall Bow,* 160–359; and United States Department of Justice, *Department of Justice Report on Internal Review Regarding the Ruby Ridge Hostage Situation and Shooting by Law Enforcement Personnel* (Washington, D.C.: Government Printing Office, 1994); National Public Radio, "White Supremacist Barricaded in Idaho," *All Things Considered,* 28 August 1992, and "Barricaded Supremacist Weaver Gives Up," *All Things Considered,* 31 August 1992; Stern, *A Force upon the Plain,* 24–41. See also Wayne D. Sneath, "The Conspiratorial Ideology of Right-Wing Extremism in the 1990s: A Cultural Analysis of Ruby Ridge, Waco, and Oklahoma City" (Ph.D. dissertation, Bowling Green University, 2000).

53. Stern, *A Force upon the Plain,* 35.

54. Dees and Corcoran, *Gathering Storm,* 32–33; Stern, *A Force upon the Plain,* 35.

55. See Chip Berlet, "Mapping the Political Right: Gender and Race Oppression in Right-Wing Movements," in *Home-Grown Hate: Gender and Organized Racism,* ed. Abby L. Ferber (New York: Routledge, 2004), 36–37.

56. Stern, *A Force upon the Plain*, 36–37; see also James Ridgeway and Leonard Zeskind, "Revolution U.S.A.: The Far Right Militias Prepare for Battle," *Village Voice*, 2 May 1995, 23; David Real, "Divide and Conquer: White Supremacists See Idaho Cabin Standoff as First Salvo in Race War," *Dallas Morning News*, 2 November 1992, A1, A10.

In the *Field Manual of the Free Militia*, the discussion about the organization of the group states that "the whole Militia must be committed to the same cause and coordinated in their joint defense of the community. ... The way a balance between these competing concerns is achieved in the Free Militia is to organize all elements into 'cells' " (85).

57. Stern, *A Force upon the Plain*, 35–36.

58. Ibid., 36. Beam had been advocating "phantom cells" for at least ten years; I found his "Leaderless Resistance" essay (part 2) in a 1983 issue of *IKNSA* (issue no. 2), 17–19, folder 1, Aryan Nations, Wilcox Collection.

59. Stern, *A Force upon the Plain*, 37; see also Philip Lamy, *Millennium Rage: Survivalists, White Supremacists, and the Doomsday Prophecy* (New York: Plenum Press, 1996), 93; David H. Bennett, *The Party of Fear*, 448–449.

60. Stern, *A Force upon the Plain*, 58–59.

61. Ibid.; Philip Lamy, *Millenium Rage*, 159; Charles B. Strozier, "Apocalyptic Violence and the Politics of Waco," *The Year 2000: Essays on the End*, ed. Charles B. Strozier and Michael Flynn (New York: New York University Press, 1997), 100–101.

62. Lamy, *Millennium Rage*, 160–161; James L. Pate, "Gun Gestapo's Day of Infamy," *Soldier of Fortune* 18:6 (June 1993), 48. The byline on this story is "Bureau of Alcohol, Tobacco & Firearms agents violate Constitution and common sense in disastrous raid on Waco, Texas religious cult, leaving four agents dead and 16 wounded."

63. Stern, *A Force upon the Plain*, 58–64.; Hamilton, *Militias in America*, 25–27; Ridgeway and Zeskind, "Revolution U.S.A.," 34–37; Joseph Shapiro, "An Epidemic of Fear and Loathing," *U.S. News and World Report*, 8 May 1995, 37–44; Gary Hunt, Press release from the Outpost of Freedom, 8 March 1993, formerly located at http://www.illusions.com/opf/opfo308.htm. Hunt has been a tireless advocate of militias since Waco. I accessed the site in March 2003. As of 2004, it was no longer available.

64. Stern, *A Force upon the Plain*, 60.

65. Ibid., 60.

66. Ibid., 60; Abanes, *American Militias*, 50–51; Mark S. Hamm, *Apocalypse in Oklahoma: Waco and Ruby Ridge Revenged* (Boston: Northeastern University Press, 1997), 104.

67. See Abanes, *American Militias*, 58–59, for evidence that there was child abuse. Most Patriot groups are convinced there was not.

68. Lamy, *Millennium Rage*, 163–164; Pate, "Gun Gestapo's Day of Infamy," 62–63; Abanes, *American Militias*, 61; Hamilton, *Militias in America*, 27. Hamm notes that two camps of public opinion sprang up following the April 1993 conflagration. One included millions of politically moderate Americans who were skeptical of the government's account, and the other was a more strident group of radical rightists. See Hamm, *Apocalypse in Oklahoma*, 104–105, and *St. Louis Post-Dispatch*, "From Boise to Waco," 13 July 1993, B6. For militia views about Waco, Hunt has a variety of right-leaning editorials on his Outpost of Freedom website (http://www.illusions.com/opf). The Freedom Page

offers links to various Patriot and militia sites (http://www.home/mindspring .com). The Militia of Montana website contains links and a few archival references to Waco (http://www. nidlink .com/~bobhard/ mom.html). Ken Vardon, another self-proclaimed Patriot, offers a section on his website about Waco (http://www. esotericworldnews .com/whywaco/html) (all sites accessed March 2003).

69. Abanes, *American Militias*, 60.

70. Ibid.; Stephen Labaton, "Outside Review Criticizes F.B.I. on Raid on Cult," *New York Times*, 16 November 1993, A7, and "U.S. Agency Defends Tactics in Assault on Sect," *New York Times*, 30 March 1993, A13; Richard Abanes, "Controversy Still Smolders A Year after Waco Disaster," *Christian Research Journal*, spring/summer, 1994, 5–6, 41; Melinda Beck et al., "Someone Dropped the Ball," *Newsweek*, 17 May 1993, 51; Douglas Frantz, "Justice Dept. Report Absolves FBI, Blames Koresh for 75 Waco Deaths," *Los Angeles Times*, 9 October 1993, A17; see also Department of Justice, "Report to the Deputy Attorney on the Events at Waco, Texas," *United States Department of Justice Report on the Events at Waco, Texas, February 18 to April 19, 1993*, redacted version; United States Department of the Treasury, *Report of the Department of the Treasury on the Bureau of Alcohol, Tobacco and Firearms Investigation of Vernon Wayne Howell Also Known as David Koresh* (Washington, D.C.: Government Printing Office, 1993).

71. One of the first protests, organized by self-proclaimed militia spokeswoman Linda Thompson, occurred 3 April 1993. See Abanes, *American Militias*, 51. Thompson, an attorney, has complained

about her lack of credibility with male militia members, but she continues to stump for the right of militias to organize. For a brief discussion about the sexism that Thompson encountered after Waco, see Stewart, *Militias*, 56–58. Thompson also circulated flyers when the Waco seige broke out, entreating people to join militias and fight for freedom: "David Koresh and every other member of the Branch Davidians is a citizen. Even a prisoner of war would deserve to be treated humanely. We simply must take a stand *now*. There is no other choice, except to be slaves, living in fear of our own government. You are already probably a member of the militia and even if you are not, please JOIN US!" Linda Thompson's call to arms was posted on the web at http://www.illusions.com/opf/ Warms .htm (accessed April 2003).

72. For McVeigh's paranoia and fascination with violence, see Hamm, *Apocalypse in Oklahoma*.

73. Accounts of the Oklahoma City Bombing are too numerous to mention, as its occurrence and impact graced every American newspaper for weeks. Local television stations carried all-day coverage of the bombing's aftermath and the efforts of rescue workers dealing with the carnage. Hamm, *Apocalypse in Oklahoma*, provides a detailed background of McVeigh and his closest confidants, James and Terry Nichols and Michael Fortier. Any study of the right—whether journalistic or scholarly—that was published after 1995 discusses the Oklahoma City Bombing and Timothy McVeigh. A few of these are Dees, with Corcoran, *Gathering Storm;* Stern, *A Force upon the Plain;* Dyer, *Harvest of Rage;* Vincent Coppola, *Dragons of God: A Journey Through Far-Right America* (Atlanta: Longstreet Press,

1996); Howard L. Bushart, John R. Craig, and Myra Barnes, *Soldiers of God: White Supremacists and Their Holy War for America* (New York: Kensington Books, 1998); Abanes, *American Militias;* Lamy, *Millennium Rage;* Neiwert, *In God's Country;* and, more recently, Lou Michel and Dan Herbeck, *American Terrorist: Timothy McVeigh and the Oklahoma City Bombing* (New York: Harper Collins, 2001).

74. Neiwert, *In God's Country,* 1–2. The idea that the federal government was responsible for the Oklahoma City bombing has been circulating in rightist circles since it happened. Ken Vardon's website links the bombing to economic fallout generated when the Japanese yen plummeted. I accessed the following sites in April 2003; many are no longer available: http://www.esotericworldnews.com/ Oklahoma; the Arc-Hive is another site offering conspiracy theories about the federal government and its role in everything (http://www.netizen.org/arc-hive/ archive.htm); the Truth Is Freedom site offers a mixed bag of Patriot, common law, and conspiracy theory, including the government cover-ups of UFOs (http://www.geocities.com/Area51/ Corridor/3007).

75. Klanwatch, "Growing in Numbers, Hardening in Attitude: Patriot Groups Pose Continued Threat to American Public," *Intelligence Report* 86 (spring 1997), 4–5. One of the rightist groups that attempted to analyze the conspiracies about Oklahoma City was Gary Hunt's Outpost of Freedom. Hunt posted a series of articles on his website that debunked the idea that the government planted a bomb inside the Murrah Building and that the government's bomb, not McVeigh's, brought the structure down

(http://www.illusions.com/opf). As of June 2005, it was no longer available. Klanwatch is part of the Southern Poverty Law Center.

76. I accessed the Patriot Knowledge Base website in March 2003, which was located at http://www.micro.com/~pkb/ index.html, the Freedom Page site, at http://freedompage.home.mindspring .com, and the Vigo Examiner, which was actually a webzine (web magazine) at http://www/thnet.com/~deckard. Over the summer of 2003, many of these sites were updated fairly frequently, so the content changed.

77. Timothy Egan, "Hiding Out Underneath the Big Sky," *New York Times,* 7 April 1996, D1. Toole was elected to the Montana state senate in 2004.

78. Egan, "Hiding Out Underneath the Big Sky," D1.

79. Jim Robbins, "Prairie Revolt: Sound and Fury but Little Fire," *New York Times,* 1 April 1996, A1.

80. Richard E. Nicholls, "'Westward I Go Free,'" *New York Times,* 12 April 1996, A31. Nicholls is an author who has written on Jack London and hydroponics.

81. *New York Times,* "U.S. Seizes 2 Leaders of a Fugitive Group," 26 March 1996, B11; Dale and Connie Jakes, with Clint Richmond, *False Prophets: The Firsthand Account of a Husband-Wife Team Working for the FBI and Living in Deepest Cover with the Montana Freemen* (Los Angeles: Dove Books, 1998), 231.

82. See Jakes and Jakes, with Richmond, *False Prophets,* 122.

83. *New York Times,* "Officials Say Montana 'Freemen' Collected $1.8 Million in Scheme," 29 March 1996, A1.

84. Laurie Goodstein, "'Freemen's' Theological Agenda," *Washington Post,* 9 April 1996, A3.

85. Carey Goldberg, "The Freemen Sought Refuge in an Ideology That Kept the Law, and Reality, at Bay," *New York Times*, 16 June 1996, A14.

86. Mark Pitcavage, "Every Man a King: The Rise and Fall of the Montana Freemen" ("Patriot" Profile #3). This web publication was part of Pitcavage's Militia Watchdog organization. The document can now be accessed through the Anti-Defamation League of B'Nai B'rith website at http://www.adl.org/ mwd/ freemen.asp.

87. Ibid. See also Tom Kenworthy and Serge F. Kovaleski, "'Freemen' Finally Taxed the Patience of Federal Government," *Washington Post*, 1, 8–9.

88. Pitcavage, "Every Man a King."

89. Ibid.; *New York Times*, "Officials Say Montana 'Freemen' Collected $1.8 Million in Scheme."

90. Pitcavage, "Every Man a King"; Kenworthy and Kovaleski, "'Freemen' Finally Taxed the Patience of Federal Government," 8–9.

91. *New York Times*, "Anti-Tax Group Prowls; Neighbors Protest," 28 March 1996, A16.

92. *New York Times*, "A Standoff in Which the Government Is Showing a Change in Tactics," 27 March 1996, A16; and "Standoff With Militants Is High-Stakes Experiment," 30 March 1996, 6.

93. Gustav Niebuhr, "Mother and Son in Standoff Surrender," *New York Times*, 12 April 1996, A14; *New York Times*, "At Montana Standoff, F.B.I. Spurns Aid of Far-Right Groups," 26 April 1996, A28; Tom Kenworthy, "Talks Fail to End Montana Freemen Standoff," *Washington Post*, 2 May 1996, A3. Agnes Stanton, fifty-two, and her son Ebert, twenty-three, were the pair who surrendered on April 11. Stanton's husband Will had already been

arrested for "criminal syndicalism," which is an old law that Garfield County Attorney Nick Murnion used to get a conviction. Criminal syndicalism, defined as advocating violence or terrorism for political purposes, was originally intended for labor protests. It was a felony punishable by as much as ten years in prison. Will Stanton was convicted in 1995. See Pitcavage, "Every Man a King."

94. Pierre Thomas, "FBI Sends Armored Vehicles, Helicopter to Freemen Ranch," *Washington Post*, 1 June 1996, A12, and "FBI Cuts Off Power to Freemen's Ranch," *Washington Post*, 4 June 1996, A9; Tom Kenworthy, "FBI Lets One of Freemen Visit Leader," *Washington Post*, 12 June 1996, A22, "Teenage Girl Leaves Freemen Compound," *Washington Post*, 13 June 1996, A3, and "Freemen Standoff Ends with Peaceful Surrender," *Washington Post*, 14 June 1996, A1.

95. *New York Times*, "Anti-Tax Group Prowls; Neighbors Protest."

96. Berlet and Lyons, "Militia Nation," 24.

97. See Frank and Deborah Popper's work in this area, including "Great Plains: Checkered Past, Hopeful Future," *Forum for Applied Research and Public Policy*, (winter 1994); and Florence Williams, "Plains Sense: Frank and Deborah Popper's 'Buffalo Commons' is Creeping toward Reality," *High Country News* 33:1 (January 15, 2001) [http:// www.hcn.org /servlets/hcn.article?article_id=10194].

98. Berlet and Lyons, "Militia Nation," 24.

99. See *New York Times*, "Sheriff Asks Tax Protestors to Surrender," 27 March 1996, A16; "Anti-Tax Group Prowls; Neighbors Protest," and "Officials Say Montana 'Freemen' Collected $1.8 Million in Scheme," A1.

100. Handbook of Texas online (http://www.tsha.utexas.edu/handbook/online/articles/view/FF/hlf24.html).

101. See Fort Davis, Texas, web site (http://www.city-data.com/city/Fort-Davis-Texas.html.)

102. Sam Howe Verhovek, "Before His Armed Standoff, Texan Waged War on Neighbors in Court," *New York Times,* 2 May 1997, A12. I have been unable to determine where McLaren attended "some college."

103. Ibid.

104. It is generally accepted that 1995 is the year of the group's debut. Atkins maintains that McLaren started the Republic of Texas's movement in 1994 in the aftermath of a dispute involving his vineyard. See Atkins, *Encyclopedia of Modern American Extremists and Extremist Groups,* 254.

105. Ibid. McLaren posted a $10,000 bond in June 1996 and promised to stop filing liens. He reneged immediately upon his release.

106. Susan Jeffords, "Popular Culture: Above the Law." Part of the symposium: Law, Morality, and Popular Culture in the Public Sphere Articles, *Indiana Law Journal* (spring 2002), 1.

107. Sam Howe Verhovek, "Serious Face on a Texas Independence Group," *New York Times,* 24 January 1997, A1; Atkins, *Encylopedia of Modern American Extremists,* 254.

108. Atkins, *Encyclopedia of Modern American Extremists,* 254.

109. Same Howe Verhovek, "Hostages Taken in Standoff With Militant Texas Group," *New York Times,* 28 April 1997, A10.

110. Ibid.; Douglas Holt, "Armed Militia Takes Captives in West Texas," *Dallas Morning News,* 28 April 1997, accessible through the Ross Institute at http://www.rickross.com/reference/republic/republic3.html (accessed 21 February 2004).

111. Ibid.

112. Sam Howe Verhovek, "Texas Swaps Jailed Militant for Hostage in Tense Siege," 29 April 1997, A1, and "Troopers Move Closer to Texas Separatists' 'Encampment,'" 3 May 1997, A8, both in the *New York Times.*

113. Sam Howe Verhovek, "Texas Standoff Continues, Next Moves Are Uncertain," *New York Times,* 30 April 1997, A1.

114. Sam Howe Verhovek, "Leader of Armed Group Breaks Off Talks on Settling Standoff in West Texas," 30 April 1997, A16, and "Troopers Move Closer to Texas Separatists' Encampment," 3 May 1997, A18, both in *New York Times.* I found a call to arms from the San Joaquin County (Texas) militia archived at http://www.iahushua.com/T-L-J/rotacla.htm (accessed 15 August 2005).

115. Sam Howe Verhovek, "Seven-Day Standoff between Texas Authorities and Republic of Texas Ends," 4 May 1997, A1; Atkins, *Encyclopedia of Modern American Extremists and Extremist Groups,* 255.

116. Sam Howe Verhovek, "One Texas Secessionist Who fled Into Mountains Is Killed," *New York Times,* 6 May 1997, A16; Atkins, *Encyclopedia of Modern American Extremists and Extremist Groups,* 255.

117. Verhovek, "Hostages Taken in Standoff With Militant Texas Group;" Thomas G. Watts, "McLaren Rarely Seen since Late '96," *Dallas Morning News,* 28 April 1997. Archived at the Ross Institute, http://www.rickross.com/reference/republic/republic4.html (accessed 22 February 2004). See also Watts, "Republic of Texas Schism

Creates Confusion," *Dallas Morning News*, 2 February 1997, A47.

118. Paul Reichert, "'Republic of Texas' Faction Misses the Big Picture on Secession, *Nationalist Times* (May 1997). Available on the web at http://www.anu.org/archives_republicoftexasarticle.html (accessed 22 February 2004). The *Nationalist Times* is a white supremacist publication put out by the American Nationalist Union, founded in 1995. Though not blatantly racist on their website or in the public rhetoric I have seen, the organization wishes to end immigration, abolish welfare, abolish homosexuality and feminism, and support a "freedom of choice" for Americans to live in a racially segregated society, fusing libertarianism and racist elements. The ANU can be accessed via the web at *www.anu.org*. The *Nationalist Times* can be accessed via this website as well.

119. Atkins, *Encyclopedia of Modern American Extremists and Extremist Groups*, 255.

120. Verhovek, "Seven-Day Standoff Between Texas Authorities and Republic of Texas Ends;" Dick Reavis, "Texas Republic Leader Plans Return to Fort Davis," *Desert-Mountain Times*, 19 February 2004. Accessible on the web at http://www.dmtimes.net/blog/News/_archives/2004/1/15/14006.html.

121. Reavis, "Texas Republic Leader Plans Return to Fort Davis."

122. McLaren was born in Missouri but graduated from high school in Wilmington, Ohio. Others, including "White Eagle Otto," McLaren's chief bodyguard, are from Idaho. Greg and Karen Paulson were from Los Angeles. Richard F. Keyes III quit his job in Kansas to move

to Texas and fight for the Republic. Mike Matson was originally from Chicago. See Verhovek, "For Leader of Separatists, A Dignified End to Siege," *New York Times*, 5 May 1997, A10.

Chapter 6

1. Michael Kimmel, "Foreword," in *Home-Grown Hate: Gender and Organized Racism*, ed. Abby L. Ferber (New York: Routledge, 2004), xii–xiii.

2. Ibid., xiii.

3. Kathleen M. Blee, *Inside Organized Racism: Women in the Hate Movement* (Berkeley: University of California Press, 2002).

4. Carol M. Swain, *The New White Nationalism in America: Its Challenge to Integration* (New York: Cambridge University Press, 2002).

5. Ibid., 4.

6. Ibid., 5–6.

7. Ibid., 16.

8. The *American Renaissance* website is located at http://www.amren.com/.

9. For interviews with Hart and Levin, see Carol M. Swain and Russ Nieli, eds., *Contemporary Voices of White Nationalism in America* (New York: Cambridge University Press, 2003). For Rushton and Whitney's views, see "Stalking the Wild Taboo" website, http:// www.lrainc.com/swtaboo/ stalkers/jpro1.html (Rushton) and http:// www.lrainc.com/ swtaboo/ stalkers/reb_gw.html (Whitney) (accessed 18 August 2005).

10. Don Black interview in Swain and Nieli, *Contemporary Voices of White Nationalism in America*, 155–157. Stormfront can be accessed at www.stormfront.org.

11. Ibid., 159.

12. The ADL has information about

Smith and Furrow on their website at www.adl.org. Most major news archives also have information about the shootings.

13. Hale is currently serving a prison sentence for obstruction of justice and soliciting the murder of Chicago federal judge Joan Lefkow. Tragically, Lefkow's husband and mother were murdered in February 2005 by a man with no known ties to Hale or any other white supremacist. See "Police Say Chicago Man Killed Lefkow's Family," at http://abclocal.go.com/wls/news/031005_ns_lefkow_van.html (19 August 2005). Hale himself holds a J.D. from Southern Illinois University and did pass the Illinois bar exam. The state bar, however, has refused to issue him a license to practice law because of his extreme bigotry. See Hale's biography at www.adl.org.

14. See "Rudolph, Unsorry, Gets Life for Abortion Clinic Bombing," in USA TODAY, 17 July 2005, available at http://www.usatoday.com/news/nation/2005-07-17-rudolph-monday-sentencing_x. htm (accessed 26 August 2005).

15. The ADL has a biography of Rudolph, accessible on their website at www.adl.org.

16. Chip Berlet, "Mapping the Political Right: Gender and Race Oppression in Right-Wing Movements," in *Home-Grown Hate: Gender and Organized Racism,* ed. Abby L. Ferber (New York: Routledge, 2004), 19.

17. The National Vanguard was founded by a group of disaffected former members of the long-running National Alliance. The National Alliance is still active, but apparently there was quite a bit of ran-

cor in the split. The Vanguard details their reasons for leaving at http://nationalvanguard.org/story.php?id=4977 (accessed 19 August 2005). Information about the formation of the WPP can also be found on the Vanguard website at http://www.nationalvanguard.org/story.php?id=5517 (accessed 18 August 2005). The WPP was originally founded as the National Socialist White People's Party in 1958 by George Lincoln Rockwell, leader of the American Nazi Party. See the Nizkor information site at http://www.nizkor.org/hweb/orgs/american/national-socialist-white-peoples-party/nswpp-0895.html (accessed 19 August 2005). Nizkor is a white supremacist watchdog/information site.

18. Steve Friess, "Vegas: White-Power Politics," *Newsweek,* 22 August 2005, 11.

19. Ibid.

20. Luria's concerns are documented in Friess, "Vegas: White-Power Politics," 11; the quotation comes from the WPP information on www.adl.org.

21. The Pennsylvania-based Aryan Nations website provides extensive "activist tips," readily available at http://aryan-nations.org/activist_tips.htm (accessed 19 August 2005).

22. Abby L. Ferber, "Afterword," in *Home-Grown Hate,* 230.

23. See, for example, the Northwest Homeland blog located at http://nwhomeland.blogspot.com/ (accessed 26 August 2005).

24. See Swain, *The New White Nationalism in America,* for references to some of the better-known separatists and their ideas.

Bibliography

A NOTE REGARDING WEBSITES: *Because I accessed so many and because some are no longer extant, I opted to leave the citations for those in the notes only and not include them in the bibliography.*

Books

Abanes, Richard. *American Militias: Rebellion, Racism, and Religion.* Downer's Grove, Ill.: InterVarsity Press, 1996.

Abel, Ernest L. *The Roots of Anti-Semitism.* Rutherford, N.J.: Fairleigh Dickinson University Press, 1974.

Adams, Jane, ed. *Fighting for the Farm: Rural America Transformed.* Philadelphia: University of Pennsylvania Press, 2003.

Adams, Les, and Buck Rainey. *Shoot-'em-Ups: The Complete Reference Guide to Westerns of the Sound Era.* Metuchen, N.J.: Scarecrow Press, 1985.

Athearn, Robert. *The Mythic West in Twentieth-Century America.* Lawrence: University Press of Kansas, 1986.

Aho, James. *The Politics of Righteousness: Idaho Christian Patriotism.* Seattle: University of Washington Press, 1994.

Alexander, Charles. *Crusade for Conformity: The Ku Klux Klan in Texas, 1920–1930.* Houston: Rice University Press, 1962.

———. *The Ku Klux Klan in the Southwest.* Lexington: University of Kentucky Press, 1966.

Anti-Defamation League of B'nai B'rith. *Extremism on the Right: A Handbook.* New York: Anti-Defamation League of B'nai B'rith, 1988.

———. *Special Report: Paranoia as Patriotism: Far-Right Influences on the Militia Movement.* New York: Anti-Defamation League of B'nai B'rith, 1995.

———. *Beyond the Bombing: The Militia Menace Grows.* Fact-Finding Report. New York: Anti-Defamation League of B'nai B'rith, 1995.

———. *Danger: Extremism—The Major Vehicles and Voices on America's Far-Right Fringe.* New York: Anti-Defamation League of B'nai B'rith, 1996.

———. *The Freemen Network: An Assault on the Rule of Law.* New York: Anti-Defamation League of B'nai B'rith, 1996.

———. *Poisoning the Airwaves: The Extremist Message of Hate on Shortwave Radio.* Research Report. New York: Anti-Defamation League of B'nai B'rith, 1996.

———. *Hate Groups in America: A Record of Bigotry and Violence.* New York: Anti-Defamation League of B'nai B'rith, n.d.

Aquila, Richard, ed. *Wanted Dead or Alive: The American West in Popular Culture.* Urbana: University of Illinois Press, 1996.

Argersinger, Peter H. *The Limits of Agrarian Radicalism: Western Populism and American Politics.* Lawrence: University Press of Kansas, 1995.

Armitage, Susan, and Elizabeth Jameson. *The Women's West.* Norman: University of Oklahoma Press, 1987.

Athearn, Robert. *The Mythic West in Twentieth-Century America.* Lawrence: University Press of Kansas, 1986.

Atkins, Stephen E. *Encyclopedia of Modern American Extremists and Extremist Groups.* Westport, Conn.: Greenwood Press, 2002.

Babcock, C. Merton. *The American Frontier: A Social and Literary Record.* New York: Holt, Rinehart, and Winston, 1965.

Bailyn, Bernard, ed. *Pamphlets of the American Revolution.* Volume 1: 1775–1776. Cambridge, Mass.: Harvard University Press, 1965.

Bailyn, Bernard. *The Ideological Origins of the American Revolution.* Cambridge, Mass.: Harvard University Press, 1967.

Barkun, Michael. *Disaster and the Millennium.* New Haven, Conn.: Yale University Press, 1974.

———. *Religion and the Racist Right: The Origins of the Christian Identity Movement.* Chapel Hill: University of North Carolina Press, 1994.

Barry, Wendell. *The Unsettling of America: Culture and Agriculture.* 1977; San Francisco: Sierra Club Books, 1986.

Bederman, Gail. *Manliness and Civilization: A Cultural History of Gender and Race in the United States, 1880–1917.* Chicago: University of Chicago Press, 1995.

Bell, Daniel, ed. *The Radical Right.* Garden City, N.Y.: Anchor Books, 1964.

Bendroth, Margaret Lamberts. *Fundamentalism and Gender, 1875 to the Present.* New Haven, Conn.: Yale University Press, 1993.

Bennett, David. *The Party of Fear: The American Far Right from Nativism to the Militia Movement.* 1988; New York: Vintage Books, 1995.

Berlet, Chip, ed. *Eyes Right! Challenging the Right Wing Backlash.* Boston: South End Press, 1995.

Berlet, Chip, and Matthew N. Lyons. *Right-Wing Populism in America: Too Close for Comfort.* New York: Guilford Press, 2000.

Billington, Ray Allen. *The Westward Movement in the United States.* New York: D. Van Nostrand, 1959.

———. *America's Frontier Heritage.* Albuquerque: University of New Mexico Press, 1966.

Black, John D. *Parity, Parity, Parity.* Cambridge, Mass.: Harvard University Press, 1942.

Blee, Kathleen M. *Women of the Klan: Racism and Gender in the 1920s.* Berkeley: University of California Press, 1991.

———. *Inside Organized Racism: Women in the Hate Movement.* Berkeley: University of California Press, 2002.

Bloch, Ruth H. *Visionary Republic: Millennial Themes in American Thought, 1756–1800.* Cambridge: Cambridge University Press, 1985.

Bold, Christine. *Selling the Wild West: Popular Western Fiction, 1860–1960*. Blooming-ton: Indiana University Press, 1991.

Boyer, Paul. *When Time Shall Be No More: Prophecy Belief in Modern American Culture*. Cambridge, Mass.: Belknap Press of Harvard University Press, 1992.

Boyte, Harry C., Heather Booth, and Steve Max, eds. *Citizen Action and the New American Populism*. Philadelphia: Temple University Press, 1986.

Braeman, John, Robert H. Bermner, and David Brody, eds. *Change and Continuity in Twentieth-Century America: The 1920s*. Columbus: Ohio State University Press, 1968.

Brauer, Ralph, and Donna Brauer. *The Horse, the Gun, and the Piece of Property: Changing Images of the TV Western*. Bowling Green, Ohio: Bowling Green University Press, 1975.

Brexel, Bernadette. *The Populist Party: A Voice for the Farmers in Industrialized Society*. New York: Rosen Publishing, 2003.

Bridges, Tyler. *The Rise of David Duke*. Jackson: University Press of Mississippi, 1994.

Brown, Richard Maxwell. *The South Carolina Regulators*. Cambridge, Mass.: Belknap Press of Harvard University Press, 1963.

———. *Strain of Violence: Historical Studies of American Violence and Vigilantism*. New York: Oxford University Press, 1975.

———. *No Duty to Retreat: An American Theme*. New York: Oxford University Press, 1991.

Browne, William P., Jerry R. Skees, Louis E. Swanson, Paul B. Thompson, and Laurian J. Unnevehr. *Sacred Cows and Hot Potatoes: Agrarian Myths in Agricultural Policy*. Boulder, Colo.: Westview Press, 1992.

Bull, Malcolm, ed. *Apocalypse Theory and the Ends of the World*. Cambridge, Mass.: Blackwell, 1995.

Bushart, Howard L., John R. Craig, and Myra Barnes. *Soldiers of God: White Supremacists and Their Holy War for America*. New York: Kensington Books, 1998.

Canovan, Margaret. *Populism*. New York: Harcourt, Brace, Jovanovich, 1981.

Carmichael, Joel. *The Satanizing of the Jews: Origin and Development of Mystical Anti-Semitism*. New York: Fromm International Publishing, 1992.

Carnes, Mark C. *Secret Ritual and Manhood in Victorian America*. New Haven, Conn.: Yale University Press, 1989.

Carnes, Mark C., and Clyde Griffen, eds. *Meanings for Manhood: Constructions of Masculinity in Victorian America*. Chicago: University of Chicago Press, 1990.

Chafe, William H. *The Unfinished Journey: America since World War II*. New York: Oxford University Press, 1986.

Chalmers, David M. *Hooded Americanism: The First Century of the Ku Klux Klan, 1865–1965* (Garden City, N.Y.: Doubleday & Company, 1965).

Chazan, Robert. *Medieval Stereotypes and Modern Antisemitism*. Berkeley: University of California Press, 1997.

Clanton, O. Gene. *A Common Humanity: Kansas Populism and the Battle for Justice and Equality, 1854–1903*. Lawrence, Kans.: Sunflower University Press, 2004.

Clawson, Mary Ann. *Constructing Brotherhood: Class, Gender, and Fraternalism*. Princeton, N.J.: Princeton University Press, 1989.

Coates, James. *Armed and Dangerous: The Rise of the Survivalist Right.* New York: Hill and Wang, 1987.

Cohn, Norman. *Warrant for Genocide: The Myth of the Jewish World-Conspiracy and the Protocols of the Elders of Zion.* New York: Harper & Row, 1969.

———. *The Pursuit of the Millennium: Revolutionary Millenarians and Mystical Anarchists of the Middle Ages.* 1957; New York: Oxford University Press, 1970.

Cohn-Sherbok, Dan. *The Crucified Jew: Twenty Centuries of Christian Anti-Semitism.* Grand Rapids, Mich.: W. B. Eerdmans/Philadelphia: American Interfaith Institute and the World Allliance of Interfaith Organizations, 1997.

Colbourn, H. Trevor. *The Lamp of Experience: Whig History and the Intellectual Origins of the American Revolution.* Chapel Hill: University of North Carolina Press, 1965.

Connell, R. W. *Masculinities.* Berkeley: University of California Press, 1995.

Coppola, Vincent. *Dragons of God: A Journey through Far-Right America.* Atlanta: Longstreet Press, 1996.

Corcoran, James. *Bitter Harvest: Gordon Kahl and the Posse Comitatus: Murder in the Heartland.* New York: Viking, 1990.

Cott, Nancy F. *The Bonds of Womanhood: "Woman's Sphere" in New England, 1780–1835.* New Haven, Conn.: Yale University Press, 1977.

Cronon, William, George Miles, and Jay Gitlin, eds. *Under an Open Sky: Rethinking America's Western Past.* New York: W. W. Norton, 1992.

Crothers, Lane. *Rage on the Right: The American Militia Movement from Ruby Ridge to Homeland Security.* New York: Rowman and Littlefield, 2003.

Daniels, Jessie. *White Lies: Race, Class, Gender, and Sexuality in White Supremacist Discourse.* New York: Routledge, 1997.

Davidson, David, and H. Aldersmith. *The Great Pyramid: Its Divine Message: An Original Co-ordination of Historical Documents and Archaeological Evidences.* 11th ed. London: Williams and Norgate, 1948.

Davidson, Osha Gray. *Broken Heartland: The Rise of America's Rural Ghetto.* Iowa City: University of Iowa Press, 1996.

Davis, David Brion, ed. *The Fear of Conspiracy: Images of Un-American Subversion from the Revolution to the Present.* Ithaca, N.Y.: Cornell University Press, 1971.

Dees, Morris, with James Corcoran. *Gathering Storm: America's Militia Threat.* New York: HarperCollins, 1996.

Diamond, Sara. *Roads to Dominion: Right-Wing Movements and Political Power in the United States.* New York: Guilford Press, 1995.

Dimsdale, Thomas. *The Vigilantes of Montana.* 1866; Norman: University of Oklahoma Press, 1953.

Dinnerstein, Leonard. *Uneasy at Home: Anti-Semitism and the American Jewish Experience.* New York: Columbia University Press, 1979.

———. *Antisemitism in America.* New York: Oxford University Press, 1994.

Dobkowski, Michael N. *The Tarnished Dream: The Basis of American Anti-Semitism.* Westport, Conn.: Greenwood Press, 1979.

Dobratz, Betty A. and Stephanie L. Shanks-Meile. *"White Power, White Pride!" The*

White Separatist Movement in the United States. 1997; Baltimore: Johns Hopkins University Press, 2000.

Donaldson, Paschal. *The Odd-fellows' Pocket Textbook,* rev. ed. Philadelphia: Moss and Co., 1867.

Drinnon, Richard. *Facing West: The Metaphysics of Indian-Hating and Empire Building.* 1980; Norman: University of Oklahoma Press, 1997.

Dudley, Kathryn Marie. *Debt and Dispossession: Farm Loss in America's Heartland.* Chicago: University of Chicago Press, 2000.

Durham, Martin. *The Christian Right, the Far Right, and the Boundaries of American Conservatism.* Manchester: Manchester University Press, 2000.

Dyer, Joel. *Harvest of Rage: Why Oklahoma City Is Only the Beginning.* Boulder, Colo.: Westview Press, 1997.

Ellis, John Tracy. *Perspectives in American Catholicism.* Baltimore: Helicon Press, 1963.
———. *Catholics in Colonial America.* Baltimore: Helicon Press, 1965.

Engelhardt, Tom. *The End of Victory Culture: Cold War America and the Disillusioning of a Generation.* New York: Basic Books, 1995.

Etulain, Richard W. *Re-Imagining the American West: A Century of Fiction, History, and Art.* Tucson: University of Arizona Press, 1996.

Farber, David. *The End of Great Dreams: America in the 1960s.* New York: Hill and Wang, 1994.

Fenster, Mark. *Conspiracy Theories: Secrecy and Power in American Culture.* Minneapolis: University of Minnesota Press, 1999.

Ferber, Abby L. *White Man Falling: Race, Gender, and White Supremacy.* New York: Rowman and Littlefield, 1998.

Ferber, Abby L., ed. *Home-Grown Hate: Gender and Organized Racism.* New York: Routledge, 2004.

Filene, Peter. *Him/Her/Self: Sex Roles in Modern America.* Baltimore: Johns Hopkins University Press, 1986.

Fite, Gilbert. *The Farmers' Frontier: 1865–1900.* 1966; Albuquerque: University of New Mexico Press, 1974.

Flannery, Edward H. *The Anguish of the Jews: Twenty-Three Centuries of Anti-Semitism.* New York: Macmillan, 1965.

Flynn, Kevin, and Gary Gerhardt. *The Silent Brotherhood: The Chilling Inside Story of America's Violent Anti-Government Militia Movement.* 1989; New York: Signet Books, 1995.

Forster, Arnold, and Benjamin R. Epstein. *Danger on the Right.* New York: Random House, 1964.

Free Militia. *Field Manual of the Free Militia.* Great Barrington, Mass.: Riverwalk Press, 1994.

Gallaher, Carolyn. *On the Fault Line: Race, Class, and the American Patriot Movement.* New York: Rowman and Littlefield, 2003.

Gardell, Mattias. *Gods of the Blood: The Pagan Revival and White Separatism.* Durham, N.C.: Duke University Press, 2003.

Gardner, Bruce L. *American Agriculture in the Twentieth Century: How It Flourished and What It Cost.* Cambridge, Mass.: Harvard University Press, 2002.

Gibson, James W. *Warrior Dreams: Violence and Manhood in Post-Vietnam America.* New York: Hill and Wang, 1994.

Gilmore, David G. *Manhood in the Making: Cultural Concepts of Masculinity.* New Haven, Conn.: Yale University Press, 1990.

George, John, and Laird Wilcox. *Nazis, Communists, Klansmen, and Others on the Fringe: Political Extremism in America.* Buffalo: Prometheus Books, 1992.

Gerber, David A., ed. *Anti-Semitism in American History.* Urbana: University of Illinois Press, 1986.

Gerlach, Larry R. *Blazing Crosses in Zion: The Ku Klux Klan in Utah.* Logan: Utah University Press, 1982.

Gerstle, Gary. *American Crucible: Race and Nation in the Twentieth Century.* Princeton, N.J.: Princeton University Press, 2001.

Glassman, Samuel. *Epic of Survival: Twenty-Five Centuries of Antisemitism.* 1943; Philadelphia: Jewish Publication Society of America, 1983.

Goetzmann, William H., and William N. Goetzmann. *The West of the Imagination.* New York: W. W. Norton, 1986.

Goldberg, Robert A. *Hooded Empire: The Ku Klux Klan in Colorado.* Urbana: University of Illinois Press, 1981.

Goodwyn, Lawrence. *The Populist Moment: A Short History of the Agrarian Revolt in America.* New York: Oxford University Press, 1978.

Gossett, Thomas F. *Race: The History of an Idea in America.* New York: Schocken Books, 1987.

Griffiths, David B. *Populism in the Western United States, 1890–1900.* 2 vols. Lampeter, Dyfed, Wales: Edwin Mellen Press, 1992.

Grossman, James R., ed. *The Frontier in American Culture.* Berkeley: University of California Press, 1992.

Hamilton, David E. *From New Day to New Deal: American Farm Policy from Hoover To Roosevelt, 1928–1933.* Chapel Hill: University of North Carolina Press, 1991.

Hamilton, Neil A. *Militias in America: A Reference Handbook.* Santa Barbara, Calif.: ABC-Clio, 1996.

Hamm, Mark S. *Apocalypse in Oklahoma: Waco and Ruby Ridge Revenged.* Boston: Northeastern University Press, 1997.

Harl, Neil E. *The Farm Debt Crisis of the 1980s.* Ames: Iowa State University Press, 1990.

Hawley, Ellis W. *The Great War and the Search for a Modern Order: A History of the American People and Their Institutions, 1917–1933.* New York: St. Martin's Press, 1979.

Heimert, Alan. *Religion and the American Mind from the Great Awakening to the Revolution.* Cambridge, Mass.: Harvard University Press, 1966.

Heimert, Alan, and Perry Miller, eds. *The Great Awakening: Documents Illustrating the Crisis and Its Consequences.* Indianapolis: Bobbs-Merrill, 1967.

Hellman, John. *American Myth and the Legacy of Vietnam.* New York: Columbia University Press, 1986.

Hennessey, James. *American Catholicism: A History of the Roman Catholic Community in the United States.* New York: Oxford University Press, 1981.

Hertzberg, Arthur. *The Jews in America: Four Centuries of an Uneasy Encounter, A History.* New York: Simon & Schuster, 1989.

Hertzke, Allen D. *Echoes of Discontent: Jesse Jackson, Pat Robertson, and the Resurgence of Populism.* Washington, D.C.: Congressional Quarterly Press, 1993.

Hicks, John D. *The Populist Revolt: A History of the Farmers' Alliance and the People's Party.* 1931; Lincoln: University of Nebraska Press, 1961.

Higham, John. *Strangers in the Land: Patterns of American Nativism, 1860–1920.* 1955; New York: Atheneum, 1975.

Hilliard, Robert L., and Michael C. Keith. *Waves of Rancor: Tuning in the Radical Right.* Armonk, N.Y.: M. E. Sharpe, 1999.

Hine, Edward. *England's Coming Glories: Being the Fourth Part of the "Identifications of the Anglo Saxons with Lost Israel."* New York: James Huggins, 1880.

———. *Forty-Seven Identifications of the Anglo-Saxons with the Lost Ten Tribes of Israel, Founded upon Five Hundred Scripture Proofs.* New ed. New York: James Huggins, 1885.

Hobsbawm, Eric J. *Primitive Rebels: Studies in Archaic Forms of Social Movement in the 19th and 20th Centuries.* Manchester: University of Manchester Press, 1959.

Hofstadter, Richard. *The Age of Reform: From Bryan to F.D.R.* New York: Knopf, 1955.

———. *The Paranoid Style in America Politics and Other Essays.* New York: Knopf, 1965.

Horn, Stanley F. *Invisible Empire: The Story of the Ku Klux Klan.* New York: W. W. Norton, 1981.

Horsman, Reginald. *Race and Manifest Destiny: The Origins of American Racial Anglo-Saxonism.* Cambridge, Mass.: Harvard University Press, 1981.

Hough, Emerson. *The Passing of the Frontier: A Chronicle of the Old West.* Vol. 26. Chronicles of America Series. New Haven, Conn.: Yale University Press, 1926.

Hughes, Richard T. *Myths America Lives By.* Urbana: University of Illinois Press, 2003.

Hurlburt, Archer Butler. *Frontiers: The Genius of American Nationality.* Boston: Little, Brown and Company, 1929.

Hurt, R. Douglas. *Problems of Plenty: The American Farmer in the Twentieth Century.* Chicago: Ivan R. Dee, 2003.

Isaacs, Arnold. *Vietnam Shadows: The War, Its Ghosts, and Its Legacy.* Baltimore: Johns Hopkins University Press, 1997.

Jackson, Kenneth T. *The Ku Klux Klan in the City, 1915–1930.* New York: Knopf, 1967.

Jaher, Frederic Cople. *A Scapegoat in the New Wilderness: The Origins and Rise of Anti-Semitism in America.* Cambridge, Mass.: Harvard University Press, 1994.

Jakes, Dale, and Connie Jakes, with Clint Richmond. *False Prophets: The Firsthand Account of a Husband-Wife Team Working for the FBI and Living in Deepest Cover with the Montana Freemen.* Los Angeles: Dove Books, 1998.

Jameson, Elizabeth. *All That Glitters: Class, Conflict, and Community in Cripple Creek.* Urbana: University of Illinois Press, 1998.

Jameson, Elizabeth, and Susan Armitage. *Writing the Range: Race, Class, and Culture in the Women's West.* Norman: University of Oklahoma Press, 1997.

Jardim, Anne. *The First Henry Ford: A Study in Personality and Business Leadership.* Cambridge, Mass.: MIT Press, 1970.

Jefferson, Thomas. *Writings.* Ed. Merrill D. Peterson. New York: Literary Classics of the United States, 1984.

Jeffords, Susan. *The Remasculinization of America: Gender and the Vietnam War.* Bloomington: Indiana University Press, 1989.

Jeffrey, Julia Roy. *Frontier Women: The Trans-Mississippi West, 1840–1880.* New York: Hill and Wang, 1979.

Joff, James R., Jr. *Fields White unto Harvest: Charles F. Parham and the Missionary Origins of Pentecostalism.* Fayetteville: University of Arkansas Press, 1988.

Johnson, Michael L. *New Westers: The West in Contemporary American Culture.* Lawrence: University Press of Kansas, 1996.

Jones, Harry. *The Minutemen.* Garden City, N.Y.: Doubleday, 1968.

Kazin, Michael. *The Populist Persuasion: An American History.* New York: Basic Books, 1995.

Kennedy, David. *Over Here: The First World War and American Society.* New York: Oxford University Press, 1980.

Kaplan, Jeffrey. *Radical Religion in America: Millenarian Movements from the Far Right to the Children of Noah.* Syracuse, N.Y.: Syracuse University Press, 1997.

Kaplan, Jeffrey, ed. *Encyclopedia of White Power: A Sourcebook on the Radical Racist Right.* New York: AltaMira Press, 2000.

Kimmel, Michael S., ed. *Changing Men: New Directions in Research on Men and Masculinity.* Newbury Park, Calif.: Sage Books, 1987.

———. *Manhood in America: A Cultural History.* New York: Free Press, 1996.

Klier, John Doyle. *Imperial Russia's Jewish Question, 1855–1881.* Cambridge: Cambridge University Press, 1995.

Kolodny, Annette. *The Land before Her: Fantasy and Experience of the American Frontiers, 1600–1860.* Chapel Hill: University of North Carolina Press, 1984.

Lamy, Philip. *Millennium Rage: Survivalists, White Supremacists, and the Doomsday Prophecy.* New York: Plenum Press, 1996.

Lane, David. *Deceived, Damned, & Defiant: The Revolutionary Writings of David Lane.* St. Maries, Idaho: 14 Words Press, 1999.

Larson, Robert W. *Populism in the Mountain West.* Albuquerque: University of New Mexico Press, 1986.

Lay, Shawn. *War, Revolution, and the Ku Klux Klan: A Study of Intolerance in a Border City.* El Paso: Texas Western Press, 1985.

Lay, Shawn, ed. *The Invisible Empire in the West: Toward a New Historical Appraisal of the Ku Klux Klan in the 1920s.* Urbana: University of Illinois Press, 1992.

Lee, Albert. *Henry Ford and the Jews.* New York: Stein and Day, 1980.

Leonard, Ira M., and Robert D. Parmet. *American Nativism: 1830–1860.* New York: Van Nostrand Reinhold, 1971.

Leuchtenburg, William. *The Perils of Prosperity, 1914–32.* Chicago: University of Chicago Press, 1958.

Levitas, Daniel. *The Terrorist Next Door: The Militia Movement and the Radical Right.* New York: Thomas Dunne Books, 2002.

Lewis, David L. *The Public Image of Henry Ford: An American Folk Hero and His Company.* Detroit: Wayne State University Press, 1976.

Limerick, Patricia Nelson. *The Legacy of Conquest: The Unbroken Past of the American West.* New York: W. W. Norton, 1987.

———. *Something in the Soil: Legacies and Reckonings in the New West.* New York: W. W. Norton, 2000.

Limerick, Patricia Nelson, Clyde A. Milner II, and Charles E. Rankin, eds. *Trails: Toward a New Western History.* Lawrence: University Press of Kansas, 1991.

Lingenfelter, Richard E. *The Hardrock Miners: A History of the Mining Labor Movement in the American West, 1863–1893.* Berkeley: University of California Press, 1974.

Lipset, Dorothy Ann. *Freemasonry in Federalist Connecticut.* Princeton, N.J.: Princeton University Press, 1977.

Lipset, Seymour, and Earl Raab. *The Politics of Unreason: Right-Wing Extremism in America, 1790–1970.* New York: Harper & Row, 1970.

Litvinoff, Barnett. *The Burning Bush: Antisemitism and World History.* London: Collins, 1988.

McAvoy, Thomas. *The Formation of the American Catholic Minority, 1820–1860.* 1948; Philadelphia: Fortress Press, 1967.

MacDonald, Andrew [William Pierce]. *The Turner Diaries.* Hillsboro, W.V.: National Vanguard Books, 1978.

———. *Hunter.* Hillsboro, W.V.: National Vanguard Books, 1989.

McGrath, Roger D. *Gunfighters, Highwaymen, and Vigilantes: Violence on the Frontier.* Berkeley: University of California Press, 1984.

McKenna, George, ed. *American Populism.* New York: G. P. Putnam's Sons, 1974.

MacLean, Nancy. *Behind the Mask of Chivalry: The Making of the Second Ku Klux Klan.* New York: Oxford University Press, 1994.

McMath, Robert C., Jr. *American Populism: A Social History, 1877–1898.* New York: Hill and Wang, 1993.

Maier, Pauline. *From Resistance to Revolution: Colonial Radicals and the Development of American Opposition to Britain, 1765–1776.* New York: Knopf, 1972.

Malone, Michael P., and Richard W. Etulain. *The American West: A Twentieth-Century History.* Lincoln: University of Nebraska Press, 1989.

Marcus, Jacob Rader. *The American Jew, 1585–1990: A History.* Brooklyn, N.Y.: Carlson, 1995.

Marsden, Victor E., trans. *The Protocols of the Learned Elders of Zion.* Union, N.J.: Common Sense, [1922].

Martinez, Thomas, and John Guinther. *Brotherhood of Murder: How One Man's Journey through Fear Brought The Order—The Most Dangerous Racist Gang in America—to Justice*. New York: McGraw-Hill, 1988.

Matsumoto, Valerie J., and Blake Allmendinger, eds. *Over the Edge: Remapping the American West*. Berkeley: University of California Press, 1999.

Marx, Leo. *The Machine in the Garden: Technology and the Pastoral Ideal in America*. New York: Oxford University Press, 1967.

McGirr, Lisa. *Suburban Warriors: The Origins of the New American Right*. Princeton, N.J.: Princeton University Press, 2001.

Mecklin, John Moffatt. *The Ku Klux Klan: A Study of the American Mind*. New York: Harcourt, Brace and Co., 1924.

Meldrum, Barbara Howard, ed. *Under the Sun: Myth and Realism in Western Popular Classics*. Troy, N.Y.: Whitston, 1985.

Mendelsohn, Kurt. *The Riddle of the Pyramids*. New York: Praeger Books, 1974.

Merk, Frederick. *Manifest Destiny and Mission in American History*. 1963; Cambridge, Mass.: Harvard University Press, 1995.

Michel, Lou, and Dan Herbeck. *American Terrorist: Timothy McVeigh and the Oklahoma City Bombing*. New York: Regan Books, 2001.

Milner, Clyde A., II. *A New Significance: Re-envisioning the History of the American West*. New York: Oxford University Press, 1996.

Mosse, George L. *The Image of Man: The Creation of Modern Masculinity*. New York: Oxford University Press, 1996.

Murdock, David Hamilton. *The American West: The Invention of a Myth*. Reno: University of Nevada Press, 2001.

Nash, Gary B. *The Urban Crucible: Social Change, Political Consciousness, and the Origins of the American Revolution*. Cambridge, Mass.: Harvard University Press, 1979.

Nash, Gerald. *The American West in the Twentieth Century: A Short History of an Urban Oasis*. Englewood Cliffs, N.J.: Prentice-Hall, 1973.

———. *Creating the West: Historical Interpretations, 1890–1990*. Albuquerque: University of New Mexico Press, 1991.

Nash, Roderick. *The Nervous Generation: American Thought, 1917–1930*. Chicago: Rand-McNally, 1970.

———. *Wilderness and the American Mind*. 1967; New Haven, Conn.: Yale University Press, 1982.

Neiwert, David A. *In God's Country: The Patriot Movement and the Pacific Northwest*. Pullman: Washington State University Press, 1999.

Nelson, Shirley. *Fair Clear and Terrible: The Story of Shiloh, Maine*. Latham, N.Y.: British American Publishing, 1989.

Neu, Charles., ed. *After Vietnam: Legacies of a Lost War*. Baltimore: Johns Hopkins University Press, 2000.

Novick, Michael. *White Lies, White Power: The Fight Against White Supremacy and Reactionary Violence*. Monroe, Me.: Common Courage Press, 1995.

Nugent, Walter T. K. *The Tolerant Populists: Kansas Populism and Nativism*. Chicago: University of Chicago Press, 1963.

Ostler, Jeffrey. *Prairie Populism: The Fate of Agrarian Radicalism in Kansas, Nebraska, and Iowa, 1880–1892*. Lawrence: University Press of Kansas, 1993.
Overstreet, H. A., and Bonaro Wilkinson. *The Strange Tactics of Extremism*. New York: W. W. Norton, 1964.

Parkes, J. *The Conflict of the Church and the Synagogue*. London: 1934.
Pleck, Elizabeth H., and Joseph Pleck, eds. *The American Man*. Englewood Cliffs, N.J.: Prentice-Hall, 1980.
Pollack, Norman. *The Populist Response to Industrial America*. New York: W. W. Norton, 1966.
Prucha, Francis Paul. *The Great Father: The United States Government and the American Indians*. Lincoln: University of Nebraska Press, 1984.
Pugh, David. *Sons of Liberty: The Masculine Mind in Nineteenth-Century America*. Westport, Conn.: Greenwood Press, 1984.

Randel, William Pierce. *The Ku Klux Klan: A Century of Infamy*. Philadelphia: Chilton Books, 1965.
Ribuffo, Leo P. *The Old Christian Right: The Protestant Far Right from the Great Depression to the Cold War*. Philadelphia: Temple University Press, 1983.
Rice, Arnold S. *The Ku Klux Klan in American Politics*. Washington, D.C.: Public Affairs Press, 1962.
Ridge, Martin, ed. *History, Frontier, and Section: Three Essays by Frederick Jackson Turner*. Albuquerque: University of New Mexico Press, 1993.
Ridgeway, James. *Blood in the Face: The Ku Klux Klan, Aryan Nations, Neo-Nazi Skinheads, and the Rise of a New White Culture*. 1990; New York: Thunder's Mouth Press, 1995.
Roche, Jeffrey. *Cowboy Conservatism: The Emergence of Western Political Culture, 1933– 1984*. New York: Peter Lang Publishing, forthcoming.
Roche, Jeffrey, and David Farber, eds. *The Conservative Sixties*. New York: Peter Lang Publishing, 2003.
Roosevelt, Theodore. *The Winning of the West*. 4 vols. New York: G. P. Putnam's Sons, 1907.
Rorabaugh, W. J. *The Alcoholic Republic: An American Tradition*. New York: Oxford University Press, 1979.
Rose, Douglas D., ed. *The Emergence of David Duke and the Politics of Race*. Chapel Hill: University of North Carolina Press, 1992.
Rotter, Andrew J., ed. *Light at the End of the Tunnel: A Vietnam War Anthology*. New York: St. Martin's Press, 1991.
Rotundo, Anthony. *American Manhood: Transformations in Masculinity from the Revolution to the Modern Era*. New York: Basic Books, 1993.

Rowe, John Carlos, and Rick Berg, eds. *The Vietnam War and American Culture.* New York: Columbia University Press, 1991.

Russell, Sharman Apt. *Kill the Cowboy: A Battle of Mythology in the New West.* Reading, Mass.: Addison-Wesley, 1992.

Sanders, Elizabeth. *Roots of Reform: Farmers, Workers, and the American State, 1877–1917.* Chicago: University of Chicago Press, 1999.

Savage, William W., Jr. *The Cowboy Hero: His Image in American History and Culture.* Norman: University of Oklahoma Press, 1979.

———. *Cowboy Life: Reconstructing an American Myth.* 1975; Niwot: University Press of Colorado, 1993.

Saxton, Alexander. *Indispensable Enemy: Labor and the Anti-Chinese Movement in California.* Berkeley: University of California Press, 1971.

Saveth, Edward N. *American Historians and European Immigrants, 1875–1925.* New York: Columbia University Press, 1948.

Saveth, Edward N., ed. *Understanding the American Past: American History and Its Interpretations.* New York: Little, Brown, 1958.

Schlissel, Lillian. *Women's Diaries of the Westward Journey.* 1982; New York: Schocken Books, 1992.

Schlissel, Lillian, Vicki L. Ruiz, and Janice Monk, eds. *Western Women: Their Land, Their Lives.* Albuquerque: University of New Mexico Press, 1988.

Schroder, Eugene, and Micki Nellis. *Constitution: Fact or Fiction.* Cleburne, Tex.: Buffalo Creek Press, 1995.

Shilts, Randy. *Conduct Unbecoming: Lesbians and Gays in the U.S. Military, Vietnam to the Persian Gulf.* New York: St. Martin's Press, 1993.

Shortridge, James R. *The Middle West: Its Meaning in American Culture.* Lawrence: University Press of Kansas, 1989.

Siedler, Victor J. *Unreasonable Men: Masculinity and Social Theory.* London: Routledge Press, 1993.

Simonelli, Frederick J. *American Fuehrer: George Lincoln Rockwell and the American Nazi Party.* Urbana: University of Illinois Press, 1999.

Simpson, William Gayley. *Which Way Western Man.* Cooperstown, N.Y.: Yeoman Press, 1978.

Singular, Stephen. *Talked to Death: The Life and Murder of Alan Berg.* New York: Beech Tree Books, 1987.

Slaughter, Thomas B. *The Whiskey Rebellion: Frontier Epilogue to the American Revolution.* New York: Oxford University Press, 1986.

Smith, Duane A. *Rocky Mountain West: Colorado, Wyoming, and Montana, 1859–1915.* Albuquerque: University of New Mexico Press, 1992.

Smith, Gerald L. K. *Beseiged Patriot.* Edited by Elma M. Smith and Charles F. Robinson. Eureka Springs, Ark.: Elma M. Smith Foundation, 1978.

Smith, Henry Nash. *Virgin Land: The American West as Symbol and Myth.* 1950; Cambridge, Mass.: Harvard University Press, 1970.

Slotkin, Richard. *Regeneration through Violence: The Mythology of the American Frontier, 1600–1860*. Middletown, Conn.: Wesleyan University Press, 1973.

———. *The Fatal Environment: The Myth of the Frontier in the Age of Industrialization, 1800–1890*. New York: Harper Perennial, 1985.

———. *Gunfighter Nation: The Myth of the Frontier in Twentieth-Century America*. New York: Atheneum, 1992.

Smith, Henry Nash. *Virgin Land: The American West as Symbol and Myth*. Cambridge, Mass.: Harvard University Press, 1950.

Stegner, Wallace. *The American West as Living Space*. Ann Arbor: University of Michigan Press, 1987.

Steiner, Stan. *The Waning of the West*. New York: St. Martin's Press, 1989.

Stern, Kenneth. *A Force upon the Plain: The American Militia Movement and the Politics of Hate*. New York: Simon & Schuster, 1996.

Stewart, Gail B. *Militias*. San Diego: Lucent Books, 1998.

Stock, Catherine McNicol. *Rural Radicals: Righteous Rage in the American Grain*. Ithaca, N.Y.: Cornell University Press, 1996.

Swain, Carol M. *The New White Nationalism in America: Its Challenge to Integration*. New York: Cambridge University Press, 2002.

Swain, Carol M., and Russ Nieli, eds. *Contemporary Voices of White Nationalism in America*. New York: Cambridge University Press, 2003.

Tompkins, Jane. *West of Everything: The Inner Life of Westerns*. New York: Oxford University Press, 1992.

Totten, C. A. L. *Our Race: Its Origins and Destiny: A Series of Studies on the Saxon Riddle*. New Haven, Conn.: Our Race Publishing, 1891.

———. *The Order of History: The Coming Crusade. Palestine Regained, or the Relation of Our Race to the Restoration of Israel: The Means towards the End*. New Haven, Conn.: Our Race Publishing, 1897.

Trachtenberg, J. *The Devil and the Jews*. New Haven, Conn.: Yale University Press, 1943.

Trelease, Allen W. *White Terror: The Ku Klux Klan Conspiracy and Southern Reconstruction*. Westport, Conn.: Greenwood Press, 1971.

Trevor-Roper, H. R. *Catholics, Anglicans, and Puritans: Seventeenth-Century Essays*. Chicago: University of Chicago Press, 1988.

Tuveson, Ernest Lee. *Redeemer Nation: The Idea of America's Millennial Role*. Chicago: University of Chicago Press, 1968.

Utley, Robert. *The Indian Frontier of the American West*. Albuquerque: University of New Mexico Press, 1984.

Volkman, Ernest. *A Legacy of Hate: Anti-Semitism in America*. New York: F. Watts, 1982.

Wade, Wyn Craig. *The Fiery Cross: The Ku Klux Klan in America*. New York: Simon & Schuster, 1987.

Walter, Jess. *Every Knee Shall Bow: The Truth and Tragedy of Ruby Ridge and the Randy Weaver Family.* New York: Regan Books, 1995.

Watkins, T. H. *The Great Depression: America in the 1930s.* Boston: Back Bay Books, 1995.

Weaver, Randy, and Sara Weaver. *The Federal Siege at Ruby Ridge: In Our Own Words.* Marion, Mont.: Ruby Ridge, 1998.

Webb, James. *The Occult Underground.* LaSalle, Ill.: Open Court, 1974.

Webb, Walter Prescott. *The Great Frontier.* 1951; Lincoln: University of Nebraska Press, 1986.

Weber, Timothy P. *Living in the Shadow of the Second Coming: American Premillenialism, 1875–1925.* New York: Oxford University Press, 1979.

White, Richard. *"It's Your Misfortune and None of My Own": A New History of the American West.* Norman: University of Oklahoma Press, 1991.

Wilkinson, Rupert. *American Tough: The Tough-Guy Tradition and American Character.* New York: Harper & Row, 1986.

Wilson, Bryan R. *Magic and the Millennium: A Sociological Study of Religious Movements of Protest among Tribal and Third-World Peoples.* London: Heineman Educational, 1973.

Wilson, John. *Lectures on Our Israelitish Origin.* 5th ed. London: James Nisbit, 1876.

Wood, Gordon S. *The Creation of the American Republic, 1776–1787.* Chapel Hill: University of North Carolina Press, 1969.

———. *The Radicalism of the American Revolution.* New York: Knopf, 1992.

Woodward, C. Vann. *Tom Watson: Agrarian Rebel.* New York: MacMillan, 1938.

Worster, Donald. *Under Western Skies: Nature and History in the American West.* New York: Oxford University Press, 1992.

Wright, James Edward. *The Politics of Populism: Dissent in Colorado.* New Haven, Conn.: Yale University Press, 1974.

Wright, Will. *Six Guns and Society: A Structural Study of the Western.* Berkeley: University of California Press, 1975.

Wrobel, David. *The End of American Exceptionalism: Frontier Anxiety from the Old West to the New Deal.* Lawrence: University Press of Kansas, 1993.

Young, Alfred F., ed. *The American Revolution: Explorations in the History of American Radicalism.* DeKalb: Northern Illinois University Press, 1976.

Young, Marilyn. *The Vietnam Wars, 1945–1990.* New York: HarperCollins, 1991.

Zhu, Liping. *A Chinaman's Chance: The Chinese on the Rocky Mountain Mining Frontier.* Niwot: University of Colorado Press, 1997.

Articles

Abanes, Richard. "Controversy Still Smolders A Year after Waco Disaster." *Christian Research Journal* (spring/summer 1994), 5–6, 41.

Adams, Herbert Baxter. "The Germanic Origin of New England Towns." Paper presented before the Harvard Historical Society, 9 May 1881.

———. "Saxon Tithing Men of America." Paper presented before the American Antiquarian Society, 21 October 1881.

Albany Democrat-Herald. "Racists Seek to Form White Homeland in Northwest." 12 June 1986.

———. "Aryans Plan NW Homeland." 14 July 1986.

Albuquerque Journal. "Tear Gas Foils Farmers' Attempts to Block Auction in Colorado." 5 January 1983.

Arizona Republic. "Secret War: 'Patriots' Have Loose Ties to Rightists Nationwide." 21 December 1986, A1, A14.

"Aryan Nationalist Army Code of Conduct." *Aryan Nations Newsletter* 18 (1980), n.p.

"The Aryan Warriors [*sic*] Stand." *Calling Our Nation* 10 (1979), n.p.

Babb, E. M. "Some Causes of Structural Change in U.S. Agriculture." *Structure Issues of American Agriculture: Setting, Farm Production, Public Policies, Marketing, Rural America, The Experience of Others.* United States Department of Agriculture Economic Report no. 490, 1979.

Baldwin, James. "On Being 'White'. . . and Other Lies." In *Black on White: Black Writers on What It Means to Be White.* Edited by David R. Roediger. New York: Schocken Books, 1998, 177–180.

Balogh, Brian. "From Metaphor to Quagmire: The Domestic Legacy of the Vietnam War." In *After Vietnam: Legacies of a Lost War.* Edited by Charles Neu. Baltimore: Johns Hopkins University Press, 2000, 24–54.

Baritz, Loren. "Military Mismanagement." In *Light at the End of the Tunnel: A Vietnam War Anthology.* Edited by Andrew J. Rotter. New York: St. Martin's Press, 1991, 330–345.

Barkun, Michael. "The Millenarian Aspects of 'White Supremacist' Movements." *Terrorism and Political Violence.* 1:4 (October 1989), 409–434.

Barnett, Andrea. "The Girl Next Door Could Be the Next Leader of the Colorado KKK." *Westword* (Denver, Colorado), 16–24 March 1994, 24–30.

Barnett, Barry J. "The U.S. Farm Financial Crisis of the 1980s." In *Fighting for the Farm: Rural America Transformed.* Edited by Jane Adams. Philadelphia: University of Pennsylvania Press, 2003, 160–174.

Baugh, Brian. "From Metaphor to Quagmire: The Domestic Legacy of the Vietnam War." In *After Vietnam: Legacies of a Lost War.* Edited by Charles Neu. Baltimore: Johns Hopkins University Press, 2000, 24–55.

Beam Louis. "Leaderless Resistance." *Inter-Klan Newsletter and Survival Alert* 2 (1983), n.p.

———. "Computers and the American Patriot." *Inter-Klan Newsletter and Survival Alert.* September 1984, n.p.

Beam, Louis, and John C. Calhoun. "The Eternal War. . ." *Inter-Klan Newsletter and Survival Alert* 5 (1984), n.p.

Beck, Melinda. "Someone Dropped the Ball." *Newsweek* 17 May 1993, 51.

Becker, Carl. "Kansas." In *Understanding the American Past: American History and*

Its Interpretations. Edited by Edward N. Saveth. New York: Little, Brown, 1958, 384–405.

Berlet, Chip. "Mapping the Political Right: Gender and Race Oppression in Right-Wing Movements." In *Home-Grown Hate: Gender and Organized Racism.* Edited by Abby L. Ferber. New York: Routledge, 2004, 19–39.

Berlet, Chip, and Matthew Lyons. "Militia Nation." *Progressive* 59:6 (June 1995), 22–26.

Bogue, Allan G. "The Significance of the History of the American West: Postscripts and Prospects." *Western Historical Quarterly* 24:1 (February 1993), 45–68.

Breen, T. H. "Ideology and Nationalism on the Eve of the American Revolution: Revisions *Once More* in Need of Revising." *Journal of American History* 84:1 (June 1997), 13–39.

Brown, Richard Maxwell. "Violence and Vigilantism in American History." In *American Law and the Constitutional Order: Historical Perspectives.* Edited by Harry N. Schreiber. Cambridge, Mass.: Harvard University Press, 1988, 171–190.

———. "Western Violence: Structure, Values, Myth." *Western Historical Quarterly* 24:1 (February 1993), 5–20.

Brown, Thomas More. "The Image of the Beast: Anti-Papal Rhetoric in Colonial America." In *Conspiracy: Fear of Subversion in American History.* Edited by Richard O. Curry and Thomas M. Brown. New York: Holt, Rinehart, and Winston, 1972, 1–20.

Browne, William P., and John Dinse. "The Emergence of the American Agricultural Movement, 1977–79." *Great Plains Quarterly* 5 (fall 1985), 221–235.

Burke, William Kevin. "The Wise Use Movement: Right-Wing Anti-Environmentalism." In *Eyes Right! Challenging the Right-Wing Backlash.* Edited by Chip Berlet. Boston: South End Press, 1995, 135–145.

Butler, Richard G. "Interview." *Calling Our Nation* 27 (1980), n.p.

———. "The Sword on the Land." *Calling Our Nation* 26 (1981), n.p.

Calhoun, John C. "The Invisible Empire." *Inter-Klan Newsletter and Survival Alert* 4 (1984), n.p.

———. "What It Means to be a Klansman." *Inter-Klan Newsletter and Survival Alert* (ca. 1983), n.p.

Chicago Tribune. "200 Farmers Protesting Foreclosures in Springfield, Colorado, Dispersed by Tear Gas." 5 January 1983, A4.

Cohen, Bronwen J. "Nativism and Western Myth: The Influence of Nativist Ideas on American Self-Image." *Journal of American Studies* 8:1 (1974), 23–39.

Cohn, Norman. "How Time Acquired a Consummation." In *Apocalypse Theory and the Ends of the World.* Edited by Malcolm Bull. Cambridge, Mass.: Blackwell, 1995, 21–37.

Cronon, William. "Revisiting the Vanishing Frontier: The Legacy of Frederick Jackson Turner." *Western Historical Quarterly* 18:2 (1987), 157–176.

Davis, Mike. "Dead West: Ecocide in Marlboro Country." In *Over the Edge: Remapping the American West.* Edited by Valerie J. Matsumoto and Blake Allmendinger. Berkeley: University of California Press, 1999, 339–369.

Denver Post. "Split Rears in Farmer Movement." 11 January 1983, B1.

———. "Farm Militants Study Bomb-Making." 13 February 1983.

Deverell, William. "Fighting Words: The Significance of the American West in the History of the American West." *Western Historical Quarterly* 25:2 (summer 1994), 185–206.

Dippie, Brian. "The Winning of the West Reconsidered." *Wilson Quarterly* 14:3 (summer 1990), 72–85.

Dyck, Reginald. "Frontier Violence in the Garden of America." In *Desert, Garden, Margin, Range: Literature on the American Frontier.* Edited by Eric Heyne. New York: Twayne Publishers, 1992, 55–69.

"Ear to the Ground." *Outside* (August 1997), 28.

Eddy, Roy N. "Evacuation Part I." *Calling Our Nation* 26 (1981), n.p.

Egan, Timothy. "White Supremacist Surrenders after 11-Day Seige." *New York Times,* 1 September 1992.

———. "Hiding Out Underneath the Big Sky." *New York Times,* 7 April 1996, D1.

———. "Siege Is Subplot in Town's Survival Drama." *New York Times,* 23 April 1996, A1.

Etulain, Richard W. "Origins of the Western." In *Critical Essays on the Western American Novel.* Edited by William T. Pilkington. Boston: G. K. Hall, 1980, 56–60.

Everitt, Elly. "A Light for the White Race." *Twin Falls News-Times,* 3 January 1983, A9–10.

Fabian, Ann. "History for the Masses: Commercializing the Western Past." In *Under an Open Sky: Rethinking America's Western Past.* Edited by William Cronon, George Miles, and Jay Gitlin. New York: W. W. Norton, 1992, 223–238.

Fafnir [Robert Miles]. "The Birth of a Nation." In *Inter-Klan Newsletter and Survival Alert,* ca. 1980, n.p.

Ferber, Abby L. "Introduction." In *Home-Grown Hate: Gender and Organized Racism.* Edited by Abby L. Ferber. New York: Routledge, 2004, 1–18.

Ferber, Abby L., and Michael S. Kimmel, " 'White Men Are This Nation': Right-Wing Militias and the Restoration of Rural American Masculinity." In *Home-Grown Hate: Gender and Organized Racism.* Edited by Abby L. Ferber. New York: Routledge, 2004, 143–160.

Finck, Charlene. "The 80s Are Over But ... Farmers Are Still Killing Themselves." *Farm Journal* 114:12 (October 1990), 36–39.

Flora, Cornelia Butler. "Presidential Address: Rural Peoples in a Global Economy." *Rural Sociology* 55:2 (summer 1990), 157–178.

Foster, David. "Demolition Clears Symbols of Hate at Former Aryan Nations Compound." 24 May 2001. Associated Press Wire.

Frantz, Douglas. "Justice Dept. Report Absolves FBI, Blames Koresh for 75 Waco Deaths." *Los Angeles Times,* 9 October 1993, A17.

Friess, Steve. "Vegas: White-Power Politics." *Newsweek,* 22 August 2005, 11.

Geranios, Nicholas K. "Richard Butler Said to Have Left the Property He Lost in Lawsuit." *Seattle Post-Intelligencer*, 24 October 2000 [http://seattlepi.nwsource.com/local/arya24.shtml].

Gibson, James W. "Is the Apocalypse Coming? Paramilitary Culture after the Cold War." In *The Year 2000: Essays on the End*. Edited by Charles B. Strozier and Michael Flynn. New York: New York University Press, 1997, 180–189.

Gitlin, Jay. "On the Boundaries of Empire: Connecting the West to Its Imperial Past." In *Under an Open Sky: Rethinking America's Western Past*. Edited by William Cronon, George Miles, and Jay Gitlin. New York: W. W. Norton, 1992, 71–89.

Goldberg, Carey. "Last of Freemen Surrender to F.B.I. at Montana Site." *New York Times*, 14 June 1996, A1.

———. "The Freemen Sought Refuge in an Ideology That Kept the Law, and Reality, at Bay." *New York Times*, 16 June 1996, A14.

Goodstein, Laurie. "'Freemen's' Theological Agenda." *Washington Post*, 9 April 1996, A3.

Grestle, Gary. "Liberty, Coercion, and the Making of Americans." *Journal of American History* 84:2 (September 1997), 536–559.

Griffen, Clyde. "Reconstructing Masculinity from the Evangelical Revival to the Waning of Progressivism: A Speculative Synthesis." In *Meanings for Manhood: Constructions of Masculinity in Victorian America*. Edited by Mark C. Carnes and Clyde Griffen. Chicago: University of Chicago Press, 1990, 183–204.

Hall, Bill. "It's Reason vs. Violence on an Idaho Mountain." *Lewiston* (Idaho) *Morning Tribune*, 27 August 1992.

Hammer, Joshua. "Trouble." *People*, 29 August 1983, 44–48.

Hansen, Susan. "A Rule of Their Own." *American Lawyer* 18:4 (May 1996), 52–63.

Hardisty, Jean. "The Resurgent Right: Why Now?" *Public Eye* (fall–winter 1995), 1–13.

Harris, John. "Hitler's Legacy." *Seattle Post-Intelligencer*, 5 January 1985, F1.

Harwood, W. S. "Secret Societies in America." *North American Review* 164 (May 1897), 620–623.

Henderson, Paul. "We're Not Saluting Hitler—We're Saluting God." In the *Seattle Times*, 17 April 1983.

Hoar, William P. "Manifest Destiny: Many 19th-Century Americans Believed Their Young Nation Was Destined to Extend the Benefits of Freedom and Opportunity across the Continent—From Sea to Shining Sea." *New American*, 19 (28 July 2003; originally published in *American Opinion*, June 1981), 33+.

Horn, Miriam. "How the West was Really Won." *U.S. News and World Report* 108:20 (21 May 1990), 56.

Horowitz, David A. "The Klansman as Outsider: Ethnocultural Solidarity and Antielitism in the Oregon Ku Klux Klan of the 1920s." *Pacific Northwest Quarterly* 80 (January 1989), 12–20.

"Huey Long's Nation-Wide Share Our Wealth Organization." *Literary Digest* 119 (16 March 1935), 12–13.

Huie, William Bradford. "Gerald Smith's Bid for Power." *American Mercury* 55 (August 1942), 147–157.

Huhn, Wilson. "Political Alienation in America and the Legal Premises of the Patriot Movement." *Gonzaga Law Review* (1998–1999), 417–443.

Hurtado, Albert L. "The Proffered Paradigm: Finding the West in Time and Space." *Western Historical Quarterly* 25:4 (winter 1994), 467–469.

Hyde, Anne F. "Cultural Filters: The Significance of Perception in the History of the American West." *Western American Quarterly* 24:3 (August 1993), 351–376.

Janofsky, Michael. "Home-Grown Courts Spring Up As Judicial Arm of the Far Right." *New York Times* 17 April 1996, A1.

Jeffords, Susan. "Popular Culture: Above the Law." Part of the symposium: Law, Morality, and Popular Culture in the Public Sphere Articles, *Indiana Law Journal* 77:2 (spring 2002), 331–336.

Jensen, Joan M., and Darlis A. Miller, "The Gentle Tamers Revisited: New Approaches to the History of Women in the American West." *Pacific Historical Review* 49 (May 1980), 173–213.

Junas, Daniel. "The Rise of Citizen Militias: Angry White Guys with Guns." In *Eyes Right! Challenging the Right Wing Backlash.* Edited by Chip Berlet. Boston: South End Press, 1995, 226–235.

Kansas City Star. "Bands of Minutemen across the Country Whet for Communist Threat." 23 January 1966. On file in Wilcox Collection.

———. "Takeover Coming From Within." 23 January 1966. On file in Wilcox Collection.

———. "Posses Take On Government." 5 September 1976. On file in Wilcox Collection.

———. "Head of Rightist Army Charged in Sex Case." 14 September 1993. On file in Wilcox Collection.

Keating, Kevin. "Die-Hard Protestors Keep Roadblock Vigil." *Spokane Spokesman-Review,* 26 August 1992, A6.

Keating, Kevin, and J. Todd Foster. "Rural Peace Shattered—and Some Blame Feds." *Spokane Spokesman-Review,* 22 August 1992, A1, A9.

Kenworthy, Tom. "A Wave of Reporters Grows Amid Montana Grain." *Washington Post,* 1 April 1996, A4.

———. "Freemen Split over Standoff, Negotiator Says." *Washington Post,* 1 May 1996, A13.

———. "Talks Fail to End Montana Freemen Standoff." *Washington Post,* 2 May 1996, A3.

———. "FBI Lets One of Freemen Visit Leader." *Washington Post,* 12 June 1996, A22.

———. "Teenage Girl Leaves Freemen Compound." *Washington Post,* 13 June 1996, A3.

———. "Freemen Standoff Ends With Peaceful Surrender." *Washington Post,* 14 June 1996, A1.

Kenworthy, Tom, and Serge F. Kovaleski. "'Freemen' Finally Taxes the Patience of Federal Government." *Washington Post,* 31 March 1996, 1, 8–9.

Kimmel, Michael. "Foreword." In *Home-Grown Hate: Gender and Organized Racism.* Edited by Abby L. Ferber. New York: Routledge, 2004, xi–xiv.

Kimmel, Michael, and Abby L. Ferber. "'White Men Are This Nation': Right-Wing Militias and the Restoration of Rural American Masculinity." *Rural Sociology* 65:4 (December 2000), 582–604.

Klanwatch. "Growing in Numbers, Hardening in Attitude: Patriot Groups Pose Continued Threat to American Public." *Intelligence Report* 86 (spring 1997), 4–6.

Koehl, Matt. "12-Point Program of the NSWPP." *White Power.* September [?] 1980, n.p.

Krieger, Lisa M. "I Love My Country—It's the Government I Hate." *San Francisco Examiner,* 7 May 1995.

Labaton, Stephen. "U.S. Agency Defends Tactics in Assault on Sect." *New York Times,* 30 March 1993, A7.

———. "Outside Review Criticizes F.B.I. on Raid on Cult." *New York Times,* 16 November 1993, A13.

Lee, Mark. "Study Shows Suicide Rate High Among Farmers." *Tulsa World,* 12 September 1989, C1.

———. "High Suicide Rate Linked to Farm Financial Stress." *Tulsa World,* 16 September 1989, A1.

Leistritz, Larry, and Steve H. Murdock. "Financial Characteristics of Farms and of Farm Financial Markets and Policies in the United States." In *The Farm Financial Crisis: Socioeconomic Dimensions and Implications for Producers and Rural Areas.* Edited by Steve H. Murdock and Larry Leistritz. Boulder, Colo.: Westview Press, 1988, 14–27.

Lenihan, John H. "Westbound: Feature Films and the American West." In *Wanted Dead or Alive: The American West in Popular Culture.* Edited by Richard Aquila. Urbana: University of Illinois Press, 1996, 109–134.

Los Angeles Times. "300 Farmers Protest Auction of Farm in Springfield." 5 January 1983, 16, 20.

McBride, Kelly. "Weaver Was Target of Arms Sting." *Spokane Spokesman-Review,* 26 August 1992, A4.

McMurtry, Larry. "Westward Ho Hum: What the New Historians Have Done to the Old West." *New Republic* 203:17 (22 October 1990), 32–39.

McVeigh, Rory. "Structural Incentives for Conservative Mobilization: Power Devaluation and the Rise of the Ku Klux Klan 1915–1925." *Social Forces* 77 (1999), 1463–1464.

Malone, Michael P. "Beyond the Last Frontier: Toward a New Approach to New Western History." *Western Historical Quarterly* 20:4 (November 1989), 409–427.

Markoutsas Elaine. "Wisconsin Posse Digs in for the 'Bloodbath' to Come." *Chicago Tribune,* 20 August 1980, 3.

Mauer, Richard. "Aryan Nations." *Idaho Statesman,* September 1980, 14–17.

Mitchell, Lee Clark. "'When you call me that. . .': Tall Talk and Male Hegemony in *The Virginian.*" *PMLA* 102:1 (1987), 66–77.

Moore, Leonard J. "Historical Interpretations of the 1920s Klan: The Traditional View and Recent Revisions." In *The Invisible Empire in the West: Toward a New Historical Appraisal of the Ku Klux Klan of the 1920s.* Edited by Shawn Lay. Urbana: University of Illinois Press, 1992, 17–38.

Morgenthau, Tom. "The Echoes of Ruby Ridge." *Newsweek,* 28 August 1995, 24–28.

Morgenthau, Tom, Frank Maier, Marily Achiron, and Jeff B. Copeland. "Again, The Fear of Foreclosure." *Newsweek,* 17 January 1983, 12–13.

Murphy, Kim. "Hate's Affluent New Godfathers." *Los Angeles Times,* 10 January 1999, A14.

———. "Last Stand of an Aging Aryan." *Los Angeles Times,* 10 January 1999.

Neu, Charles. "The Vietnam War and the Transformation of America." In *After Vietnam: Legacies of a Lost War.* Edited by Charles Neu. Baltimore: Johns Hopkins University Press, 2000, 1–23.

New York Times. "Links of Anti-Semitic Band Provoke 6-State Parley." 12 December 1984, B7.

———. "Officials Say Montana 'Freemen' Collected $1.8 Million in Scheme." 19 March 1996, A1.

———. "U.S. Seizes 2 Leaders of a Fugitive Group." 26 March 1996, B11.

———. "Sheriff Asks Tax Protestors to Surrender." 27 March 1996, A16.

———. "Anti-Tax Group Prowls; Neighbors Protest." 28 March 1996, A16.

———. "Standoff With Militants Is High-Stakes Experiment." 30 March 1996, A6.

———. "At Montana Standoff, F.B.I. spurns Aid of Far-Right Groups." 26 April 1996, A28.

"News Media Interview." *Calling Our Nation* 27 (ca. 1980), n.p.

Nicholls, Richard E. " 'Westward I Go Free.' " *New York Times,* 12 April 1996, A31.

Niebuhr, Gustav. "Creed of Hate Called Christian Identity Is the Heart of the Freemen's Beliefs." *New York Times,* 12 April 1996, A14.

———. "Mother and Son in Standoff Surrender." *New York Times,* 12 April 1996, A14.

Norton, Dee. "Fugitive Guards Family, Beliefs Atop Sheer Cliff." *Seattle Times,* 25 August 1992, A1 [archived at www.seattletimes.com].

Novick, Michael. "Was Hitler an Ecologist?" In *White Lies, White Power: The Fight Against White Supremacy and Reactionary Violence.* Monroe, Me.: Common Courage Press, 1995, 203–224.

Oregonian. "Meeting Draws Leaders of Neo-Nazi Groups." 12 July 1986, B7.

O'Sullivan, John. "The Great Nation of Futurity." *United States Democratic Review* 6:23 (November 1839), 426–430.

———. "Annexation." *United States Magazine and Democratic Review* 17:1 (July 1845), 5–10.

Pate, James L. "Bo Knows Politics: Klansmen, Christics, Clowns, and Gritz's Populist Party." *Soldier of Fortune* 17:9 (September 1992), 40–43, 74.

———. "Standoff in Idaho: The Randy Weaver Incident." *Soldier of Fortune* 18:3 (March 1993), 63–65.

———. "Gun Gestapo's Day of Infamy." *Soldier of Fortune* 18:6 (June 1993), 48.

———. "Amateurs and Assassins II." *Soldier of Fortune* 21:1 (January 1996), 56–61, 84–87.

Penn, J. B. "The Structure of Agriculture." *Structure Issues of American Agriculture: Set-*

ting, *Farm Production, Public Policies, Marketing, Rural America, The Experience of Others*. United States Department of Agriculture Economic Report 438, 1979.

Peraino, Kevin. "Aryan Nations in the Dock." *Newsweek* 136:10 (4 September 2000), 26.

Pitcavage, Mark. "Common Law and Uncommon Courts: An Overview of the Common Law Court Movement." Militia Watchdog website: http://www.militia watchdog .org/common.htm. July 1997, 1–22.

———. "Every Man a King: The Rise and Fall of the Montana Freemen" ("Patriot" Profile #3). [This web publication was part of Pitcavage's Militia Watchdog organization. The document can now be accessed through the Anti-Defamation League of B'Nai B'rith website at *http://www.adl.org/mwd/freemen.asp*.]

Pomeroy, Earl. "Computers in the Desert: Transforming the Simple Life." *Western Historical Quarterly* 25:1 (spring 1994), 7–20.

Popper, Frank, and Deborah Popper. "Great Plains: Checkered Past, Hopeful Future," *Forum for Applied Research and Public Policy,* winter 1994, 89–120.

Real, David. "Divide and Conquer: White Supremacists See Idaho Cabin Standoff as First Salvo in Race War." *Dallas Morning News,* 2 November 1992, A1, A10.

Ribuffo, Leo P. "Henry Ford and the International Jew." *American Jewish History* 69:4 (June 1980), 437–477.

Ridgeway, James, and Leonard Zeskind. "Revolution U.S.A. The Far Right Militias Prepare for Battle." *Village Voice,* 2 May 1995, 23.

Ritz, William R. "Farmers to Protest Debt Sale, 300 Gather to Block Court-Ordered Auction of Farm." *Denver Post,* 4 January 1983, A1, A14.

———. "Farmers Jailed After Protest At Springfield, Deputies' Tear Gas Subdues Crowd at Auction of Land." *Denver Post,* 5 January 1983.

———. "Bad Debts Followed Ag Activist, 11 Suits Filed in Last 14 Years." *Denver Post,* 6 January 1983, A1, A10.

Robbins, Jim. "Prairie Revolt: Sound and Fury but Little Fire." *New York Times,* 1 April 1996, A1.

Roche, Jeffrey. "Cowboy Conservatives." In *The Conservative Sixties.* Edited by Jeffrey Roche and David Farber. New York: Peter Lang Publishing, 2003, 79–92.

Ross, Wayne A. "Join a Militia—Break the Law?" *Soldier of Fortune* 20:4 (April 1995), 52–53.

Rotundo, Anthony. "Body and Soul: Changing Ideals of American Middle-Class Manhood, 1770–1920." *Journal of Social History* 16 (1983), 23–35.

Sager, Mike. "A Journey to the Heart of Whiteness." *Gentleman's Quarterly* 66:3 (March 1996), 246–254, 278–280.

Salina Journal. "Colorado Farmer Sought on Explosives Charges." 18 February 1983, 3.

———. "'Posse' Philosophy Raises Fears." 20 February 1983, 3.

———. "Weskan Training School Taught 'Killer Team' Tactics?" 20 February 1983, 1, 3.

Schlatter, Evelyn A. "'Extremism in the Defense of Liberty': The Minutemen and the Radical Right." In *The Conservative Sixties.* Edited by David Farber and Jeffrey Roche. New York: Peter Lang Publishing, 2003, 37–50.

Scott, Jim. "The Vigilantes are Back!" *Argosy* 281:2 (February 1975), 30–32.

Shapiro, Joseph. "An Epidemic of Fear and Loathing." *U.S. News and World Report,* 8 May 1995, 37–44.

Shulman, Stuart W. "The Origin of the Federal Farm Loan Act: Issue Emergence and Agenda-Setting in the Progressive Era Print Press." In *Fighting for the Farm: Rural American Transformed.* Edited by Jane Adams. Philadelphia: University of Pennsylvania Press, 2003, 113–128.

Smith, Thompson. "The Patriot Movement: Refreshing the Tree of Liberty with Fertilizer Bombs and the Blood of Martyrs," *Valparaiso Law Review* (fall 1997), 269–347.

Smolowe, Jill. "Enemies of the State." *Time.* 8 May 1995, 5–68.

Starr, Mark, and George Raine. "Violence on the Right: A Handful of New Extremists Disturbs the Peace." *Newsweek* 4 March 1985, 23–26.

St. Louis Post-Dispatch. "From Boise to Waco." 13 July 1993, B6.

Strozier, Charles B. "Apocalyptic Violence and the Politics of Waco." In *The Year 2000: Essays on the End.* Edited by Charles B. Strozier and Michael Flynn. New York: New York University Press, 1997, 97–111.

———. "Introduction." In *The Year 2000: Essays on the End.* Edited by Charles B. Strozier and Michael Flynn. New York: New York University Press, 1997, 1–12.

Thomas, Judy L. "New Farm Parity Movement Quickly Encounters Criticism." *Kansas City Star,* 24 March 1999, A9.

Thomas, Pierre. "FBI Sends Armored Vehicles, Helicopter to Freemen Ranch." *Washington Post,* 1 June 1996, A12.

———. "FBI Cuts Off Power to Freemen's Ranch." *Washington Post,* 4 June 1996, A9.

Toll, William. "Progress and Piety: The Ku Klux Klan and Social Change in Tillamook, Oregon." *Pacific Northwest Quarterly* 69 (April 1978), 75–85.

Trillin, Calvin. "I've Got Problems." *New Yorker,* 18 March 1985, 109–118.

Turner, Frederick Jackson. "The Significance of the Frontier in American History." In *History, Frontier, and Section.* Edited and with introduction by Martin Ridge. Tucson: University of New Mexico Press, 1993, 59–92.

———. "The Significance of the Frontier in American History." In *The American Frontier: Opposing Viewpoints,* American History Series. Edited by Mary Ellen Jones. San Diego: Greenhaven Press, 1984, 24–40.

Vann, Richard T. "The Free Anglo-Saxons: A Historical Myth." *Journal of the History of Ideas* 19 (April 1958), 259–272.

Verhovek, Sam Howe. "Serious Face on a Texas Independence Group." *New York Times,* 24 January 1997, A1.

———. "Hostages Taken in Standoff with Militant Texas Group." *New York Times,* 28 April 1997, A10.

———. "Texas Swaps Jailed Militant for Hostage in Tense Siege." *New York Times,* 29 April 1997, A1.

———. "Texas Standoff Continues; Next Moves Are Uncertain." *New York Times,* 30 April 1997, A16.

———. "Leader of Armed Group Breaks Off Talks on Settling Standoff in West Texas." *New York Times,* 1 May 1997, A16.

———. "Before His Armed Standoff, Texan Waged War on Neighbors in Court." *New York Times,* 2 May 1997, A12.

———. "Troopers Move Closer to Texas Separatists' Encampment." *New York Times,* 3 May 1997, A18.

———. "Seven-Day Standoff between Texas Authorities and Republic of Texas Ends." *New York Times,* 4 May 1997, A1.

———. "One Texas Secessionist Who Fled into Mountains Is Killed." *New York Times,* 6 May 1997, A16.

Wagner, Steven P. "Prof Says Theology Links Hate Groups." *The Forum.* 10 February 2003 [available online at http://in-forum.com/specials/gordonkahl.index.cfm?id= 27460]; accessed 30 December 2005.

Washington Post. "U.S. Alleges Overthrow Plot ... White Supremacists Linked to Scheme to Take Over Government." 12 December 1984, A3.

Watts, Thomas G. "Republic of Texas Schism Creates Confusion," *Dallas Morning News,* 2 February 1997, A47.

———. "McLaren Rarely Seen Since Late '96," *Dallas Morning News,* 28 April 1997.

West, Elliott. "Selling the Myth: Western Images in Advertising." In *Wanted Dead or Alive: The American West in Popular Culture.* Edited by Richard Aquila. Urbana: University of Illinois Press, 1996, 269–291.

———. "Reconstructing Race." *Western Historical Quarterly* 34:1 (spring 2003), 7–26.

White, Richard. "The Current Weirdness in the West." *Western Historical Quarterly* 28:1 (spring 1997), 5–18.

Williams, Florence. "Plains Sense: Frank and Deborah Popper's 'Buffalo Commons' is Creeping Toward Reality," *High Country News* 33:1 (January 2001) [archived at http://www.hcn.org].

Williams, Mike. "Citizen Militias: '. . .Necessary to the Security of a Free State. . .' " *Soldier of Fortune* 20:4 (April 1995), 48–53, 81–82.

Wilson, John. "British Israelism: The Ideological Restraints on Sect Organization." In *Patterns of Sectarianism: Organization and Ideology in Social and Religious Movements.* Edited by Bryan R. Wilson. London: Heinemann, 1967.

Woodward, C. Vann. "Tom Watson and the Negro." In *Understanding the American Past: American History and Its Interpretations.* Edited by Edward N. Saveth. New York: Little, Brown, 1958, 339–359.

Wooten, Terry. "Economic Woes Lead Movement to Another Winter of Discontent." Wichita *Eagle-Beacon,* February 1983.

Worster, Donald. "Beyond the Agrarian Myth." In *Trails: Toward a New Western History.* Edited by Patricia Nelson Limerick, Clyde Milner II, and Charles E. Rankin. Lawrence: University Press of Kansas, 1991, 3–25.

———. "Freedom and Want: The Western Paradox." In *Under Western Skies: Nature and History of the American West.* New York: Oxford University Press, 1992, 79–92.

Zeskind, Lenny. "The Far Right." *Shmate: A Journal of Progressive Jewish Thought* 11–12 (summer 1985), 17–20.

Unpublished Sources

Akins, John K. "God, Guns, and Guts: Religion and Violence in Florida Militias. Ph.D. dissertation, University of Florida, 1998.

Ferber, Abby. "Regulating Interracial Sexuality: The Production of Racialized, Gendered Subjects in Contemporary White Supremacist Discourse." Ph.D. dissertation, University of Oregon, 1994.

Frereichs, Rebecca L. "Christian Patriots: A Comparative Historical Analysis." M.A. thesis, University of New Mexico, 1996.

Harper, Suzanne. "The Brotherhood: Race and Gender Ideologies in the White Supremacist Movement." Ph.D. dissertation, University of Texas, 1993.

Price, Isabel B. "Gerald L. K. Smith and Anti-Semitism." M.A. thesis, University of New Mexico, 1965.

Sneath, Wayne D. "The Conspiratorial Ideology of Right-Wing Extremism in the 1990s: A Cultural Analysis of Ruby Ridge, Waco, and Oklahoma City." Ph.D. dissertation, Bowling Green State University, 2000.

Snyder, Rebecca C. "Citizens' Militias and Armed Masculinity: The Citizen Soldier Ideal and Gender in the Civic Republican Tradition." Ph.D. dissertation, Rutgers University, 1997.

Newspapers/Periodicals

Albany (Oregon) *Democrat-Herald*

Argosy

Arizona Republic

Albuquerque Journal

Chicago Tribune

Christian Research Journal

Dallas Morning News

Denver (Colorado) *Post*

Desert-Mountain Times (Fort Davis, Texas)

Wichita (Kansas) *Eagle-Beacon*

Gentleman's Quarterly

(Boise) *Idaho Statesman*

Instauration (white supremacist)

Kansas City (Kansas) *Star*

Lewiston (Idaho) *Morning Tribune*

Los Angeles Times

The Nationalist (American National Union publication; rightist)

New York Times

Newsweek

Northwest Magazine (*Oregonian* insert)

The (Portland) *Oregonian*

Outside

People

Playboy

The Progressive
Salina (Kansas) *Journal*
San Francisco Examiner
Seattle Post-Intelligencer
Seattle Times
Soldier of Fortune
Spokane (Washington) *Spokesman-Review*
St. Louis News-Dispatch
The Talon (Euro-American Alliance)
Time
Tulsa (Oklahoma) *World*
Twin Falls (Idaho) *News-Times*
U.S. News and World Report
Washington Post
Wasau (Wisconsin) *Herald*
Westword (Denver, Colorado)
White Power (National Socialist White People's Party)
Village Voice (New York City)

  Newsletters
Calling Our Nation (Aryan Nations)
Inter-Klan Newsletter and Survival Alert (Aryan Nations/Ku Klux Klan)
Aryan Nations Newsletter (Aryan Nations)

  Government Documents
Congressional Record. Volume 86, pt. 10, 76th Congress, 3rd Session, 19 August 1940.
   Washington, D.C.: Government Printing Office, 1940.
John Doe vs. O. Edward Schlatter. Colorado State Case No. 98-D-1196. Objection to
   order dismissing complaint and request to correct order and issue judgment,
   22 June 1998.
The Ku Klux Klan, 67th Congress, 1st Session. House Committee on Rules, 11–17
   October, 1921. Washington, D.C.: 1921.
United States Department of Agriculture, Economic Research Service. "The Current
   Financial Condition of Farmers and Farm Lenders." *Agriculture Information Bulletin*
   490 (March 1985).
———. Economics, Statistics, and Cooperative Service, *Structure Issues of American
   Agriculture: Setting, Farm Production, Public Policies, Marketing, Rural America, The
   Experience of Others.* Agricultural Economic Report 438, 1979.
United States Department of Justice, Federal Bureau of Investigation. "Unknown
   Subjects; Members of Aryan Nation [*sic*], Coeur d'Alene, Idaho." Report filed
   20 October 1983.
———. *Report on the Events at Waco, Texas, February 18 to April 19, 1993.* Washington,
   D.C.: Government Printing Office, 1993.
———. *Department of Justice Report on Internal Review Regarding the Ruby Ridge
   Hostage Situation and Shooting by Law Enforcement Personnel.* Washington, D.C.:
   Government Printing Office, 1994.

United States Department of the Treasury. *Report of the Department of the Treasury on the Bureau of Alcohol, Tobacco, and Firearms Investigation of Vernon Wayne Howell, also Known as David Koresh*. Washington, D.C.: Government Printing Office, 1993.

United States Senate. *Hearing Before the Committee on Agriculture, Nutrition, and Forestry*. 96th Congress, 1st Session, 9 February 1979. Washington, D.C.: Government Printing Office, 1979.

United States Senate. *Examination of Problems Affecting the Farm Community*. Hearings before the Committee on Agriculture, Nutrition, and Forestry. 100th Congress, 1st Session. 9 February 1987. Washington, D.C.: Government Printing Office, 1988.

Interviews and Correspondence

Berlet, Chip, senior research analyst, Political Research Associates, Somerville, Mass. 10 March 1999.

Butler, Pastor Richard. Former head of Aryan Nations, Hayden Lake, Idaho. E-mail correspondence, 8 August 2003.

Kemp, Richard, former member of The Order, Federal Corrections Institution, Sheridan, Oregon. Correspondence, 14 July 2003 and 6 August 2003.

Lane, David, former member of The Order, U.S. Penitentiary, Florence, Colorado. Correspondence, (postmarked) 6 August 2003.

Scutari, Richard, former member of The Order, U.S. Penitentiary, Florence, Colorado. Correspondence, 26 July 2003, 15 October 2003, and 13 December 2003.

Vanderhees, Captain Robert "Bob." Department of Public Safety, Albuquerque, New Mexico. Telephone interview, 23 March 1999.

Wright, Colonel R. J. 1st New Mexico Militia, Hobbs, New Mexico. Dinner, 12 January 1999.

Radio

National Public Radio. "White Supremacist Barricaded in Idaho." *All Things Considered*. 28 August 1992.

———. "Barricaded Supremacist Weaver Gives Up." *All Things Considered*. 31 August 1992.

Archives

Ku Klux Klan Collection, Western History Collections.

Denver Public Library, Denver, Colorado.

Keith Stimely Collection, Knight Library, University of Oregon, Eugene, Oregon.

Wilcox Collection, Spencer Research Library, University of Kansas, Lawrence, Kansas.

Index